KOFFSKI

FUND SELECTIONS
EVERETT PUBLIC LIBRARY

Top left & right: Eliza Ann McAuley at two moments in her life. At left in her wedding picture with husband Robert Seely Egbert, on November 20, 1856, in Sacramento. At right in later years, date unknown.
Courtesy, Thomas Macauley, Reno, Nevada, a great-nephew of Eliza.

At left: Lucy R. Cooke, date unknown.
Courtesy, R.S. Cooke, Taylorsville, CA.

Covered Wagon Women

Diaries & Letters from the Western Trails
1852

Volume 4

The California Trail

Edited and compiled by
KENNETH L. HOLMES

Introduction to the Bison Books Edition
by Glenda Riley

University of Nebraska Press
Lincoln and London

Introduction to the Bison Books Edition © 1997 by the University of Nebraska Press

⊛ The paper in this book meets the minimum requirements of American National Standard for Information Sciences—Permanence of Paper for Printed Library Materials, ANSI Z39.48-1984.

First Bison Books printing: 1997
Most recent printing indicated by the last digit below:
10   9   8   7   6   5   4   3   2

Library of Congress Cataloging-in-Publication Data
The Library of Congress has cataloged Vol. 1 as:
Covered wagon women: diaries & letters from the western trails, 1840–1849
/ edited and compiled by Kenneth L. Holmes; introduction to the Bison Books editon by Anne M. Butler.
p. cm.
Originally published: Glendale, Calif.: A. H. Clark Co., 1983.
"Reprinted from volume one . . . of the original eleven-volume edition"—T.p. verso.
:Volume I."
Includes index.
ISBN 0-8032-7277-4 (pa: alk. paper)
1. Women pioneers—West (U.S.)—Biography.   2. West (U.S.)—History.
3. West (U.S.)—Biography.   4. Overland journeys to the Pacific.
5. Frontier and pioneer life—West (U.S.)   I. Holmes, Kenneth L.
F591.C79   1996
978—dc20   95-21200   CIP

Volume 2 introduction by Lillian Schlissel.
ISBN 0-8032-7274-X (pa: alk. paper)
Volume 3 introduction by Susan Armitage.
ISBN 0-8032-7287-1 (pa: alk. paper)
Volume 4 introduction by Glenda Riley.
ISBN 0-8032-7291-X (pa: alk. paper)

Reprinted from volume four (1985) of the original eleven-volume edition titled *Covered Wagon Women: Diaries and Letters from the Western Trails, 1840–1890*, by the Arthur H. Clark Company, Glendale, California.

Introduction to the Bison Books Edition

Glenda Riley

During the past few years the concept of "western trail" has become increasingly complicated. Scholars have pointed out that numerous trails led to the American West, including a variety of overland routes, the trek across Panama, roads heading north from Mexico, and the Pacific and Atlantic oceans. These not only brought Anglo-Americans and African Americans westward, but Mexicans northward, and Europeans and Asians to the West.

This volume represents one of the most common routes: the one motion pictures and television have drawn upon for thousands of stories. The women who traversed the Oregon Trail, and offer their accounts here, were stock characters as well. They were largely Anglo-American and had a modicum of education, which allowed them to record their observations and experiences for posterity.

Because these women lacked exposure to television, especially the nightly news, they had little knowledge of other migrants taking different trails to a similar destination. In twentieth-century terms, they suffered from a want of global and cultural awareness. But, in nineteenth-century parlance, they had purpose.

For them, "the trail" was the Oregon Trail, invested with the demands, hardships, and adjustments they had to face to reach the far West. Despite the difficulties, thousands were willing to challenge the obstacles to finding new homes. In 1852, the number of migrants on the Oregon Trail increased notably over the previous year. The *Missouri Republican* of July 1, 1852, claimed that by May alone, 8,174 men, 1,286 women, and 1,776 children had departed for points west. The newspaper also commented that the migration included a marked increase in the number of women.

In the selections that follow, some of these women relate their reluctance to leave kin and friends behind, express their dread or curiosity about meeting their "first" Indian, wonder how they will survive striking climatic changes, and question their abilities to deal with natural and other disasters. They clearly anticipate the transformation of their known world.

Oregon Trail women were right to worry. Besides forsaking kin, friends, and others, they could expect to encounter peoples of vastly different cultures from their own. Moreover, before leaving home women absorbed confusing and conflicting images of Native Americans from the press and popular literature. On the one hand, Indians were seen as friendly, kind, and courageous; on the other, native peoples were described as bad, hostile, and vicious. Because the likeness of the "bad" Indian dominated during the 1850s, however, women's initial expectations tended to be negative rather than positive.

Too, embellishments abounded at every turn. These included family stories about "murderous savages," myths involving "barbarians," and inflated rumors about Indian "atrocities" and "uprisings." Along the trail, women encountered additional horror stories about Indian "depredations" and alarms of various sorts, including printed circulars and bleached skull bones inscribed "danger—Indian troubles" or "Indian uprising," sometimes accompanied by a crude drawing of a skull and crossbones.

Presumably, Indians also heard rumors and gossip about the oncoming immigrants. Consequently, both sides were, at best, uninformed— and, at worst, horribly misinformed—about the other. As Francis Sawyer put it, "We are now in the Indian country, and we suspect that it will not be many days before we see some of these wild natives" (89).

When they finally met, migrants and natives alike were primed for trouble. In addition, because meetings were unplanned and feared, no protocol for proper behavior existed. Both Anglos and Indians asked invasive questions, picked up and laughed at other peoples' possessions, and were curious to the point of rudeness. In some cases, anxiety and suspicion caused an encounter to turn into an armed confrontation. In other cases, people met—and even liked—each other. Inevitably, however, some amount of conflict ensued, for settlers seemed intent on imposing their ways on American Indians. For example, even though most Indian cultures believed in sharing, Anglos tried to convince Native Americans that resources existed to be exploited. Women travelers had their own criticisms of Indians. They especially lamented the Indians' lack of clothing, inability to speak English, and practice of plural marriage.

Native peoples who resisted Anglo invasion and expressed their opinions about the changes occurring became, in Anglo eyes, "savage," "hostile," and "barbaric." In one way, Indians were victims of encroaching settlers who tricked, cheated, and relied on the military to clear their way. In another, however, American Indians retained their dignity, if not their lands. In their own quiet fashion, Indians often expressed their wills. For instance, one traveler liked to tell the story of naive, childlike Indians who showed off by shooting arrows at nickels and other coins. Since the Indians kept the nickels—and spent them later—one has to wonder who was the gullible party.

Because of such cultural differences, the women in this volume sometimes demonstrate what are today termed imperialist or colonialist attitudes. Often, women not only censured American Indians but hoped to "civilize" (that is, bring white customs to) the native peoples they met. Although some cared more about their own problems than those of Native Americans, others dreamed of the ways in which their religions, laws, policies, and culture would improve the Indians' way of life. In this, they were unfortunately products of their era and thus created problems that later generations still have to solve.

As they progressed along the trail, however, women often altered their views of Indians. Because women traded with Indians, visited with Indian women and children, and borrowed such helpful knowledge as which roots to dig and what herbal medicines to use, women often grew sympathetic with Indians. As trail women came to know and appreciate American Indians, many lamented the natives' deteriorating situations and questioned why a once proud, self-sufficient people increasingly lived in poverty and begged scraps of food from migrants.

Besides relationships with native peoples, climate also posed a huge problem for travelers. The mountains the settlers climbed, the rivers they forded, and the storms they survived accounted for many trail disasters, which in themselves became commonplace. Drowning, accidental shootings, and getting lost were a usual part of trail life. When her party reached Starvation Camp and Donner Lake, Eliza Ann McAuley recalled the 1846 tragedy that occurred on that spot. "It is," McAuley wrote, "the most desolate, gloomy looking place I ever saw" (78–79).

Because of the high drama and sometimes low chicanery along the trail, the journey has been mythologized. For most migrants the trip was neither as harsh nor as happy as legend portrayed it. Generally, trail women made the crossing with hope, energy, and even grace. Also, they coped with their problems in myriad ways, four of which were so universal that they beg notice.

First, women served as transitional forces on the westward journey. The importance of this time on the trail has been overlooked. The trip provided a time for people to adjust from the known to the new, to learn fresh skills, and to develop ways of managing unexpected situations.

As wives and mothers, trail women especially played a crucial role by providing moral guidance in a situation that involved drinking, swearing, missed Sabbath observances, loose sexual practices, polygamy, and near nudity on the part of some natives. Typically, women's magazines urged women to act as "correctives of what is wrong." Serving as moral guides on the trail could convince women of their importance and give them a reason to endure.

Women also led the way in testing new behaviors along the trail. For instance, they visited Native American women and regularly gained entrance to Indian homes. Such friendly occurrences not only eased female migrants' anxieties regarding Indians, but frequently led to an exchange of important information. On other occasions, such meetings provided social contact or what one woman called "quite a dish of conversation."

Second, women survived the trail because they had the tenets of women's culture to guide them. Women's customary roles and domestic ideologies in chaotic circumstances gave women a sense of meaning and purpose. For example, women kept "standards" in place. Despite exhaustion and the difficulty of laundering clothes, women often donned clean dresses to attend an often hastily improvised Sabbath meeting.

Clearly, the care needed by children offered women a larger purpose than simply reaching the end of the trail. Lucy Rutledge Cooke touched on the importance of motherly care when she wrote "my little babe is so sick I was up all night with her she takes little or no nourishment & what she does she throws up directly."

In addition, trail women contributed medical and apothecary skills. Long taught they were "gifted to excel" at nursing and doctoring, women served as the medical practitioners for many overland trains. They knew how, or learned how, to manage everything from trail accidents to ague, poison ivy, and poison oak.

Another part of nineteenth-century women's culture involved the formation of reciprocal relationships with other women. Encouraged to practice "union and cooperation," trail women often joined with their counterparts to get a job done, whether it be laundry, cooking, or childcare. Childbirth provided yet another opportunity for women to help one another. When women were "confined" or "in a poor fix to travel," midwives or other women usually delivered babies and even cared for mother and child afterwards.

Such collaboration between trail women provided stability for them and their families. It also created a common bond, so that a woman did not feel alone or lost. From exchanging recipes to assisting at childbirth, women felt they had mothers, sisters, and friends to take the place of the ones they left behind.

Third, Oregon Trail women served as dispensers of food. Although men occasionally took over culinary tasks, it was not the norm. Francis Sawyer noted that "the men do all the cooking in bad weather" but that she cooked otherwise (88–89).

Even though food preparation may sound commonplace, it played a critical role. In various ways, food sustained pioneers as they crossed the Oregon Trail: besides supplying physical and psychological nourishment, it established a pattern of success.*

Because the outcome of migration depended on the health and strength of the migrants, meals had to be plentiful and nourishing. Women carried food supplies in wagons, such as the "dried fruits and vegetables, also a quantity of light bread cut in slices and dried" that Eliza Ann McAuley described (37). Also, men hunted and fished along the way. Francis Sawyer rejoiced when her husband killed a deer: "This was very acceptable to all of us, as fresh meat is quite a treat on a trip like this" (89). Women and children also fished and gathered berries.

Not only did food provide nutrition but it could boost morale as well. Meals supplied warmth and comfort when the migrants grew tired, wet, cold, discouraged, or ill. Food could also be a reward—for a stream forded, a hill ascended, or a long day completed. Or food might suggest a connection to something known and familiar. To provide structure amid upheaval, many women continued pre-migration mealtime routines. They prepared favorite foods, Sunday dinners, and holiday dinners along the trail.

Trail women also kept spirits up by supplying unexpected mealtime treats. These included wild strawberries, currants, and huckleberries, as well as pies and soda fritters. To an exhausted and downhearted traveler such delicacies represented a tie with home, a fact that encouraged some women to stay up stewing apples rather than get much-needed sleep.

Tasty, regular meals also suggested success to emigrants. If they ate, they survived. If they survived, they could not only expect to reach their goal—their own particular promised land—but to eat and survive there as well. Women proved incredibly adaptable and creative in this realm.

*N. Jill Howard and Glenda Riley, "Thus You See I Have Not Much Rest," *Idaho Yesterdays* 37 (fall 1993): 27–35.

Frequently, they even turned obstacles into advantages. Instead of riding in the back of bumping wagons, women placed butter churns inside them. Because of the swaying, mixing motion of the wagon, by the end of the day women had fresh butter for dinner. They might even have enough to sell to local farmers, the cash paying for bridge tolls and incidental expenses. Other women dug trenches in the ground and lit open fires in them. Balancing the pots and pans across the trenches on their edges, women made bread, bean soup, boiled bacon, mush, and tea.

Clearly, women's ability to endure boded well for the years ahead. If they could feed their families on the trail, and even earn extra money, they could do so in their new homes. Also, filling the crucial role of cook gave more than one woman enough purpose and determination to hurdle all obstacles.

Finally, many trail women possessed hardy spirits and cheery personalities. They could glory in a sunrise, laugh at a mishap, and appreciate the beauties of the landscape. Mariett Foster Cummings wrote: "Arose early and passed over two of the most beautiful prairies I ever saw" (123). Later, although she was a more seasoned traveler, Cummings still reveled in "the wildest and most magnificent scenery, surpassing anything I ever dreamed of" (149). Even teenager Elizabeth Keegan, who found the overland journey to Sacramento "tedious in the extreme," waxed lyrical about "rolling praries . . . covered with verdure" (24).

Light-hearted, optimistic women further leavened their trips by joining in the fun that marked many camps. They sang spirituals and other songs, celebrated such holidays as the Fourth of July, and danced to the music of fiddles, banjos, and bones in the light of the campfire. Sarah Pratt punctuated her diary with such notations as "circus expected here tomorrow," "music in the evening," and "good company—lively times" (178–79) while Lucy Rutledge Cook noted "dancing" and "considerable merriment" (240).

Of course, women's efforts to cope with the hazards of the Oregon Trail demanded great energy, stamina, and fortitude. Traversing the Oregon Trail was a twenty-four-hour, every-day-of- the-week undertaking. Thus, in all likelihood, even if Oregon Trail women had been aware of travelers on other trails they would have continued to focus on their own travails. While they might have had sympathy for the migrants who streamed from all parts of the world across a wide variety of trails, they had little energy to spare. They had mountains to climb, rivers to ford, and thousands of miles to cross before they could unload their baggage and begin the work of building new homes.

Contents

Illustrations

Introduction to Volume IV

If, as we pointed out in the introduction to Volume III of this series, the number of emigrants to all destinations in 1851 was at its lowest level, exactly the opposite is true for 1852. During that season the number traveling to western destinations exceeded that of any previous or following year. On July 1, 1852, the correspondent of the *Missouri Republican* newspaper of St. Louis reported from Fort Kearny that up to late May, 8174 men, 1286 women, 1776 children, 3533 horses, 2316 mules, 26,269 oxen and cows, 2654 wagons, 500 sheep – "together with a hog and a hand cart" – were on their way.[1]

The most accurate estimate, that of John D. Unruh, Jr., in *The Plains Across,* indicates that the number of those going to California increased from 1,100 in 1851 to 50,000 in 1852. Those going to Oregon rose from 3,600 to about 10,000. The number to Salt Lake City rose from 1,500 to about 10,000.[2]

The *Republican* also reported in an April 15, 1852, editorial that "A marked feature of the emigration this year is the number of women who are going by the land routes."[3]

There were more turn-arounds in 1852 also. These were the travelers who for one reason or another turned back from the tedious and dangerous journey. Ezra Meeker, who traveled part of the way with Tom

---

[1] *Publications of the Nebraska State Historical Society,* xx (Lincoln, 1922), p. 239.

[2] (Urbana, Illinois, 1979), p. 120.

[3] *Publications of the Nebraska State Historical Society,* xx p. 238.

and Eliza McAuley in 1852, wrote of the following
experience:

> One of the incidents that made a profound impression upon
> the minds of all; the meeting of eleven wagons returning and
> not a man left in the entire train; – all had died, and had been
> buried along the way, and the women were returning alone from
> a point well up on the Platte below Fort Laramie.[4]

Another feature of the emigration was that as with
the Oregon and Utah overlanders, there were many
going to California to engage in farming or "ranching" as it was called there. Others wanted either to
enter into trades or professions in the growing com-
munities in the new state. It was a family migration.
There were still many single men out to seek gold as
well, of course. George R. Stewart, in *The California
Trail,* pointed this out.[5] He also suggested "The most
striking difference in the appearance of the migration
was supplied by the great herds of cattle and sheep,
totaling about 100,000 head." These animals needed
forage, as did the draft animals, and were often taken
some distance away from the wagon trail to feed on
greener pastures.

The presence of disease, especially Asiatic cholera,
was overwhelming. Entire families would die and have
to be buried along the trail. This was true both of
the California and Oregon overlanders. There is a
clipping from an unnamed newspaper in a scrapbook
in the Oregon Historical Society which quotes Joaquin
Miller, the California poet who crossed the plains as
a teenager with his parents in 1852. The newspaper
clipping, undoubtedly from a 1905 paper, quotes Miller in a speech given at the Lewis and Clark Exposi-

4 Ezra Meeker, *The Busy Life of Eighty-Five Years* (Seattle, 1916), p. 46.
5 (New York, 1962), p. 307.

THE BLOOMER COSTUME
A Currier & Ives lithograph which appeared in 1851.
Courtesy, Museum of the City of New York.

tion in Portland: "It is a sad story. There was but one graveyard that hot, dusty, dreadful year of 1852, and that graveyard reached from the Missouri to the Columbia."

Some of our diarists were "grave counters." They would note each day or every few days the number of graves they saw along the trail. Cecilia Adams, after listing five, seven, twenty-one or more "new made graves" day after day, added, "If we should go by all the camping grounds we should see five times as many graves as we do now." (Ms. 1508, Oregon Historical Society.)

One of the best treatments of this subject for the entire span of trail travel is that of Merrill J. Mattes in *The Great Platte River Road* in his section, "Disease and Death." Mattes suggests that a conservative figure for the number of deaths from disease for the years 1842-1859 for the California Trail would be "20,000 for the entire 2,000 miles, or an average of ten graves to each mile." [6]

Another feature of the 1852 migration for women was that many of them wore the "Bloomer Costume."

6 *Nebraska State Historical Society Publications*, Vol. xxv (Lincoln, 1979), pp. 81-89. The particular quote is from page 82. A great deal more study of the cholera factor might well be made. What was its relationship to the presence of cholera in the eastern states during the great epidemic of 1849-1854? Charles E. Rosenberg in *The Cholera Years* is quite helpful in this. Were there more deaths in New York City due to the coming of the disease on immigrant ships? Tantalizing questions are also raised by the fascinating study by the French scholar André Siegfried in his *Routes of Contagion* (New York, 1965). It always began in India and spread over trade routes to Europe. The Moslem road to Mecca was very important. Then it traveled overseas on shipboard. Was the overland trail one of these routes? How did the spread relate to the washing of clothes by the women in sources of drinking water as it did along the Ganges? The best short treatment of the history of cholera in the United States is an article, "Cholera," by Harold W. Jones, M.D., in the 1962 edition of *The Encylopedia Americana*, Vol. vi, pp. 585-86.

This had been invented in 1850 by Elizabeth Smith Miller. She named it for Amelia Bloomer, a well known women's rights leader of the time. This lady also made the new costume famous in her paper, *The Lily*.[7] There is a manuscript written by Elizabeth Miller in the New York Public Library that quotes her as saying that she had gotten tired of "years of annoyance in wearing the long, heavy skirt," so she thought up a combination of a short skirt to be worn with "Turkish trousers."[8] The new costume made it possible for women to stride a horse rather than riding side-saddle on the long overland journey.

The bloomers had already made their appearance on the west coast. In its September 2, 1851, edition the *Oregon Statesman* of Salem reported:

> THE "BLOOMERS" IN OREGON. — A couple of our down town ladies appeared in the Bloomer costume (short dress and trousers) one day last week. We was not "there to see," but we understand the demonstration created an intense excitement in that quarter.

The Portland *Oregonian* also noted the new kind of dress in its edition of February 14, 1852. The quote, which has somewhat of a "male chauvinistic" bent, was written as an editorial:

> LAPS AND BLOOMERS. — Does not the Bloomer do away with the feminine peculiarity known as the lap? Are laps and Bloomers co-existent? You remember that the heroine in "One and a Thousand"[9] was detected, when disguised as a page, by a simple

---

[7] Aileen S. Kraditor, *Up From the Pedestal* (Chicago, 1968), pp. 123-24.

[8] *Ibid.* See also D. C. Bloomer, *Life and Writings of Amelia Bloomer* (Boston, 1895), new edition with introduction by Susan J. Kleinberg (New York, 1975).

[9] George P. R. James, *Works*, Volume IV, *One in a Thousand* (London, 1845). This reference has not been found by the editor. James was an inveterate revisor of previous editions of his books. Perhaps that is what happened, or else it could be an incorrect reference by the writer in the

process. Somebody tossed her a jack-knife, as she was sitting upon a door step. She doing as a young lady would do under similar circumstances, spread out her knees in order to form a large surface for the reception of the missile. But the missile fell through, in company with her attempt to travel incognito. Now, what we want to know is this. Can a bloomer catch a jack-knife?

There are several apt references to bloomers in the diaries here published. The following travelers to California wrote about them in 1852:

Eliza Ann McAulcy declared on April 7, "My sister and I wear short dresses and bloomers and our foot gear includes a pair of light calf-skin topboots for wading through mud and sand" (p. 37 below).

Mariett Foster Cummings wrote near Peru, Illinois that "in passing one house the women came out and laughed at me and my dress, I did not ask which, but find it much more convenient for traveling than a long one" (p. 120, below).

Francis Sawyer told in her diary on May 23 about a family observed by her, "The daughter is dressed in a bloomer-costume – pants, short skirt and red-top boots. I think it is a very appropriate dress for a trip like this. So many ladies wear it, that I almost wish that I was so attired myself" (p. 90, below).

In publishing the diaries and letters written by 1852 travelers in *Covered Wagon Women,* so many items have been found that it is necessary to expand the year's collection to two volumes: Volume IV will contain those of women on the way to California; while Volume V will make available those of women going to the Pacific Northwest.

Oregonian. Mark Twain described a similar method of distinguishing someone dressed in women's clothes in *Huckleberry Finn.* But that was many years later.

The California diaries and letters are arranged, as in previous volumes, in chronological order from the date they crossed the Missouri River. The sequence is as follows: Elizabeth Keegan, early May; Eliza Ann McAuley, May 15-16; Francis Sawyer, May 20; Mariett F. Cummings, May 21-22; Sarah Pratt, June 8. Lucy R. Cooke has been placed last because her's was a two-year journey, with a winter stop-over in Salt Lake City.

Again for those who have not read the introduction to the first volume of this series, we reiterate some salient points which have been used to guide the editorial hand. It is a major purpose to let the writers tell their own story in their own words with as little scholarly trimming as possible. The intent is to transcribe each word or phrase as accurately as possible, leaving mis-spellings and grammatical errors as written in the original.

Two gestures have been made for the sake of clarity:

1. We have added space where phrases or sentences ended and no punctuation appeared in the original.

2. We have put the daily journals into diary format even though the original may have been written continuously line by line because of the writer's shortage of paper.

There are numerous geographic references that are mentioned over and over again in the various accounts. The final volume in the series will include geographical gazeteer, in addition to an index and bibliography to aid the reader.

The scarce and unusual in overland documents have been sought out. Readily available accounts are not included, but they will be referred to in the final volume along with the bibliography. If the reader knows of such accounts written while on the journey, please let us know. Our goal is to add to the knowledge of all regarding this portion of our history – the story of ordinary people embarked on an extraordinary experience.

KENNETH L. HOLMES

Monmouth, Oregon, 1984

The Diaries, Letters, and Commentaries

A Teenager's Letter from Sacramento
∮ Elizabeth Keegan

INTRODUCTION

They arrived in Marysville, California, on September 17, 1852. Two months later, on December 12, Elizabeth Keegan wrote the letter we now publish to her brother and sister back in St. Louis. Her companions on the journey were her mother, also named Elizabeth, a servant girl named Kate, an an un-named hired man. Nearly eighty years later, in 1930, her great-granddaughter, Mrs. Dorothy Sims, presented to the manuscript collection of the California Historical Society in San Francisco a typescript of the letter with the note, "I have copied it word for word." Mrs. Sims indicated that Elizabeth was twelve years old at the time of the covered wagon journey. That figure is justified by the 1900 Federal Census which lists her as being sixty years old, born in Canada.[1]

In an accompanying letter Mrs. Sims shared other family memories about Elizabeth Keegan as she commented, "The daring feat of three women, one practically a child, with only 1 male escort, I think was quite a feat of note." The teenager "rode her pony all the way," being a good horse-woman.

The brother and sister to whom the letter was addressed, James B. and Julia Keegan, followed their mother and sister overland two years later.

By the time of the 1860 Federal Census,[2] Elizabeth had

---

[1] Information from the Federal Census for 1900 by Lorraine M. Lineer, genealogical researcher, Sacramento, in response to a request for information by the author. This is noted here with gratitude.

[2] United States Bureau of the Census, Manuscript Records of the Eighth Census of the United States, 1860.

been married to William Ketchum, a 35-year-old carpenter. They were listed by the census-taker on August 23, 1860, as living in Sacramento, their personal property being worth $700. Elizabeth was noted as being the mother of two children, a girl named Missouri, four years old, and a year-old baby boy named Harry.

The information on Elizabeth Keegan is sparse, but there emerges more than twenty years after the above census records a series of references in the Sacramento City Directories from 1882 to 1895.[3]

The 1882 directory listed her, with a minimum of punctuation, as "Ketchum Mrs E J C, furnished rooms, Masonic Building, res same."

In the 1884-1885 Directory she was "KETCHUM E J C Mrs, proprietress Metropolitan House, res 427 K [Street]."

Then in 1895 there was a half-page advertisement for "THE METROPOLITAN" with "Mrs. E. J. C. KETCHUM, Propr." The rooming house was at the "N. W. Corner Fifth and K Sts.," and the ad told how "Electric Cars pass the door to all parts of the City." There was also a "Restaurant in the Same Building." Advertising was raised to the heights in the following list of statements in Italics:

Handsomely Furnished Rooms, Single or En Suite.
Centrally Located.
Strictly First-Class.
Special Attention to Transients.

In the 1895 Directory her son, Harry W. Ketchum, who had been a year old at the time of the 1860 census, is recorded as residing in the Metropolitan with his mother.

It was on May 2, 1907, in Alameda, California, that Elizabeth died of "Senility" and "Cerebral Hemorrhage."

---

[3] These quotes from the directories were kindly located and passed on to us by Thomas Fante of the California State Library, Sacramento.

The funeral was to take place in Sacramento two days later on May 4.[4] She had been living with another son, William Ketchum, a detective, at the time.

We are grateful to the California Historical Society Library in San Francisco for permission to publish this dynamic 1852 letter. It is part of their manuscript collection.

THE LETTER OF ELIZABETH KEEGAN

Sacramento Dec. 12th 1852.

My Dear Sister and Brother

Having written to you twice before and not receiving any answer I am beginning to feel impatient I do not attribute the non-receival of a letter to your not writing but to the errigularities of the mail. I will send this one by express and I sincerely hope it will reach its destination in safety and find you both in the enjoyment of that inestimable blessing good health as this leaves all at pressent.

Our journey across the plains was tedious in the extreme We were over four months coming it is a long time to be without seeing any signs of civilization, we left the Baptist Mission[1] on 3rd May and arrived in Marysville on 17th Sept. at which place we remained three weeks and then came on here. I

---

[4] Original Certificate of Death, California State Board of Health, Bureau of Vital Statistics, Sacramento, California. The person who gave the information on the death certificate signed her name as "Zuri" Hawks. This was Elizabeth Ketchum's daughter, Missouri, listed above in the 1860 census.

[1] This would probably have been the Shawnee Baptist Mission founded by Isaac McCoy in the summer of 1831. It was on the south side of the Kansas River just before it joined the Missouri in present Johnson County, Kansas, in Mission township. The Shawnee Baptist Mission was in operation until the mid-1850's. Louise Barry, *The Beginning of the West* (Topeka, 1972), many references, particularly on pages 204-205.

like this place very well. But I must first tell you something of the route. The first part of it is beautiful and
the scenery surpassing anything of the kind I have
ever seen large rolling praries stretching as far as
your eye can carry you covered with verdure. The
grass so green and flowers of every discription from
violets to geraniums of the richest hue. Then leaving
this beautiful scenery behind, you descend into the
woodland which is composed mostly of Oak and interspersed with creeks. some of them very large there
was one we crossed called the Big Vermillion whose
banks were so steep that our wagons had to be let down
by means of ropes. I rode through on horseback and
I had a fine opportunity to see and examine everything
of note on the way. We did not meet any sickness
nor see any fresh graves until we came in on the road
from St Joseph. I forgot to say in its proper place that
Kansas was our starting point which was on the 17th
of May [2] from that out there was scarsely a day but
we met six and not less than two fresh graves. We
were camped one night next to a train and they were
digging a grave for one of their companions. Another
night a man was taken ill and his cries of agony drove
sleep from many a pillow that night. All from Aseatic
Cholera in its worst form from the beginning to the
end of the journey. "Thanks be to God" we did not
have one sick amongst us. After we passed the first
desert our road was uniformly the same thing every
day passing across wide dreary wastes covered only
with sage and greenwood this last mentioned is a
small shrub resembling evergreen. This is mostly the
kind of road untill you arrive at the last desert. This

---

[2] This is at odds with the May 3rd reference above mentioned.

desert is very heavy and difficult of travel, it is forty-five miles across and must be performed in one stretch as there is no good water or grass on it. There is some boiling springs about the middle part of it you can see the steam a good distance off it was in the night when we passed them and I did not see them. I heard a woman and a boy were badly scalded. They went to look in at it and went to near and the earth caved in. The woman was so badly scalded that her life was dispared of. Many teams go in on this desert but few come out of it We had great difficulty to get across the desert. The mules we had in our carriage gave out when we were about ten miles in on it. We had to take a yoke of oxen out of large wagon which so weakened the other that when we were within about twelve miles of being across we were compeled to leave the carriage behind and put all our force to one. When we got across we laid up for a week and sent back for the carriage. We then started for to cross the mountains. The crossing of the plains is nothing to the crossing of the mountains. Some of them are so high and steep that you would scarsley think if you turned the cattle loose they could scarcely get up. We were one whole day getting up four miles having to double teams putting nine yoke to a waggon. After you cross the last of the mountains you descend into the Sacramento Valley long looked for by the weary emigrant. the heat can scarcely be enduered particularly so on the first coming down from the mountains. It is very cold on them. One night it froze so hard that water in the bucket had half an inch thick of ice. After we got down into the valley all our difficulties were at an end We met houses at every turn of the

road and flourishing farms, called here ranches   When
we came within five miles of Marysville we stopped at
one of the ranches and engaged ranching for our cattle.
We turned all our cattle out but one yoke. We then
went into Marysville like a flash.

We slept that night in our wagons and the next day
doffed our plains habilments and went down town,
how that word sent a thrill through my frame   no
one can picture the feelings of those who have come
that wearisome journey   the joy they feel at once more
beholding and mingling with their fellow creatures.
Church we had not to go to, but we thanked God
from the bottom of our hearts for preserving through
our trials and temptations,   on the following sunday
mass was celebrated in the house of a private family
at which we attended. Rev. Dr. Arcker [3] officiated. We
procured a house and the second night of arrival in
Marysville we slept inside of a house for the first time
since we left the states   We remained as I said before
in Marysville three weeks but hearing we could do
better here, we came on. We started in our wagons
again   came within four miles of the city   we could
not get a house to go into and had to remain camped
out on a ranch for three weeks. When the rains set in

[3] This was Father Acker about whom precious little is known. He min-
istered both at Marysville and at Downieville. Father Henry L. Walsh in
his *Hallowed Were the Gold Dust Trails, The Story of the Pioneer Priests
of Northern California* (Santa Clara, California, 1946) pp. 220-221, says
simply that "all accounts of his missionary labors have been lost or for-
gotten." T.H. Thompson and A.A. West in their *History of Yuba County*
(Oakland, 1889), p. 94, say of him, "Catholic Services were held here
[Marysville] in 1852, by Rev. Father Acker. While on his way to Downieville his mule was accidentally killed, and he stopped at the bar. The services were held in a canvas store belonging to James Lawrence. From the
collection taken the reverend gentleman was enabled to replenish his ward-
robe that had been seriously damaged by the accident."

on us, we started again and came in in the pouring rain. Altogether we are not two months inside of a house. You must know we do not have a drop of rain during nine months of the growing season. the raining season sets in about the first day of Nov. and terminates about the first of Feb. The rains are very heavy in the mountains, so that it raises the river very high. There is a slough on one side of the city which comes and goes with the tide Since the rains have set in it swollen produgrously so much that they apprehend an overflow like in "49. There is nothing to keep the water out but a clay enbankment. Our city has been visited with destructive fire which destroyed the principal part of the city, leaving only a few houses in the suburbs but it is almost built up again. I will tell you a little how houses are built here. they are all mostly frame, lined with furniture calico or canvas There is no such thing as plastering except in very few cases. There is no pavements here but plank walks. We have public places of amusement of every kind and description.

Dear Sister and Brother here I have written and thought over and over about filling this little book the task looks easy but it is hard to perform. I thought what I had to say would fill it full but here I have almost exhausted my store and it is half full. If I were writing to a friend I would feel obliged to offer some apology but as it is to a loving sister and brother I know they can more readily excuse the tediousness and sameness of its contents. I have not made any acquaintances so I cannot give you any account of the usages or manners of the people. Society is at a very low ebb though I must say there are some families here of the highest respectability, but they keep no company. One word to young ladies who are aspiring, that if they wish to be comfortable and enjoy society they had better stay where they are. Though I am one of the nondescripts who neither cares or is cared for, for I do not court society. All I ask is to live peaseful and retired that I can do here without any remarks. for never did you see a place where there are like remarks passed than there is in this place. If I was back in St Louis now, I would not come here, but as I am here the wealth of mines could not purchase me to return save to see you my dear Sister and brother and we may see each other e'er long sooner than was expected. I want you to write me such a long letter never was and write as I have done and do still write the first and fifteenth of every month regardless of any answer of the last.

I want you to let Kate O'Shea see this letter. Tell her that I would not encourage her to come here. For there is no encouragement for females here. Whatever there is for them to do in the states. Tell her if she was here and married I presume she could do well then. I had a grand seranade when we were on the ranch   Better voices and as good music as ever I heard. Some one I never knew untill I made their acquaintance in this place gave it. I would give anything to see Kate at the present moment. Tell her I mean to write to her a voluminous letter wherein I will let her know all the gossip. We have the greatest lot of chinese here that ever were. I cannot say that ever you seen, for you never saw one in your life. They are very smart clean and tidy set of people   I cannot say anything about intelligence for I do not know how to determine

by their features. Wether or not there is nothing han-
some about them but their feet and they have the
smallest as well as the prettiest feet I have ever seen.
There is every class of people here in California the
rich and poor of every nation of the world.

See what gold can do it brings men from all na-
tions here to this distance shore to make their fortune many go home worse than when they came
others have wealth countless wealth thus it is some
must fall that others may rise. It is night now and I
labored seslously at this writing I must lay by til
morning for I have to be up at half past four.

Dec 13th I am now endeavoring to think of something else to write but in vain I have well nigh exhausted my stock of news. This day is very cold and
raining hard. I fear we will be flooded the water
has risen frightfully. If it does overflow it will flood
the entire business part of the town. Though we need
not fear much for those who have little to lose The
whole of the lower part of Marysville called the plazer
is inundated when it rains here no ladies can put
their feet outside, those who are foolhardy to do it
have to wear boots that reach almost to their knees.
I must tell that mud and mire is so bad that it [is]
with the greatest difficulty wagons can get along. We
are in sight of the snowy peaks of the Sierra Nevada
mountains visible all the time. On the plains we met
snow several times and we had a severe hail storm on
4th July the largest I have ever seen. Little did I think
when I was learning and posing those mountains that
I would ever behold them. I also seen Fremonts Peak
down from whose snowy top runs the sweet water
river it has the coldest water in it I have ever tasted.

The only curiosity I thought worthy of note was singularity of hot and cold water almost within reach of each other There was some of them so hot that they make coffee in a few minutes. Though we are very greve and demure yet we laugh when we think of your singing "Bright Alvarta" and the turning of the word to play a trick on Kate. We have her along and you would scarcely know her she grone such a big girl. Girl did I say no she is a woman now in size. We are all altered for the better if getting fleshy is any sign. but Mother she has gone very thin so much has she altered you cannot say "My big Mother" she frets a great deal about not hearing from you both. I have written so many times that I have almost despaired of getting an answer if I do not receive an answer I shall certainly think something has happened. Mother particularly requests you both to write the 1st and 15th of every month without fail if you wish to keep her alive until she sees you both again. Mother also requests that if either of you or both are in need of anything just mention it in your letter and it shall be speedily and punctualy supplied. How much I wish to see you both. No one knows the strength of kindred love untill it is tried. Perhaps you would like to know the prices of articles of every kind and description sell here in this land of gold. Where it is said fortunes are made. It is true the money can be made easier than it could be made in any part of the states. But the thing is how to keep it after you make it. Expenses are so high I mean in the way of Eating and Drinking. Clothing is cheap enough. Flour ranges from $20 to 22 per cwt Potatoes 5 & 7¢ per lb. Sugar same. rents are extravagently high. for a house con-

taining two rooms you will have to pay $300 per
month   that is [in] the business part of town   however a little outside of the limits you will for a 1 story
frame hardly fit for cattle containing 2 rooms $75
per month   it will cost $800 to put up such a shanty
as I have named. Now you will see how money is
saved and spent in this far famed country. Every thing
is written and said about how much money you can
make here but not one word about expenses. Enough
have I said to weary the most patient reader. I think
I must give up writing but Mother and Kate cry at
me fill it   they will be glad to read it.

Mother Mary and Kate join in sending their most
affectionate love to you both   accept my Dear Sister
and Brother the sincere love of your affectionate sister.

E. J. C. Keegan.

Iowa to the "Land of Gold"

ᖷ Eliza Ann McAuley

INTRODUCTION

> Shortly after leaving the [Des Moines] river we were over-
> taken by an old man who rode along talking to us for some
> time. When he went home he told of a train he had seen. He
> said there was an old man, two boys, a lady and a little girl, Tom
> being the "old man" and I the "little girl." Five years difference
> in our ages. *Diary entry for April 15, 1852.*

This is a diary written by a 17-year-old girl: Eliza Ann
McAuley, born December 2, 1835.[1] The "old man," Tom,
who was 22 in 1852, was the acknowledged leader of their
wagon train and Eliza's older brother. The two boys were
Winthrop and Merrick Cheney, nephews of the J. P. Tif-
fanys' whom the travelers had visited on the first night of
their journey, in Mt. Pleasant. Winthrop was twenty, and
Merrick was 16 years of age.[2] The "lady" was Eliza's older
sister, Margaret, who was 28. They had left mother,
Esther McAuley, and sister Catherine (Kate), wife of
James Robinson, home in Mt. Pleasant, Henry County,
Iowa. Now they ventured forth over the plains to meet
their father, James McAuley, who had preceded them to
California. He was listed in the 1850 California U.S.
Census as living in Placerville, El Dorado County, "57
yrs. old, b. Ireland."

The young people started their long journey on April 7,
and they reached northern California in mid-September,
1852.

---

[1] Certificate of Death, California State Board of Health, Sacramento,
Eliza Ann Egbert.

[2] Much of the information here comes from the "Forward" of the typewritten copy of the diary. Some information was given, too, by Thomas R.
Macaulay, Reno, Nevada.

It was on April 24th that their party was joined by the "Eddyville company," as Eliza called it. These were William Buck and Oliver and Ezra Meeker. With Ezra were his wife, another Eliza, and a baby of six weeks named Richard.

It is our good fortune that this was the same Ezra Meeker who many years later, as a very ancient gentleman living in Seattle, would become a prime mover in the marking of the overland trails, and who would travel the overland route in 1924 by airplane from Seattle to Dayton, Ohio.[3]

In Meeker's book, *Ventures and Adventures of Ezra Meeker,*[4] he told of his family's overland journey in 1852 and described in soaring words the three McAuley overlanders:

> Thomas McAuley became by natural selection the leader of the party, although no agreement of the kind was ever made. He was, next to his maiden sister [Margaret], the oldest of the party, a most fearless man, who never lost his head, whatever the emergency, and I have been in some pretty tight places with him. While he was the oldest, I was the youngest of the men folks of the party and the only married man of the lot, and, if I do have to say it, the strongest and ablest to bear the brunt of the work. . . and so we got along well together until the parting of the way [to California and Oregon] came. This spirit, though pervaded the whole camp both with the men and women folks to the end.[5]

Meeker wrote that Margaret McAuley was "resolute and resourceful and almost like a mother to Eliza, his wife and their young baby." He wrote the following about the younger McAuley sister, Eliza:

> Eliza, the younger sister, a type of the healthy handsome

---

[3] "Ezra Meeker, the Pioneer," *Washington Historical Quarterly,* XX, No. 2 (April, 1929), p. 124.

[4] (Seattle, Washington, 1908).

[5] *Ibid,* p. 54.

American girl, graceful and modest, became the center of attrac-
tion upon which a romance might be written, but as the good
elderly lady still lives [1909], the time has not yet come, and
so we must draw the veil.[6]

Two years after her arrival in California, Eliza Ann
McAuley was married in Sacramento to Robert Seely
Egbert, who had been a Forty-Niner.[7] He had emigrated
to the Far West from Milford, Indiana, having been
born in New York State on November 17, 1825. He had
engaged in some mining in the Illinoistown area of Placer
County in the gold region. Then he went into freighting
of merchandise out of Sacramento to supply the mining
camps. For another period he contracted with the Central
Pacific Railroad to saw lumber and to build snow sheds
through the mountains. In later years the Egberts owned
a large ranch in Solano County in the Rio Vista area.

During the years immediately following their marriage,
the Egberts lived in Illinoistown.[8] They had seven children,
five boys and two girls. They are listed in a report at the
California State Library as Charles, Effie, Alvin, Walter,
Amy, Warren, and Norman, from oldest to youngest.[9]

Robert Seely Egbert died in Rio Vista July 20, 1896.
Eliza lived on many years. She died in Berkeley on November 16, 1919, at the age of 83 years, 11 months, and
14 days.[10]

For several years we thought that we would publish
this remarkable document as it appears in typescripts both
at the Library of the University of California at Los Angeles and at the California State Library in Sacramento.

[6] *Ibid,* p. 55.

[7] Notes on back of wedding picture supplied by Thomas William Macaulay, Reno, Nevada, also Nevada County, California, book of marriages,
Book 1, p. 9, Searls Historical Library, Nevada City, California.

[8] Thomas R. Macaulay, letter of April 1, 1984.

[9] Daughters of the American Revolution, "Records of Families of California Pioneers," VI (San Francisco, 1938), pp. 241-44.

[10] Certificate of Death, California State Board of Health, Sacramento,
Eliza Ann Egbert.

These are duplicate copies made by Warren Egbert, the next to the youngest son, in January 1935. He evidently sent copies to several libraries.

Then we had the good fortune to contact the Searls Historical Library in Nevada City, California, associated with the Nevada County Historical Society. Librarian Edwin L. Tyson wrote to tell us of a Thomas Macaulay of Reno, Nevada, who had visited them in connection with their family history.

Since that letter we have been in contact with the Thomas Macaulays in Reno. The elder, Thomas William Macaulay, now 88 years old, is the son of the Thomas who made the journey with his little sister, Eliza. His son is Thomas R. Macaulay. They have opened the Macaulay world to us. Incidentally, the Thomas Macaulays had changed the spelling of their former name, McAuley.

It turns out that they have the actual hand-written diary, 5" x 7", a little red book. These new friends have obliged us by comparing Warren Egbert's typewritten copy with the original and noting down all discrepancies, and there were mighty few. It is with the permission, nay the encouragement, of the Macaulay clan that the diary is here published as a major dynamic record by a bright young woman of the family's crossing of the plains in 1852.

Incidentally, they inform me that part of the way through the original diary Eliza ran out of ink, so the latter part of the journey is described with ink she made from plants along the way.

THE RECORD OF ELIZA ANN McAULEY

Wednesday, April 7th, 1852.   Bade adiew to home and started amid snow and rain for the land of gold. Our outfit consists of two light strong wagons drawn by oxen and cows, one yoke of heavy oxen for wheelers and a lighter yoke for leaders, with one or two yokes of cows between. We have two saddle horses and a drove of twenty dairy cows, a good sized tent and a sheet iron camp stove which can be set up inside, making it warm and comfortable, no matter what the weather outside.

We have a plentiful supply of provisions, including dried fruits and vegetables, also a quantity of light bread cut in slices and dried for use when it is not convenient to bake. Our stove is furnished with a reflector oven which bakes very nicely. Our clothing is light and durable. My sister and I wear short dresses and bloomers and our foot gear includes a pair of light calf-skin topboots for wading through mud and sand.

The first night we spend in Mt. Pleasant with our friends, Mr. and Mrs. Tiffany.

Thursday April 8th.   After a sad parting with Mother, sister Kate and numerous friends we made the real start of our journey.

Crossing Skunk River we stopped at the little town of Rome for the night, making but eight miles.

Friday, April 9th, 1852.   Roads very bad, but pleasant overhead until just as we were stopping for the night at a farmer's house it began to rain and continued all night.

Saturday, April 10th.   Cleared off about nine o'clock and we resumed our journey. Stopped for the night at Fairfield, the county seat of Jefferson County [Iowa].

Sunday, April 11th.   This morning the church bells were calling to worship, but we heeded not their gentle summons and hitching up our teams started onward, leaving church and Sabbath behind us. Road very bad all day. About three o'clock we came to an impassable mud hole in a lane. The only way was to lay down the fence and go through a field. While doing this the owner rushed out in great wrath, ordered us off and began laying up the rail fence, threatening all the while to go and get his gun and shoot us. Tom cooly laid his hand on the handle of his pistol, when the fellow suddenly changed his mind and went home and we left him to nurse his wrath and lay up his fence, which otherwise we should have put up as we found it. His object, it seems, was to compel us to stay over night at his place, and buy grain of him. About a mile farther on we stopped with an old Dutchman, who had plenty of grain, though the other one had told us there was no grain to be had for a long distance.

Monday, April 12, 1852.   Immediately after starting, we had Cedar Creek to cross. The ford is very bad, and the Dutchman very kindly volunteered the services of himself and two or three boys and horses to assist us in crossing. Margaret and I walked across on the mill-dam. Tonight we pitch our camp for the first time. Our campground is a beautiful little prairie, covered with grass and we feel quite at home and very independent.

Tuesday, April 13th.   This morning we passed through the old Indian Agency where we mailed a letter home. Soon after we struck the Des Moines River and traveled up the north bank, passing through Ottumwa, the prettiest place we have yet seen and have decided to come here and make our home when

we return from California with a fortune. Camped
this evening on the bank of a little stream. While we
were eating supper a lady who lives close by came in
to see, as she said, how campers did. On learning our
name she and her husband, who are Scotch people,
claimed acquaintance with our family in Scotland, and
insisted on our going to their house to spend the night.
They entertained us with the history of the McAuleys
in Scotland, which we had never known before.

Wednesday, April 14th.   Still travel up the Des
Moines River. Roads very bad. In one place we had
to double teams, take one wagon ahead a mile or so
and then return for the other wagon. While struggling
through the mud we were overtaken by two men from
Eddyville, Meeker and Buck,[1] who told us they intend
to start in a few days for Oregon. We camped at the
foot of a bluff about a mile from Eddyville.

Thursday, April 15th, 1852.   Crossed the Des Moines
at Eddyville. Ferriage seventy-five cents per wagon.
This is a pretty little place of some business. Shortly
after leaving the river we were overtaken by an old
man who rode along talking to us for some time. When
he went home he told of a train he had seen. He said
there was an old man, two boys, a lady and a little girl,
Tom being the "old man" and I the "little girl." Five
years difference in our ages. Camped on a little prairie
near timber. Grass is very good so we do not have
to buy grain for the stock.

---

[1] The "two men from Eddyville" were Ezra Meeker and William Buck.
Ezra Meeker became one of the most famous of the overlanders in later
life. This was to be the "Eddyville company" of 1852. Later Ezra wrote a
number of books about his own life with special emphasis upon his journey
over the trail and many references to the McAuleys. He pioneered in his
late life the marking of the trail. "Ezra Meeker the Pioneer," *Washington
Historical Quarterly*, xx, No. 2 (April, 1929) pp. 124-28.

Friday, April 16th.   Soon after starting we passed a
farm house where we traded the little white cow for
a larger one better suited for the journey. This is a
very pretty part of the country. The prairie is high
and rolling. Toward evening we passed the house of
the man who gave such a comical description of us.
He advised us to camp for a few days, as farther on the
grass is not good yet, and there is no grain to be had.

Crossed another Cedar Creek which was difficult
to ford, went a half mile farther and camped.

Saturday, April 17th, 1852.   Spent the day in camp,
washing and baking.

Sunday, April 18th.   Today we keep Sunday and write
letters home. The cattle have fine grass and are doing
well.

Monday, April 19th.   This morning Tom made me
practice target shooting with his pistol. I was very
expert at missing the mark, but managed to hit the
tree three times out of five.

Tuesday, April 20th.   Today the boys went out hunting and brought in a little squirrel for a pet.

Wednesday, April 21st.   A lazy day spent in camp.

Thursday, April 22nd.   Got up the teams to start, but
Mr. Slater [2] came along and wanted to go with us,
so we will wait a few days for him to get ready. He
has a pretty wife and a dear little baby.

Friday, April 23rd, 1852.   We all have the blues
today, having nothing to do.

---

[2] The only Slater we have found on record as having traveled over the
trail was S. S. Slater, whose name was inscribed without date on Independence Rock. Natrona Historical Society, Casper, Wyoming, *Independence
Rock, the Great Record of the Desert,* R. S. Ellison, Editor (Casper, 1930),
p. 37.

Saturday, April 24th. Margaret and I went over to
Slater's to help make his clothes. This evening the
men who overtook us in a mud hole near Eddyville
came to our camp for milk. They are Mr. Buck [3] and
the two Meeker brothers,[4] one of them having a wife
and six weeks old baby. They started today.

Sunday, April 25th. Today Margaret and I washed
and baked and Tom bought some corn to take along
for feed as we intend to start tomorrow. Mr. and Mrs.
Slater came over this evening and it rained so they
could not get home, so we all camped in the tent
together, making quite a tent full.

Monday, April 26th. This morning Solan Yeoman,
a neighbor of ours at home, came across our camp
while looking for his cattle. He tells us his child is
very sick. He laid by three weeks and is just starting
again. It has been drizzly all day and the road is awful.
Tom is so tired tonight that he can't whistle. We have
a beautiful camp ground near a little stream on the
prairie. The Yeomans camp with us and the Eddyville
company is about a mile back.

---

[3] Ezra Meeker described his dear friend, William Buck, as "One of
Nature's noblemen," *Ventures and Adventures of Ezra Meeker* (Seattle,
Washington, 1908), pp. 54-55. With soaring words he went on to speak
of him as "Always scrupulously neat and cleanly, always ready to cater to
the wants of his companions and as honest as the day is long, he has always
held a tender place in my heart. It was Buck who selected our nice little
outfit, complete in every part, so that we did not throw away a pound of
provisions nor need to purchase any. The water can was in the wagon, of
sufficient capacity to supply our wants for a day, and a 'sup' for the oxen
and cows besides. . ."

[4] Ezra and Oliver Meeker. Ezra was the one with the young wife, Eliza
Jane, whose maiden name had been Sumner. The baby boy, Richard, was
born in March, 1852. *Ventures and Adventures,* pp. 37-40. It is hard to find
the correct dates for these events. The *Washington Historical Quarterly*
article (*op. cit.*) says they were married on May 13, 1851, which leaves
some interesting questions unanswered.

Tuesday, April 27. Fair weather today and a good road. We camp this evening just west of a little town called Sheridan Point, on the highest hill that we can find. The rest of the company went down the creek about a mile and camped. Some of them visited us this evening. Before starting this morning, one of our best cows got mired and died in a few minutes.

Wednesday, April 28th. Traveled about four miles this morning when we came to Grave Hollow, so named from the circumstances of a woman and child being killed there. In coming down a steep hill a woman attempted to jump from the wagon with the child in her arms. Her dress caught in the wheel and she was drawn under and crushed to death. Here we came up with the Yoemans again. Their child died about daylight and they were just preparing a grave for it. We stopped and remained with them until after the burial.

The weather is fine and road good. We are traveling on a dividing ridge today, and in some places it is barely wide enough for the wagon road with ravines sloping off on each side, and again it widens out to the extent of several miles. In one place we crossed the vast chasm, stretching north and south as far as the eye can reach, leaving barely one place in which a wagon can cross. The country looks as if it had been torn asunder by some violent convulsion of nature. A singular feature of it is that on the eastern side is quite a growth of timber, while on the western side not a tree is to be seen. Tom's theory of it is, that when the boys were sent down to plant trees, they got to quarreling about the ground, so they divided it off and dug a trench between them, and the boys on one side planted trees, while the others pitched quoits on the prairie.

Thursday, April 29th. Slater did not start with us and has only this morning overtaken us. Today we came through a place called "The Narrows." It is a narrow strip of prairie, running for several miles between two bodies of timber. Here we traded one of our cows for another. Camped on White Breast.

Friday, April 30th. A very disagreeable day. A cold west wind blew all day. In making camp this evening, we placed the wagons so as to break the wind, and then by fastening each corner of the tent to a wagon wheel and putting an ox yoke and chain to each tent pin, we managed to keep it standing. The Meekers, not having any tent as yet, are camping with us tonight. One of their steers got snake-bitten on the nose this evening. It swelled very fast and gave the animal much pain, but an application of tobacco and whiskey soon relieved him. That is the only use our party makes of those articles.

Saturday, May 1st. Calm and pleasant again and roads good. Our friends Buck and the Meekers stopped at noon on a little creek for the rest of the day. We kept on the Grand River which by the way is a very small river. Passed through Mt. Pizgah, an old Mormon town, which is merely a collection of huts. Here we traded cows again.

Sunday, May 2nd. Spent the forenoon in washing and baking. At noon the rest of the party came up and we traveled on. Got to the half-way place between Eddyville and Cainsville [Kanesville]. Toward evening it began to threaten a thunder storm. By the time we stopped to make camp it was pouring rain. The boys set up the tent and held it over themselves, while Margaret and I each took a wagon and tried to keep things dry, but most of them got a pretty good soaking. For two hours it hailed and rained and blew a perfect gale. When it slacked up a little we got out the provision box and ate a cold supper. Then each one rolled up in a wet blanket and slept until morning.

Monday, May 3rd. It rained all night and fuel being scarce in this camp, we yoked up and traveled till noon, when we camped to dry our things.

Tuesday, May 4th. Pleasant weather and good road today. As we are crossing a large prairie, we have to haul our fuel for cooking.

Wednesday, May 5th. Today we crossed the East and Middle Nodaway. On the bank of the latter is a wayside directory, that is a tree with the bark peeled off and many names with the dates of those who have passed here written on it. Some of our boys left theirs on it also for a record. The road today has been quite hilly. Weather pleasant in the early part of the day, but this evening it is threatening rain.

Thursday, May 6th. Rained a little last night. Cloudy and misty this morning, but cleared off about ten o'clock. This afternoon we crossed the West Nodaway. This is a very bad creek to cross, the banks being high and steep. We got across safely and were very glad to leave it.

Friday, May 7th. It was quite foggy this morning and after it cleared away it was very warm and sultry. Shortly after noon we passed the grave of a child. It is an unusual sight here and there is a well beaten path to and from the grave. Some emigrant mother has left her little one behind.

This afternoon we crossed the East Fork of the Nishnabotna. This is a large stream, but we forded it without any difficulty. On the west bank is Indian Town, a mere collection of delapidated huts containing a few miserable looking inhabitants.

Saturday, May 8th. Got up this morning and found ten head of cattle missing. The boys found part of them at a Dutchman's camp and him trying to yoke them up. Good roads today with the exceptions of the crossing of some sloughs, which were miry.

Sunday, May 9th. Started early. Two miles travel brought us to the West Nishnabotna. Here we ferried the wagons and swam the cattle across. This evening we came to settlements again. Bought some corn at 20 cents per bushel and potatoes at 60 cents.

Monday, May 10th. Got to Kanesville [Iowa], four miles from the Missouri River about noon. After a short delay we went on to the river and camped as near the ferry as we could get. There are thousands of wagons waiting to be ferried over.

Tuesday, May 11th. Got up early and took the wagons down a little nearer the ferry, so as to take advantage of the first opportunity to cross.

A dreadful accident happened here today. A boat manned by green hands was taking a boat of cattle across. The cattle rushed to one end of the boat, causing it to tip and in a moment there was a mass of struggling men and animals in the water. One man was drowned. Another, who was a good swimmer, remembered that he had left his whip, and cooly turned around and swam back after it.

Wednesday, May 12th. Wind blew furiously today and the ferry could do very little business.

Thursday, May 13th. Wind still blowing very hard. Some of our men are using the boat that sunk with the cattle and are having the privilege of using it for a few days.

Friday, May 14th. Another ferry boat sunk today, but no lives were lost. The boys are busy raising the boat.

Saturday, May 15th. Got one of Meeker's wagons across and one of ours this morning, leaving the rest of our train on the eastern side. Mrs. Meeker and I crossed with them and were left alone to guard the wagons while the men were at work repairing the boat. Some Pawnee Indians came around, and getting impudent and troublesome, we pointed empty pistols at them and told them to "pucachee" or we would shoot them. The ruse succeeded and they soon left us. In the afternoon, having nothing else to do we amused ourselves by shooting at a mark. Had a light thunder shower this evening.

Sunday, May 16th. This morning was very cold and disagreeable, the wind blowing a perfect gale and the sand flying in clouds. After breakfast the boys took the wagons back from the river to a thicket of cottonwood and willow, where they are more sheltered.

The boys launched their boat this morning and have been ferrying all day, bringing the rest of our train across this evening. While we were getting supper, the Pawnee chief and twelve of his braves came and expressed a desire to camp with us. Their appetites are very good and it takes quite an amount of provisions to entertain them hospitably, but some willow boughs strewn around the camp fire suffices them for a bed.

Monday, May 17th. At break of day the Indians awoke us, singing their morning song. The old chief started the song and the others chimed in and it was very harmonious and pleasing. After breakfast when the boys went down to the river our guests went along and asked to be taken across. Margaret and Mrs. Meeker are washing today and I am to get dinner for the boys and take care of little Dickie.[5]

Tuesday, May 18th. Starting out this morning, we followed a bend of the river about three miles when we came to a beautiful little lake, with an island in the center covered with cottonwood trees. Here we found good grass and stopped for the day, as our cattle have fared poorly for several days. The wind blows a gale. Soon after we stopped, an old Indian riding an old pony came along, with a begging letter written by some white man, asking people to treat him well and give him something.

The boys went back to the river to run their ferry another day.

Wednesday, May 19th. The boys were late in getting to camp last night and some of them got lost in the bushes. We have now got a good "ready" and this morning made a fresh start. We soon came to the old Mormon winter quarters, where they stayed for two

---

[5] Richard Meeker, the baby boy.

years after leaving Nauvoo. There is a large graveyard here.

We found a quantity of wild mustard and picked a mess for greens. The road was quite rough this morning, but grew better toward evening. We found a good spring of water and use willow roots for fuel.

Thursday, May 20th.   Quite cool today. Road good. We passed over some beautiful prairie, which reminds of the prairies at home. There were a few scattering cottonwoods along the sloughs and river banks. Today we passed some Indian burial grounds, a large one with a small one on each side. The large one had been dug into, so that we could see the skeleton in a sitting posture. At two o'clock we came to Elk Horn River and had to wait about three hours to be ferried across. After crossing we drove about a mile, crossed a very bad slough and camped. There is a large camp here and there are many Indians around.

Friday, May 21st.   Three of our cows were missing this morning, notwithstanding we had a guard out. Last night some of the Indians talked and traded with the emigrants to attract their attention, while others drove away their cattle, and as the night was dark and rainy they had a good chance.

We traveled through a drizzling rain till noon, when we struck Platte River and camped. There is a very large camp here and grass is scarce. Here we fell in with the Sand Hill boys, Mead [6] and Crass from Wisconsin. They have a light wagon and two yokes of cattle that can travel as fast as horses.

Saturday, May 22nd.   Weather clear and pleasant.

---

[6] There was an H. H. Mead who inscribed his name on Independence Rock, *Independence Rock*, (*op. cit.*), p. 34.

Road good with the exception of sloughs, which are very bad. We now travel up the north side of Platte River. On our right stretches a beautiful rolling prairie, on our left flow the muddy waters of the Platte. The north side is destitute of timber, while the south side has a light growth of cottonwood. In places there are steep bluffs with a stunted growth of cedar on them.

The camp is full of Indians this evening, who under the guise of trading buffalo robes for blankets are watching opportunities to steal.

Sunday, May 23rd. Weather warm and pleasant. Roads bad. We had several deep, miry sloughs to cross. Two miles travel brought us to Shell Creek, which is thirty-one miles from the Missouri River. Here is a good bridge built by some emigrants, but the Indians have taken possession of it and demand toll.

This afternoon we met about a hundred Pawnees, returning from a hunt with sixty-seven ponies, laden with furs and dried meat. They passed by our little band of two wagons and three young boys with a civil "howdydo" but meeting the rest of our train, three wagons and eight men, they relieved them of most of their clothing, knives and tobacco and stampeded a team with Mrs. Ballard in the wagon.

Monday, May 24th. Pleasant weather and good roads today. About nine o'clock we came to Loup Fork of the Platte, but as the ferry is unsafe we decided to travel upstream, until we can ford.

Tuesday, May 25th. Today we crossed several tributaries of the Loup Fork. This afternoon we passed a Sioux village in ruins, also a stockade fort, probably used by trappers years ago. Found no grass for the cattle tonight, as this is a late burn. Mosquitoes in abundance.

Wednesday, May 26th. Started before breakfast and traveled a mile when we came to a ford, thirty-two miles from the ferry on Loup Fork. Here we stopped and got breakfast, while the boys examined the stream and decided to cross. Had to raise the beds of the first wagons, but as the bottom is quicksand, it soon raised high enough by the sand being stirred up. Went out a mile and stopped to let the cattle graze and dry out things, which got wet in crossing. Started at two o'clock traveled five miles and camped.

Thursday, May 27. Warm and pleasant. Traveled this forenoon over low wet prairie. At noon found a little stream and some grass. This afternoon there is nothing but sand hills. We camped among these without a stick of wood or a drop of water, except what we brought along.

Tom and Slater went out hunting and shot an antelope but did not get it. They found some prickly pear and a prairie dog village. They brought in a prairie dog, the first we have seen.

Friday, May 28th. Soon after starting we came to a ford of strong alkali water, which our cattle, being very thirsty drank of and it came nearer killing some of them. It also makes their feet sore and we have to make leather shoes for them. After the sand hills came a marsh, in which heavy wagons would sink to the hub. Found good grass at noon. This afternoon we crossed two creeks, both rather miry. Road sandy most of the day. This morning we camped near Wood River.

Saturday, May 29th. Crossed Wood River. Fair

weather and good roads. Camped early on a branch of the Platte, a fine little stream of pure cold water. Here we came up with the Sand Hill boys. They left us several days ago.

Sunday, May 30th. There is a very large camp here and most of them are remaining for the day. There was preaching this afternoon and it seems more like Sunday than any since we left home. It has been very hot today. We hitched up about four o'clock and traveled six miles.

Monday, May 31st. Road good today. Camped in the open prairie tonight. There is some prickly pear near our camp, the first we have come to, and a new variety of cactus which is in bloom.

We all are gathered in Ezra's [Meeker] tent this evening and had a merry time.

Tuesday, June 1st. Dock Ballard and I went horseback riding this morning down to the river where we saw a train that had just crossed from the south side of the Platte. They report a great deal of sickness and a scarcity of grass on that side, so we feel that we did well to stay on the north side. We saw a fresh grave, the first one since leaving the Missouri River. Nooned on Elk Creek where the water is scarce and bad. Tonight the feed is scant too and our poor stock are faring badly. We use buffalo chips for the first time. Two of our party went out hunting this morning and have not returned. Today we met three teams taking the back track. One of the men died and the others got discouraged even this far out.

Wednesday, June 2nd. Struck Platte River this afternoon and found a well of good water. This afternoon

we found a spring of the best water we have had on
the road. It has been exceedingly hot today and the
road is so dusty that we were obliged to stop often
and water the teams. As there was the appearance of
a storm we camped early, though the water is scarce.
Presently the storm broke in all its fury. I had lain
down on a pile of bedding in the tent and when I
awoke the bed was nearly afloat, and two of the boys
were trying to hold the tent up. Finding the attempt
useless, they abandoned the tent and all took to the
wagons, which were anchored to stakes driven in the
ground.

Thursday, June 3rd.   This morning we found every
tent in camp and one wagon blown over. In consequence of the storm we made a late start. Today we
have passed a number of fresh graves. Grass tolerably
good tonight.

Friday, June 4th.   Our hunters came in before breakfast. Their friends had been very anxious about them.
They saw no buffalo, but brought in a couple of stray
ponies they had found.

Travelled but a short distance when we came to
some high sand bluffs. We climbed to the top of these
and had a fine view of the River and of the teams on
the south side. We have found a new plant which is
very beautiful. The stem has a waxy appearance, with
three smooth peach colored leaves clustering together
in a canaidal [conoidal?] shape, enclosing a little
berry or seed.

At noon we crossed Skunk Creek and left the road,
which goes around by the foot of the bluffs, and took
a cut-off across Pawnee Swamp. This in high water

is impassable, but at present is dry and filled with a luxuriant growth of grass. At the upper end of the swamp is Pawnee Spring, a very large spring of fine water. Camped this evening on Platte River, but found no grass.

Saturday, June 5th.   Went ahead two miles and found some grass. stopped to graze the cattle and get break-fast. Crossed two creeks this forenoon. About three o'clock a light shower came up and we stopped until it was over. While waiting we witnessed a buffalo chase. Three of those noble animals were slain and in the fray a valuable dog was severely wounded.

The rain over we again started, crossing two creeks. Good grass tonight.

Sunday, June 6th.   Crossed two more creeks and then came to steep, sandy hills, among which are many buffalo wallows. These hills are quite barren and sup-port neither animal or vegetable life, except a little sand lizard. Later, we found giant cactus and several other new plants. One of our men killed two deer. Crossed two more creeks and camped for the night. Had to drive the cattle back to the hills for grass. While out with the cattle the boys *Caught a little antelope and brought it to camp.*

Monday, June 7th.   Crossed three creeks in ten miles and struck into sandy hills again. At noon came into the river bottom again, but the road is still sandy. Wind blowing hard today.

Tuesday, June 8th.   Crossed three creeks in about nineteen miles and take to the hills again for a few miles, then descend and cross another creek and come to Lone Tree. This is the only tree for two hundred

miles on the north side of the River. We are now
travelling from twenty to thirty miles a day.

Wednesday, June 9th.   Traveled about two miles and
camped on Castle River until three o'clock.

This afternoon we met an express to "the states" and
wrote a letter home and sent back by it. Camped this
evening by a prairie dog village. They are very active
little fellows, and look very saucy sitting up in their
doorways.

Thursday, June 10th.   Had to cross a very bad alkali
swamp and had to rush the cattle through to keep
them from drinking the water. When they get alkalied
the remedy is a good dose of whiskey. After noon the
road was sandy. We had to camp without any grass.

Our antelope, Jenny, is a great pet in camp and is
equally fond of Margaret and me. She bleats and cries
if either one is away from her.

Friday, June 11th.   Hitched up at daylight and traveled six miles before we found grass for the cattle.
We then stopped to get breakfast and let the cattle
feed. Tom goes out on horseback and looks for a camping place where there is grass and water. This afternoon we passed "The Ancient Bluff Ruins" on the
south side of the River, a picturesque mass of rocks,
resembling castles and fortifications in ruins. Here a
crumbling turret, there a bastion, and in other places
portions of a wall, with portholes, making the illusion
complete. Near this we find wild southern wood, rue,
tansy and several other garden herbs in their wild
state, also some beautiful carnations and roses. At
noon we camped in sight of the "Court House" rock
on the south side. By the aid of our spy glass we can

see plainly the cracks and crevices in the walls of the "Court House."

Saturday, June 12th. Traveled over low sand bluffs again. At noon we were nearly opposite the "Chimney Rocks" also on the south side of the River. Camped near the River. Buffalo chips scarce and no other fuel to be had.

Sunday, June 13th. Traveled along the River until we were in sight of the "Capitol Hills" or "Scott's Bluffs." They received the later name from a tragical incident connected with the place. A company returning from Oregon in 1846 had got this far when one of their number, a Mr. Scott, was unable to travel further, and they being short on provisions, he begged them to go on and leave him to his fate, which they were reluctantly compelled to do and the poor fellow was left. These legends are related in our guide book.

Weather cool this morning, but got very warm toward noon. Camped on Spring Creek, a stream abounding in fine trout. Had good grass and water but no fuel. In such cases our dried bread comes in very handy, with milk from the cows. We have a tin churn in which the morning's milk is put and by noon or evening we have a nice little pat of butter and some good buttermilk.

Monday, June 14th. Road very bad for two miles. After that it became better. Camped this evening near the Platte. Good grass and some timber. Had a fine shower this evening.

Tuesday, June 15th. The rain laid the dust and improved the road very much. This morning we met some Indians, the first in four hundred and fifty miles.

They are of the Sioux tribe and are much better looking than any we have seen. About three o'clock we
came opposite Fort Laramie. Some of the boys went
over to the fort to mail letters. There are two or three
nice looking houses in the fort, the first we have seen
since leaving the Missouri River. Traveled about four
miles further and camped. Here the River becomes
narrow and swift.

Wednesday, June 16th. Early today came to steep
rocky hills covered with a growth of scrubby cedar
and pine. About ten o'clock found a little spring at
the foot of a hill where we stopped for dinner and
at four o'clock descended to the River again where
we camped, all tired enough.

Thursday, June 17th. Road hilly but not so steep as
yesterday. The country looks very wild and rough.
In the evening found a fine spring and good grass.

Friday, June 18th. Weather very warm; road smooth;
hills long but not very steep. We can see the Black
Hills and Laramie Peak to the left, across the River.
As our guide book crosses to the south side of the River
at Fort Laramie, and we keep up the north side, we
are following the trail without knowing what is ahead
of us. Stopped at noon in a very wild looking place
where the surrounding hills, worn by torrents of rain,
resemble buildings in ruins. Struck the River about
four o'clock, where we watered the cattle and took in
some water for the night, then crossed some bluffs and
camped in a little valley with good grass.

Saturday, June 19th. Soon struck the River and good
road again. Laramie Peak has appeared to be directly
opposite us for several days.

Sunday, June 20th. Road very hilly and sandy. While the wagons skirted around the bluff, Margaret and I cut across and saw many new plants and curiousities and had quite an adventure. Following carelessly along a gulch that had been washed out, we soon found ourselves hemmed in by perpendicular walls, from six to fifteen feet high. We had either to turn back and retrace our steps or go on and run the chance of getting out. We chose the latter and after following it for half a mile found a place where we could scramble out just before it terminated abruptly in the River. Tonight we heard that the body of a woman, who had been murdered, was found hidden in a clump of rose bushes near where we had been. Camped both noon and at night on the River, but grass is scarce.

Monday, June 21st. Shortly after starting we caught up with the Sand Hill boys. They left us on Thursday last, and yesterday lay by waiting for us. Road sandy all day. Grass scarce.

Tuesday, June 22nd. Very heavy sandy roads. No grass at noon. About three o'clock a shower came up. At the same time we found some good grass, so we camped for the night. When it cleared off above, one could still see the clouds below us in the valley. It was a grand, and to me, a novel sight.

Wednesday, June 23rd. Cool and cloudy. At noon we came to the ferry on Platte River, which is one hundred and fifty miles from the fort. This is an average of over twenty-one miles a day. The trail crosses here and we now have the use of our guide book again. Until noon the road was very sandy, but the sand was so wet it was not heavy wheeling. This afternoon the road is hard and smooth and we had a long but not very steep hill to climb. Found good grass and water where we expected none. There is a great deal of mineral and alkali water about here. We heard today the particulars about the tragedy across the River. There were two men and a woman concerned. The woman's husband attacked the other man and stabbed him to death. He was tried, convicted and hung, and the woman was sent back to the fort.

Thursday, June 24th.   Were delayed a few hours this morning by rain. During this time some of the boys went out and killed three buffalo, and brought in what meat they could carry. This is the first buffalo meat that we have had. Hilly road today. Camped tonight at Willow Springs. Grass and water good, but fuel scarce. That is, very few willows.

Friday, June 25th.   Cool and cloudy. Rained a little at noon Sandy road this afternoon. Traveled twenty-one miles and camped at Independence Rock. This name was given it by Fremont who arrived here on the fourth of July, on his first exploring expedition. His party climbed to the top of the rock and partook of a fine dinner, which the ladies of St. Louis had prepared for them for this occasion. The name seems in every way appropriate. It is an immense granite rock, from six-hundred to seven-hundred yards long and one hundred and twenty to one-hundred and fifty yards wide, rising from the level plain, entirely isolated and independent of any other rock or hills. It is almost covered with the names of emigrants, chiseled in the rock or painted on its surface, with the date of their arrival. We saw the names of some of our friends, who had passed here in 1849 and 1850.

Saturday, June 26th. Crossed the Sweetwater one mile from the rock. Here we saw the graves of Mrs. Cole's and Mrs. Dart's babies, two sisters, acquaintances of ours, on their way to Oregon. Five miles farther we came to the Devil's Gate. This was also named by Fremont's party. It is a gorge through which the river has cut its way through perpondicular walls of rock about four hundred feet high. It is a mile west of the road and we went over to see it. Beyond this the valley widens out and is covered with luxuriant grass as far as the eye can reach We could see rain on the mountains on each side of us. But we got none. Traveled about sixteen miles today and camped early to do some washing.

Sunday, June 27th. Soon after starting this morning one of our team cows gave out from the effect of alkali water. We gave her salt pork and vinegar and she soon recovered sufficiently to travel again. Made twenty-one miles today. Poor grass tonight.

Monday, June 28th. Sandy road. We met a returning Californian with papers for sale. We bought a copy of the El Dorado News for fifty cents. Heard of some mountain fever today. No grass nor water tonight.

Tuesday, June 29th. Started before breakfast, traveled five miles, when we came to grass and water and camped till noon. Started after dinner and crossed the Sweetwater three times. Traveled about twelve miles and camped on the River. Tolerably good grass. Very windy today.

Wednesday, June 30th. Made thirteen miles this forenoon. Very rough, hilly road, and windy and dusty. Traveled only 3 miles this afternoon and camped on

McAchrem's branch of the Sweetwater. There is still snow in this hollow. Grass good and water plenty. While the boys were out with the cattle this evening, the mare Fan was suddenly found to be missing. We suspect a set of traders that are stopping here.

Thursday, July 1st. Traveled on seven miles to the River and camped while Tom went out to hunt for the missing animal. Found good grass. Wind blew hard all afternoon.

Friday, July 2nd. Remained in camp. Tom returned without Fan, but found where she had been secreted. We have heard of a company ahead that had taken her from the traders or thieves.

Saturday, July 3rd. Tom started again in pursuit. We moved on, crossing Sweetwater for the last time. Ate luncheon on the south pass of the Rocky mountains. Altitude seven thousand, four hundred feet, but the ascent is so gradual, that one scarcely knows when one is at the summit. The headwaters of the streams flowing eastward to the Mississippi and those flowing westward to the Pacific are but a few feet apart. Traveled twenty-four miles today and camped on Dry Sandy Creek. Got a little water and no grass.

Sunday, July 4th. Hitched up and went ahead two miles and found a little dry grass and stayed to get breakfast and let the cattle feed. Four miles brought us to the forks of the Salt Lake and California roads. We took the Sublett cut-off, leaving Salt Lake to the south. Made eighteen miles today and camped on Big Sandy. Had to drive the cattle about six miles toward the hills for grass. It has been so windy and dusty today that some times we could scarcely see the length of the team, and it blows so tonight that we cannot set the tent or get any supper, so we take a cold bite and go to bed in the wagons. The wagons are anchored by driving stakes in the ground and fastening the wagon wheels to them with ox chains. Merrick,[7] Margaret and I are the only ones in our camp tonight. Winthrop P.[8] and Slater are out about six miles with the cattle, and Tom – we know not where he is.

We came near losing our pet antelope this evening. As she was frisking about the camp, a man from another camp was about to shoot her, thinking she was a wild one. She ran to another camp where a woman got hold of her and held her, and would scarcely believe that she belonged to me, though the poor little thing was struggling to get away and bleating piteously for me. Finally she got away and came bounding to me and followed me home.

Monday, July 5th. Just after daylight Tom came in. He got into camp last night but it was so dark he could not find our wagons. As we have a fifty mile desert to cross we lay by today to recruit the teams for it. Heard of our mare on the Salt Lake road and Tom started after her. Still very windy, cold and disagreeable.

Tuesday, July 6th. Started about noon, crossed Big Sandy and traveled part of the night before stopping to camp. Just before dark a thunder shower came up, which laid the dust and improved the road very much.

Wednesday, July 7th. Started before daylight and traveled until sunrise, when we found good grass and

7 Merrick Cheney. "Forward" to typescript of the diary, written by Warren Egbert, Knights Landing, California, January, 1935.
8 Winthrop P. Cheney, brother to Merrick. *Ibid.*

stopped to get breakfast. Road today rather hilly and sandy. At sundown we arrived at Green River, fifty miles from Big Sandy. In getting to the River we have to climb a very steep hill, and then slide down the other side of it. Green River is a very pretty stream, rather narrow and with a very swift current, which we have to ferry across. Ferriage, six dollars per wagon.

Tom met us this evening with the horses, our own and another, which he stole from the horse theives. He found them very cunningly hidden in a small, open space surrounded by thick brush. He came up the River from the Mormon ferry. He thinks the Fort Bridger road much better than this.

Tuesday, July 8th.   Started out from our camp about two miles below the ferry. We had to climb a very sharp bluff. On the bluff along the road are thousands of names cut in the soft rock. Among the rest we noticed that of Asa Rodgers, a neighbor of ours, dated June 8th and McCully and Linn [9] of New London dated June 11th and of course left our own record. Traveled about thirteen miles to Lost River and turned down it about three miles to camp. Good grass and water.

Friday, July 9th.   Remain in camp today. Warm and pleasant once more. There was a heavy dew last night.

Saturday, July 10th.   Sold one of the steers that has got lame for three dollars. Traveled three miles back to the road and three more to the ford of Lost River. Rather hilly road. Weather warm and pleasant. Camped near a pine grove ten miles from Lost River. Just at dusk our old traveling companions Buck and

9 J. I. and C. E. Linn inscribed their names on Independence Rock on June 15, 1852. *Independence Rock* (*op. cit*), p. 33.

the Meekers came up and camped with us. We left them on Platte River and have not seen them since. Ezra has been very sick with the mountain fever, but is better now. O. P. also has been sick, but is now about well. They report a great deal of sickness back.

Sunday, July 11th. Very rough, hilly road. Made only nine miles this forenoon and nooned on Crow Creek. This afternoon traveled seven miles to Ham's fork of Bear River. This is a very pretty stream but quite small. Good grass.

Monday, July 12th. We have a very long, steep mountain to cross, two miles to the summit. In places it is very steep and difficult and we see the wrecks of several wagons and carriages, that have broken down in attempting it. The descent is quite easy. This afternoon we passed through a beautiful grove of fir and quaking aspin. Shortly after that we had some very steep rough road, mostly descending. Crossed Stony Creek. This is half way between the Missouri River and Placerville. Three miles from this we strike the Bear River Valley. We camped in the hills just at the edge of the valley. Grass and water tolerably good. Mosquitoes abundant.

Tuesday, July 13th. Traveled six miles today and camped on Bear River. Here is splendid feed, the cattle wading in wild oats up to their eyes, while we have fun making pop corn candy. Margaret is baking cookies, but the boys steal them as fast as she can bake them. Soon after camping, we saw a company of returning Californians, but they were too far off to get to speak with them. We are having a gentle shower this evening, while it is raining hard in the mountains around us.

Wednesday, July 14th. Have to go through a miry swamp this morning to get to the road. After traveling about two miles we came to fork roads. The right hand goes up around the mountain and crosses Smith's Fork and four branches; the left, keeps down the river bottom, and crosses Smith's Fork of the Bear River on a toll bridge which was just completed this morning. We took the latter, paying fifty cents a wagon toll. After leaving the bridge we saw to the right a very singular looking mountain. At first it appeared like a sugar loaf, but on coming nearer we found it to be connected to the main ridge. The rains have washed its sides in regular ridges and so true and even are they that it looks more like a work of art than a freak of nature. Road good, grass fine. Plenty of trout and other fish.

Thursday, July 15th. Traveled ten miles today and camped on Bear River. Just before coming to the River we had the hardest mountain to cross on the whole route. It was very steep and difficult to climb, and we had to double teams going up and at the summit we had to unhitch the teams and let the wagons down over a steep, smooth sliding rock by ropes wound around trees by the side of the road. Some trees are nearly cut through by ropes. Rained a little this evening. Mosquitoes very bad. The boys fished awhile and then took a ramble around the country and discovered a pass, by which the mountain can be avoided by doing a little road building.

Friday, July 16th. The boys took another look at the pass and concluded to stop and make a road around the mountain.

Saturday, July 17th. The Meekers resume their

journey to Oregon, Mr. Buck remaining with us. We part with them with much regret.

Sunday, July 18th. Notwithstanding it is Sunday, the boys continue their work and have hired some men to assist for a day or two, to cut brush. In the afternoon there was the appearance of a heavy rain but it all went around us.

Monday, July 19th. We have settled down to regular housekeeping and this being Monday it is of course washday. In cutting a way for the road, the boys find thickets of wild currants. There are several varieties, the black, the red and the white. The boys cut the bushes, some of them ten feet long and loaded with ripe currants, which we strip off and make into jelly, currant wine and vinegar, dried currants and currant pie.

Tuesday, July 20th. Had a light shower last night. Today is extremely warm. Our camp is in a pretty little valley, with the hills on one side and Bear River on the other. The Indians brought fish today to trade for bread.

Wednesday, July 21st. We have met with a sad loss today. Our pet antelope, Jennie, was playing around the camp and the dogs belonging to a large camp of Indians espied her and gave chase. The Indians tried to rescue her, but could not. They then offered to pay for in skins and robes. We told them it was an accident and they were not to blame, but they immediately packed up to go, saying they were afraid the men would shoot them when they came.

At dinner time a very intelligent Indian named Poro, came to our camp. He says he has been to the Missouri River and seen steamboats and explained by signs what they were like. He seems to understand the customs of the whites very well. His name is Poro. In the afternoon he came again, bringing his little boy, four or five years old. He interpreted a number of Indian words for us.

Thursday, July 22nd. Very hot today. Mosquitoes troublesome in the evening. The Indians are very friendly and visit us often. We have engaged Poro to make us some moccasins, or rather his squaw is to make them.

Friday, July 23rd. Poro visited us again today and brought his friend Pavee to see us.

Saturday, July 24th. We had a call this morning from Iowa neighbors, John and Robert Wallace. Moved the camp up the River about three miles on the road and camped in a beautiful place on the river bottom. We have eight or nine hands today to work on the road. The boys want to get it finished to save people from having to cross that dreadful mountain and also that we may get away sooner.

Sunday, July 25th. This is the most like Sunday of any day since we left home, and we feel very much at home here. Old Poro came along about ten o'clock and stayed a long time, teaching us his language. It pleases him very much to see us try to learn it. There are a great many geese and cranes about the river.

Monday, July 26h. Wash day.
Tuesday, July 27th. Ironing and baking today. Poro brought our moccasins. They are very neatly made. His little boy came with him. I offered a gay plaid shawl in payment for the moccasins. Poro was quite pleased with it and inclined to accept it, but refered

the matter to the boy. He talked to his father, who explained that he thought it was very pretty but he could not eat it. He wanted bread and sugar, so we gave him what he wanted.

Wednesday, July 28th. Poro came again today and brought a nice mess of service berries. He has been counting the "sleeps" before we go away, and regrets our going very much. He said today, "One sleep more and then wagons go away to California," and we have parted with white folks that did not regret so much.

Thursday, July 29th. Poro came twice today to bid us goodbye and feels very sad about our going. After dinner we started on, leaving Thomas and Mr. Buck to remain on the road a week or two to collect toll and pay the expenses of making it. Traveled thirteen miles and found good grass but no wood nor water.

Friday, July 30th. Started early and had good road. Crossed several fine streams. Made twelve miles this forenoon and camped on a small stream near a spring. Pretty good grass. This was according to the guide book, the last good water for seventeen miles, but we found several good springs this afternoon and have the best of grass and water to camp on. Our teams are so well rested and recruited that they travel right along. Had a light shower this evening. Mosquitoes very bad. Made twenty-two miles today.

Saturday, July 31st. About eleven o'clock we came to Soda Springs. Here are many curious formations, caused by the overflow of water from the springs. Six miles beyond we passed the Oregon and California roads. The Oregon road appears to be traveled much the more. Twenty-two miles today. Some grass but no water.

Sunday, August 1st.   Rained a little last night which wet the grass and laid the dust. Traveled seven miles and came to a beautiful spring branch. After watering here we drove on for a mile and a half and stopped for noon. Grass rather scarce. Shortly after starting again a heavy thunder storm came up and we stopped in the shelter of some bushes. The rain made the road slippery and when we started again it was with difficulty that we got to the top of the hill. Seventeen miles today. Drove the cattle across a creek to pasture.

Monday, August 2nd.   Took in a man who stayed with us last night to help drive the cattle. He is from Ohio and his name is Dougherty. He gave his part of the team to his partner, who has a family to bring through, and had been walking until he became so footsore and tired he could go no further, so we furnished him a horse to ride and he helps to drive the loose cattle. There was a heavy dew last night. Weather fine today. Excellent grass all along the road this fornoon. We traveled ten miles and nooned on a branch of Panack [Bannock] River. Had a long but not very steep hill to climb this afternoon. We met a wagon from Salt Lake selling vegetables and treated ourselves to a supply.

Good camping place this evening.

Tuesday, August 3rd.   Road rather hilly this morning. Nooned on a little creek where there are two trading posts, having among other things fresh vegetables for sale. We bought some potatoes at twelve and a half cents a pound. We here enter upon a stretch of twenty-five miles without water. Traveled nineteen miles today.

Wednesday, August 4th.   Very hilly road this morning. One very bad hill to descend. Found good grass at noon. We stopped about sundown, got supper and rested awhile and then drove until ten o'clock when we got through to a beautiful spring and good grass.

Thursday, August 5th. Lay by until noon, then hitched up and traveled about ten miles and camped on the top of a mountain. We carried water along from a spring about a mile back, and found plenty of good dry grass on the mountain side. Two packers are staying with us tonight. A heavy rain has laid the dust nicely.

Friday, August 6th, 1852. Weather pleasant and road good, though somewhat hilly. Had a very bad creek to cross and came very near upsetting a wagon. Traveled fourteen miles this forenoon and found but little grass. This afternoon traveled six miles and camped early on Sinking Creek. Had fine grass.

Saturday, August 7th. Fine roads today. Traveled two miles and crossed Sinking Creek again and went on to east branch of Raft River, twelve miles. Good grass here. This afternoon we passed the junction of Fort Hall and California roads. Traveled twenty-one miles today and found a good camping place tonight.

Sunday, August 8th. Traveled eleven miles and camped for the rest of the day. Found good grass and water.

Monday, August 9th. Traveled eight miles when we entered Pyramid Circle. This is one of the greatest curiosities on the road. In some places a piller rises to a height of one hundred and fifty feet, with smaller ones piled on the top and sides, looking as though a breath of air would hurl them down. These pyramids are of various colors. The sides have been washed by the rains in all manner of fantastic shapes, giving the place a most romantic and picturesque appearance. The circle is five miles long and three miles wide, level within the wall around and entirely surrounded by these pyramids or cliffs except an inlet at the east end of about fifty yards, and an outlet at the western end just wide enough to permit the wagons to pass through. The rocks are covered as far up as one can reach or climb, with names of emigrants. We left ours with date in a conspicuous place for the boys behind. We saw the names of some of our acquaintances who passed here two years ago.

Tuesday, August 10th, 1852. Had some very rough road today. Came near getting our wagons smashed coming down the mountain to Goose Creek. Traveled fifteen miles today and camped on Goose Creek. Good grass and water.

Wednesday, August 11th. Fine road this morning with the exception of some very bad sloughs. Several wagons in the train were broken in crossing them. Good grass at noon but had to travel until after dark to find any tonight. Made about twenty-four miles today.

Thursday, August 12th, 1852. Windy and dusty. Road hilly. No grass at noon. About three o'clock struck Thousand Spring Valley. At the head of the valley is a fine spring, but after a few miles we could find neither grass nor water. Made about twelve miles. Got some fresh beef tonight.

Friday, August 13th. Traveled until eleven o'clock when we found some excellent grass and a little water.

Two or three little birds have followed us all the morning, and when we camped came chirping fearlessly about the camp. Started at two o'clock. Traveled thirteen miles today. Grass good but water poor.

Saturday, August 14th. Soon after starting we met the Indian agent with two carriages and seven or eight horsemen. They gave encouraging news about the grass and water ahead. About ten o'clock we came to the boiling springs. Here several large springs boil up in the middle of the valley, forming a large stream at a temperature of one hundred and seventy degrees with a nauseous, sickening smell. A distressing accident occurred here about two hours before we arrived. Two brothers, who had been out hunting, stopped here to wait for their train. As they were sitting on the ground, they heard a gun fired off across the stream, and thinking there were Indians about, one of them sprang to his feet, at the same time catching up his gun, which was lying on the ground before him, with the muzzle toward him and it went off, the ball passing through his lungs. He was still alive but sinking rapidly when we left. We gave them all the fresh water we had, which was all that we could do for them, as their train had come up.

By noon we reached the end of the valley where we found two good springs, but no grass. Passed through a canon and again over the hills for eight miles and again struck a valley, which is covered with the best of grass that looks like ripe grain. We camped here near some good sulphur springs. There are a great many camped here and a merrier set I never saw. Just after dark we were treated to a variety of barnyard music in various parts of the camp. Roosters crowed, hens cackled, ducks quacked, pigs squeeled owls hooted, donkeys brayed, dogs howled, cats squalled and all these perfect imitations were made by human voices. Made twenty-one miles today. Road dusty. Weather warm.

Sunday, August 15th, 1852. We soon came to another canon very rough and rocky. Through it runs a creek which we crossed seven times. The first crossing we had to raise the wagon beds. The others were not so deep, but the last one was very stony. At one place there was a fine looking spring bubbling out from under a rock, but what was our disappointment to find it lukewarm. After leaving the canyon we came to a fine valley covered with grass. We camped on a dry creek but got water by digging in the bed of the creek. The road has been very dusty today.

Monday, August 16th, 1852. This morning we struck the head waters of the long-talked-of and much-dreaded Humboldt, but were agreeably surprised to find splendid grass and water, and good road. Traveled twenty miles today.

Tuesday, August 17th. Today we had a slight recurrence of the old sand hills, but the road generally is very good. Rather windy and dusty, which makes disagreeable travelling. Distance twenty miles.

Wednesday, August 18th. Nothing of interest today. Road very dusty. We crossed the river once.

Thursday, August 19th. Quite cool this morning and still grew cooler until it was very disagreeable. We crossed the river three times within two hours. The fords are very good. Grass scarce at noon. This afternoon we had a mountain to climb, nine and a half miles to the summit. Here we are obliged to camp without any grass, but found a good spring near the road.

Friday, August 20th. Went on about two miles and found some grass. Here we stopped, fed the cattle and got breakfast. We then descended the mountain ten miles to the Humboldt again, crossed it and traveled two miles and stopped for noon. Kept the river bottom this afternoon. Good grass and plenty of water.

Saturday, August 21st, 1852. Crossed over the point of a stony hill. We then crossed the river and took a bottom road instead of keeping the south side over the hills. Good road and good grass.

Sunday, August 22nd. Passed around a stony point, struck the river and then left it for seven miles, taking across a bend over a sandy alkali plain. We then struck the river again and nooned. Camped early tonight on good grass. Just after we stopped nine men came up and asked for supper. They had been out hunting some horses that were stolen by the Indians, and had eaten nothing since yesterday. They found one horse alive and the Indians eating another. The rest were scattered through the mountains so that they could not be found.

Monday, August 23rd. Sandy, dusty road. Weather very warm. Grass good.

Tuesday, August 24th. Most of the emigrants cross to the south side of the river, but we keep to the north side as the road is better. This afternoon we had some tedious sand hills to cross. When we got into the valley again we found no grass for several miles, and then it was very dry.

Wednesday, August 25th, 1852. Soon after starting Thomas overtook us. His first salutation was "Well you have traveled like the devil. I thought I should never overtake you." He left Mr. Buck Sunday morning. We camped at noon waiting for Mr. Buck to come up.

Mr. Holmes killed a deer this evening and we got a piece. It is very fat and nice.

Thursday, August 26th. Remained in camp today.

Friday, August 27th. Moved down the river about a mile and camped for the day.

Saturday, August 28th. Hearing from Mr. Buck we moved on. Just after dinner he came up. He has been past us down the river and saw Father [10] out looking for us. Crossed the river again after dinner.

Sunday, August 29th, 1852. After traveling about six miles we met Father. Oh wasn't it a joyful meeting. He had been waiting at a trading post, which was also a relief station, one of several that had been established by the State of California for the relief of destitute emigrants and as a bureau of information. We crossed to the north side of the river again. Road dusty, but grass is good.

Monday, August 30th, 1852. Traveled until ten o'clock when we stopped to cut some grass to take along. Camped tonight without any grass, so we found use for our hay. High wind all day.

Tuesday, August 31st. Started out early. Struck the river and watered, but found no grass, so we drove on a short distance and fed the rest of our hay. Found some grass tonight.

---

10 James McAuley, listed in the 1850 census of Henry County, Indiana, as fifty-six years old, a farmer, born in Ireland. The mother was Esther, forty-six years of age, born in New York.

Wednesday, September 1st, 1852. Very hot and dusty today. By driving late tonight we reached the Big Meadows.

Thursday, September 2nd. Lay by until three o'clock and cut grass for the cattle. We then drove down the river about four miles where we found good grass and water.

Friday, September 3rd, 1852. The bottom is covered with a thick growth of cane, which the cattle eat greedily. Found good grass at noon, but no water until we came to the river again at four o'clock. Before reaching it we crossed a very barren, desolate plain, the wind blowing very hard and raining a little. Near the river is a trading post and relief station. We crossed here but were obliged to cross back on account of a miry place at the sink of the Humboldt. Found pretty good grass this evening but the water is pretty bad.

Saturday, September 4th. After feeding some hay we started into the desert. Had to make quite a bend to get around the sink. Weather cool and pleasant. We met a man hauling water from the Truckee for the relief station, who gave us some drinking water. We stopped at noon, fed and watered from the store in our wagons and drove again and rested until ten-thirty. We then started and drove the rest of the night, passing the boiling springs about midnight. These springs boil up with great noise, emitting a very nauseous smell, but as it was dark we could not examine them very closely. We hear that a woman and child have got scalded very badly by stepping into one of them.

Sunday, September 5th. Made our breakfast on bread and milk having no wood to cook with, and

one of the cows stole all of the water we had, so we
are obliged to put up with light diet. We are now
seven miles from the Truckee River, but the road here
becomes very sandy and heavy. After traveling three
miles the teams begin to give out, so we had to unhitch them from the wagons and send them on to grass
and water. The boys went on with the cattle, leaving
Mr. Daugherty, Margaret and myself with the wagons. After resting awhile, Margaret and I started on,
taking with us a cow that had given out and been
kept behind.We took a bucket a short distance before
her, and the poor thing, thinking there was water in
it would get up and struggle on a few steps and then
fall exhausted. After resting a few minutes we would
get her on a few steps. In this way we had gained
about a mile, when we met Thomas returning with
a canteen of water. We took a drink and gave the rest
to the poor cow, which revived her so that she was
able to get to the River.

Thomas said that when the cattle were within three
miles from the River they smelled the water, and lift-
ing their heads started on a run for the river and never
stopped until they had plunged in and rushed half
way across. It was about noon when Thomas returned
with the water, and Margaret and I then lay down
on the bare sand, with the hot sun pouring down on
us and slept until the boys returned with the teams.
We then started for the river which we reached about
five o'clock. This is a delightful stream of pure, cold
water, about two rods wide and two feet deep. The
current is swift and the banks are lined with a fine
growth of cottonwood, which is quite refreshing after
such a long tedious desert. There are several trading

posts here and a relief station. After crossing the river we went up it about two miles and found good grass.

Monday, September 6th, 1852. Lay by today to rest.

Tuesday, September 7th. For a short distance up the river the road is good, but it soon becomes sandy and then rough and hilly. Crossed the river just before noon and again after noon, and had very rough road most of the day. In places huge rocks rise several hundred feet, some of them of the most beautiful colors, deep crimson, red, pink, blue and green, most beautifully shaded and blended. Others are a conglomeration of crystals, quartz, mica and sand. Camped on the river this morning and found good grass. The water is delightful, being the opposite extreme from that in the sink of the Humboldt, and we drink for the pure pleasure of drinking.

Wednesday, September 8th. Started immediately into a canyon and had very good road until we arrived at the summit. It was then rough and rocky down to the river, a distance of about three miles. The road was then in the bottom until we camped at noon. We ate dinner on the bank of the river under the shade of a large cottonwood, which overhangs the water. This afternoon we again took to the hills and rocks and traveled till late to reach Truckee Meadows. Crossed the river again before camping.

Thursday, September 9th, 1852. Went up the river about three miles when we came up with Mr. Holmes our Arkansas acquaintance, with a drove of beef cattle. We bought some fresh beef of him and camped for the rest of the day on the bank of the river.

Friday, September 10th. Crossed the river at a good

ford. Had a very heavy sandy road till noon. It was then hilly and rough the remainder of the way.

Saturday, September 11th. Drove a few miles till we came to some good grass and stopped until noon. We then drove on over hills until toward evening, when we came to the father of all hills. Here, we went about two miles to get three hundred yards, but we could not ford the river so had to take the mountain. Mr. Holmes' train here came up and we all went up the river about two miles and camped.

Sunday, September 12th, 1852. Today we take the Sierra Nevadas. Got over the first range by noon, and found the road much better than we expected, the hills being quite gradual. The scenery here is magnificent. High mountains rising on every side, covered with pine, fir and arbor-vitae.

We nooned in a little valley, covered with grass and had good road all afternoon. Camped on a branch of the truckee River.

Monday, September 13th. Very cold this morning, but became quite pleasant when the sun got above the mountain tops. Had very good road this forenoon and nooned in a little valley with excellent grass and water. This afternoon we passed Starvation Camp, which took its name from a party of emigrants, who, in 1846 attempted to reach Oregon by a southern route, but getting belated in the mountains, the snow came on and buried up their cattle. Here they were forced to remain several weeks, and were, it is said, reduced to the terrible extremity of cannibilism, and but six were living when relief came to them. It is the most desolate, gloomy looking place I ever saw. There were the ruins of two or three cabins down in a deep dark canyon, surrounded by stumps ten to fifteen feet high, where they were cut off above the snow.

Donner Lake, a beautiful sheet of water, not far from here, was named in remembrance of the party. We camped in a small valley, about three miles west of this place.

Tuesday, September 14th, 1852. This morning we began the accent of the main ridge, which is very steep and rough. About nine o'clock we doubled teams and began the ascent of the summit, and by one o'clock we all arrived in Summit Valley on the western slope, where we remained the rest of the day.

While the teams were toiling slowly up to the summit, Father, Mr. Buck, Margaret and I climbed one of the highest peaks near the road, and were well repaid for our trouble by the splendid view. On one side the snow-capped peaks rise in majestic grandeur, on the other they are covered to their summits with tall pine and fir, while before us in the top of the mountains, apparently an old crater, lies a beautiful lake in which the Truckee takes its rise. Turning our eyes from this, we saw the American flag floating from the summit of one of the tallest peaks. We vented our patriotism by singing "The Star Spangled Banner" and afterward enjoyed a merry game of snow ball. Turning to descend, the mountain side looked very steep and slippery, and Margaret and I were afraid to venture it. Father, who is a very active man for his age (about sixty)[11] volunteered to show us how to descend a mountain. "Just plant your heels firmly in the snow, this way," he said, but just then, his feet flew from under him and he went sailing down the

11 If the 1850 census was correct, James McAuley would have been fifty-eight in 1852.

mountain side with feet and hands in the air. After a minute of horrified silence we saw him land and begin to pick himself up, when we gave way to peals of laughter. We found an easier way down and rejoined the train, and tonight we camp in Summit Valley on the western slope of the Sierra Nevadas, and are really in California.

Wednesday, September 15th, 1852. Traveled down the valley a mile or two and again took the mountains. The road was mostly descending and rough. There are a number of pretty little lakes, nestled in among the mountains, which give a most charming effect to the landscape. Drove until late and had to camp without any grass.

Thursday, September 16th. This forenoon the road was very rough. In one place we had to let the wagons down by ropes over a smooth rock several yards long where the cattle could not stand. This afternoon the road was better. We camped in Yuba Valley where the grass is very good.

Friday, September 17th. The road was very good for a few miles until we came to Bear River Mountain. This was very steep and bad to descend, but we managed to get down safely, and camped in Bear Valley. Here our stock soon found their way into a ranch where they fared finely.

Saturday, September 18th, 1852. We started down the valley, passing a house on the way, which I must describe as it is the first California house we have seen. It is three logs high, about six feet long, and four wide, one tier of clapboard or shakes as they are called here, covering each side of the roof. Leaving this, and

passing through a gate we soon came to another cabin
of larger dimensions. Here the road forks, one leading
to Nevada City, the other, which we took, leading to
Little York. About four o'clock we came to Mammoth
Spring. This is most delicious water. Finding some
good grass about a mile from here we camped for the
night, this being our last camp on the journey.

Sunday, September 19th. We passed Mule Springs
this morning. There are some mines at this place, also
a tavern and a small ranch. About noon we arrived at
Father's cabin, where we consider our journey ended,
after traveling almost constantly for more than five
months.

Our first impression of Californians is that they are
a very delicate people, as their complexions contrast
so strongly with those of the sun-burned travelers
on the plains. Several called to pay their respects to
"Father Mac" as he is affectionately called by the
miners, and to get a glimpse of his two daughters, a
woman being a rare sight here. One enthusiastic miner
declared he would give an ounce of gold dust for the
sight of a woman's sunbonnet.

We have been so long without fresh vegetables that
we found that cold, boiled vegetables a great luxury,
and Margaret and I devour all that are left between
meals.

.

Kentucky to California
by Carriage and a Feather Bed
◊ Francis Sawyer

INTRODUCTION

Mr. Sawyer bought a single-horse carriage for my use and one more mule. . . My mule and carriage go along so nicely and comforably. She never stops for mud holes. She is the best animal we have, Mr. Sawyer bought her of Dr. Scott, of Cloverport, and she is named for the Doctor's daughter. Jennie. . . I sleep in my carriage every night on a feather bed, and am not exposed in any way in bad weather. The boys sleep either in the wagon or in the tent. . . The men do all the cooking in bad weather, though I never have to do anything but make up the bread.

In this way Francis Sawyer faced the rigors of the overland trail to California in 1852. The quotes are all from the first few pages below.

It was on June 13, 1852, that she wrote in her diary, "Sabbath day, and my birthday too — just twenty one." She and her husband Thomas Sawyer, who was nine years her senior, were from Cloverport, Kentucky, near the northern boundary of that state on the south bank of the Ohio River. Thomas was listed as a "boatman" in the 1850 United States Census of Kentucky, so he undoubtedly worked on the river. There was also listed a baby boy, Henry, who was nine months old. Evidently the child died, for there is no mention of him in Francis' 1852 diary.

Their neighbors, according to the census, were Tom's parents, Jonathan and Nancy Sawyer. Jonathan was an English-born farmer. Nancy was a daughter of Kentucky.

One would think that, according to the practice we are used to, our diarist's first name would have been "Frances," the feminine version of the name. That is not true, however, for in every reference to her in the diary typescript and in a covering letter given by her daughter, Nancy S. Wills, to the Bancroft Library, it is always written "Francis."

Tom Sawyer was a young man of the frontier, always on the move. In a concluding note probably added later to her diary, Francis tells that he had already made two journeys to the "Land of Gold." The first was overland in 1849. He returned to Kentucky in the autumn of 1850. Then she says, "He could not content himself to stay in Kentucky, however, and concluded to go back again. So in the spring of 1851 he, in company with my brother, B. B. Lamar and George Bruner . . . went out by water, by the way of New Orleans and the Isthmus. He soon got homesick again and came back in the fall of '51, thinking that he would either settle here in Kentucky, or move with his wife to California. He chose the latter course, hence our overland trip in 1852."

Now look again at the census information given above. Undoubtedly Tom Sawyer, himself, was away when the 1850 census was taken, and baby Henry was, in the census-taker's language, "9/12" of a year old. This nine months, plus the nine months of Francis' pregnancy would indicate that they had been married before the time Tom left on his first 1849-1850 journey. So it was that Francis had spent many lonely hours and days since their marriage.

Francis and Thomas spent the next twelve years in California. During that time there were five children born, three girls and two boys. They were Lula, b. 1854; Emma, b. 1856; Charles, b. 1858; John, b. 1859, and Amelie, b. 1861. They are all thus listed in the 1870 United States Census of Kentucky. In 1864 they took their long trek to their "Old Kentucky Home." One child, Nannie, was born that year. Where the birth took place we don't know, whether in California, on the way east, or in Kentucky

after the return to Cloverport. In later years this would
be the Nancy Wills who donated the typewritten copy
of the diary to the Bancroft Library in 1937. The 1870
census lists two more daughters born to the family in Kentucky: Mary, b. 1867, and Susan, b. 1869. In the 1870
census the father, Thomas, is identified as a "Painter."

We wish to thank the Bancroft Library of the University
of California in Berkeley for permission to publish this
important record of overland travel. We are also grateful
to the Kentucky Historical Society in Frankfort, and especially to Librarian Anne McDonnell, for sharing with
us information about the family's Kentucky years.

THE JOURNAL OF FRANCIS SAWYER

We left Louisville, Ky., on the 25th day of April,
1852, passengers on the steamer, "Pike No. 9," bound
for St. Louis.

Mr. Sawyer [1] bought his wagon and two mules and
some of the supplies which we would need on our long
and tedious journey across the western plains, in Louisville. He bought two more mules, and the steamer
stopped at his father's farm in Hancock county, Ky.,
to take these animals aboard. At St. Louis we changed
on to a small Missouri-river steamboat, and came up
that river to St. Joseph. Here it was necessary to lay in
the remainder of our supplies, so Mr. Sawyer bought
a single-horse carriage for my use and one more mule.

There are four persons in our company, Mr. Sawyer
and myself and two young men, Burk Hall and Ben-
jamin Sampson from Hancock County, Ky. Mr. Sampson is my cousin. He is a consumptive, and is going,

---

[1] Her husband is always referred to as "Mr. Sawyer." His first name
was Thomas, "Tom Sawyer" nonetheless.

hoping that the trip may benefit his health. These gentlemen pay my husband for the expense of their trip, and he furnishes everything except one mule bought by Burk Hall.

This is not the first trip for Mr. Sawyer. He was in the great California rush of '49, and went over with a large pack train. In this train was one wagon loaded with medicine, to be used in case of sickness. He drove this wagon all the way himself, and was thus the first white man who ever drove a wagon over the Sierra Nevada mountains. He knows just what we will need on this trip and has made his purchases accordingly.

Two days after our arrival in St. Joseph, all the preparations for our long overland journey were completed, and we came out and camped six miles from the city.

May 9. – We left camp this morning, and soon found that our road was as hard to travel as the proverbial one that leads to Jordan. The mud was so deep and tough that our teams of four mules mired down and stuck tight on two different occasions, and we were greatly delayed in having to stop and get them out. Our progress was very slow. We passed through Savannah, a small village, and went into camp one mile and a half beyond that place. We intend to travel in Missouri until we reach old Fort Kearney, where we expect to cross the Missouri river. Grass for our mules is very short here tonight. Distance traveled to-day eight miles.

May 10. – We started out this morning with renewed courage, hoping that we might not be visited by similar trials and difficulties to those of yesterday, but our hopes and desires went to naught. Our mules mired again before we went far, and our progress was very much impeded. We find some very bad branches, brooks and ravines to cross. It seems that the farmers in this section take no interest in improving their roads, and this makes it so disagreeable for emigrants. It commenced raining this evening, and everything is very gloomy and unpleasant. We pitch our camp by a flowing creek of good water where the grass is very plentiful. Distance traveled to-day, twelve miles.

May 11. – We came to the Nodaway, a small river, before noon to-day, crossed the stream, and are in camp on its bank. We were informed at the ferry that there was no more grass for a distance of twelve miles, and as it is plentiful here, we want our mules to get a good feed and be well rested before we start over the long barren stretch. Distance traveled ten miles.

May 12. – We got along without much difficulty to-day, as our roads are improving somewhat. Our way lay over a beautiful prairie. My mule and carriage go along so nicely and comfortably. She never stops for mud-holes. She is the best animal we have, Mr. Sawyer bought her of Dr. Scott, of Cloverport, and she is named for the Doctor's daughter, Jennie. We have but little grass to-night. Distance traveled, twenty miles.

May 13. – Ben Sampson was so unfortunate this morning as to meet with a painful accident. In crossing a deep hollow he got his foot caught between the double-tree and wagon box and the member was severely sprained. He has suffered greatly all day. We have had several showers of rain this afternoon, but I keep dry and comfortable. I sleep in my carriage every night on a feather bed, and am not exposed in any way in bad weather. The boys sleep either in the wagon or in the tent. Distance traveled, twenty miles.

May 14. – We arrived within one mile of old Fort Kearney this evening, and Mr. Sawyer sent to the ferry to register his name. To our discomfiture we learned that there were a great many before us waiting to cross, and it will probably be several days before our turn will come. Our road has been over a prairie to-day and it was very good. We passed through Linden, another small village, and crossed several large creeks on bridges and ferried one. Ben's foot is better, though he is not yet able to walk. We have pitched our camp on the edge of the prairie in a grove of timber. Distance traveled, twenty-two miles.

May 15. – One of our mules got away last night and Mr. Sawyer has had a chase for it to-day. He had to go back six miles before he caught her. She is so wild and hard to break to work. We sent to the ferry to-day to learn when we could cross, and were informed that we could not possibly get over before to-morrow or the next day. Mr. Sawyer dislikes having to wait here so long. He is anxious to be traveling all the time, and I prefer it myself. We have had more rain to-day, and the indications are that it will continue to-night. The grass is not good here.

May 16. – Sabbath day. I have been in bed in my carriage all day, for it is very disagreeable out. The wind commenced blowing at a high rate last night and it has continued to blow a perfect gale ever since. Mr. Sawyer got up in the night and pulled the carriage, with me in it, out into the prairie, for fear that timber would fall on us. The men do all the cooking in bad weather, though I never have to do anything but make up the bread.

May 17. – We are still in camp, waiting and watching for our time to come to cross the Missouri, but it seems to be very uncertain when that will be. Mr. Sawyer went out hunting this morning and killed a deer. This was very acceptable to all of us, as fresh meat is quite a treat on a trip like this.

May 18. – The wind is blowing very hard to-day and the waves are rolling so high in the river that the ferry cannot run. This camp is growing monotonous and we are all so anxious to get away and continue our journey. Up to this time, 906 wagons have crossed the river here this year.

May 19. – We drove up to the ferry this afternoon thinking that probably we might get over. However, we soon learned that we would have to content ourselves 'till morning. The old fort is on the opposite side of the river, but there is not much of it left, to be seen. The ferryman has a log cabin here and keeps some groceries and whiskey to sell at high prices.

May 20. – After having been delayed a week, we succeeded in getting safe across the river this morning. And here we make another start on our long journey, hoping that we will not again be delayed for so long a time. We are now in the Indian country, and we suspect that it will not be many days before we see some of these wild natives. We are in camp to-night with a small company of emigrants, among whom are several ladies. These, like myself, were engaged in helping to cook supper, and I have no doubt, but that they all enjoyed it heartily, as I did. There is an abundance of grass. Distance traveled, sixteen miles.

May 21. – Mr. Sawyer was taken sick last night with a hard chill and he has a high fever to-day. I felt very uneasy about him and sincerely hope that he will not have a hard spell of sickness, for on the plains is a bad place to be sick. We have a good supply of all kinds of medicine with us, but doctors are very hard to find. It began to rain last night and it has continued to pour down nearly all this day. We did not leave camp 'till nearly 3 o'clock this afternoon. Distance traveled, eight miles.

May 22. – Mr. Sawyer is some better to-day, and he has hopes to soon be well again. We picked some nice prairie peas to-day, but they cannot be considered as much of a luxury, as they are only good for making pickles. The roads are very good now and we go along with ease, making good time. Distance traveled, twenty-six miles.

May 23. – Sabbath. We camped this afternoon at 3 o'clock, to rest the remainder of the day. We have been traveling, for several days, in company with an old gentleman, and his family. He has with him, his wife, two sons, daughter and daughter's husband. The daughter is dressed in a bloomer costume [2] – pants, short skirt and red-top boots. I think it is a very appropriate dress for a trip like his. So many ladies wear it, that I almost wish that I was so attired myself. The old lady wears a short skirt and pantletts. She is fifty years old. Her health was not good when she started, but it is improving now. Distance traveled, sixteen miles.

---

2 On "bloomer costume," see Introduction to this volume, pp. 13-14.

May 24. – Today has been a very warm one, but nothing startling has occurred to break the monotony of the trip. The roads, however, continue good, and we are making rapid strides toward the far West. Mr. Sawyer guards his mules of nights now, for fear that the Indians may steal them. Distance traveled to-day, thirty miles.

May 25. – We came to the Platte river to-day. It is a wide and shallow stream, and its water is warm and muddy. There is some timber on its banks and on the islands. Some Indians are in camp near us to-night, and they came over to our camp, begging for something to eat. They are not pleasant looking guests, though they seem to be friendly and peaceable. Distance traveled, twenty-five miles.

May 26. – A large party of Pawnee Indians passed us this morning going on to their hunting grounds after buffalo, and this afternoon we met them returning. They had met a party of Sioux, and the result was a battle took place. The Sioux had whipped them, killing and scalping two of the party and wounding several others. The Pawnees were very angry and badly frightened. Some were armed with bows and some with guns. I met some ladies that saw the fight, and they said they were scared almost to death themselves. The Pawnees had made a poor fight. There were only thirteen Sioux and they whipped sixty or seventy Pawnees. When we came to where the battle had been fought, Mr. Sawyer and I drove off the road a short distance to see one of the Indians who had been killed. It was the worst horrible sight I ever saw. Four or five arrows were sticking in his body and his scalp was gone, leaving his head bare, bloody and ghastly.

I am sorry I went out to look at him. I have had the blues ever since. We are in camp with a large company of emigrants, to-night, and have out a strong guard. So we women are safe and secure from danger, and may rest in peace and comfort, if we don't dream of dead Indians. The grass is good here, but mosquitoes are very bad. Distance traveled, twenty-two miles.

May 27. – Morpheus cozily wrapped us all in his arms last night, and the pleasant dreams of our faraway Kentucky home were not disturbed by the Indians, either dead or alive. I have plucked some beautiful prairie flowers to-day. The prairie is very pretty, dressed in its many bright colors, and the atmosphere is sweet with its fragrance. The flowers somewhat resemble the bloom of the sweet pea. Distance traveled, twenty-five miles.

May 28. – Nothing of startling importance happened to-day. The same old monotony – endless prairies. Distance traveled, thirty miles.

May 29. – We arrived at new Fort Kearney at 2 o'clock this afternoon and went into camp near it. We wrote some letters home and mailed them at the Fort. The Fort is a neat little place, kept in the best of order, and the best of order is kept in it. There are several ladies here with their husbands who are officers. They keep an account of the number of emigrants who pass this place, and a soldier came out this afternoon to get our names to register. Distance traveled to-day, fifteen miles.

May 30. – Sabbath. We passed the Fort this morning and kept the bank of the Platte river till we arrived at a point ten miles above, where we forded the stream.

The Platte is a mile wide at this point, and our wagons pulled very hard in the quick-sand. Mr. Sawyer went over in the carriage with me. The water was so deep that our mule had to swim in some places. I was greatly frightened and held on tightly to my husband. When we got over Mr. Sawyer took the mule out of the carriage and went back on her to help the boys over with the wagon. The mules stopped once and the wagon settled down so, that oxen had to be procured to help to start it again. At last they got over safe, and as the wagon box had been propped up, everything kept dry, though in this were more fortunate than any others who were crossing today. Many had their effects badly damaged by water. We went into camp on the bank of the river where we had crossed.

May 31. – We have traveled all day in heat and dust. It is quite warm and dusty now, and the grass is not good. Distance traveled, twenty-eight miles.

June 1. – We heard of three very sudden deaths this morning, and the disease is supposed to be cholera. The emigrants, in traveling over the plains, dig shallow wells to procure cold water. This water is strongly impregnated with alkali, and it is thought, that by drinking this, these unfortunate, people have been taken seriously sick and died. We are making good time now. Distance traveled, twenty-eight miles.

June 2. – We are now in the Buffalo Regions, and the only fuel we have is buffalo chips. These make a good hot fire. We are in camp near the Shawnee Springs. The water is very fine, cold as ice and clear as crystal. We enjoy this treat very much, after having been compelled to use the unwholesome water contained in the shallow wells of the plains for several days past. The grass is also very good here. Distance traveled, twenty-five miles.

June 3. – We had a hard rain and thunderstorm last night, and it is cool and pleasant to-day. We camp by a creek of good, clear water tonight. This is to our liking, as the water of the Platte is so warm that we avoid its use whenever it is possible to do so. Distance traveled, twenty-five miles.

June 4. – To-day we have passed a great many new made graves, and we hear of many cases of cholera. We hear of so much sickness that we are becoming fearful for our own safety. Distance traveled, twenty miles.

June 5. – One of the men in the camp of the old gentleman who is traveling with us, was taken sick with cholera last night, and it is thought that he will die. We have not left camp to-day, though the doctors say that it is much better to be traveling.

June 6. – Sabbath day. The sick man is some better, but other members of the company have similar symptoms. The disease is very bad among the emigrants, being more prevalent among the ox teams than the others. There was more rain last night, and it is still cooler to-day. It is hoped that this will check the disease somewhat. Distance traveled, twenty-two miles.

June 7. – It rained again last night and is still cool and windy. Mr. Sawyer has slight symptoms of cholera this evening, but hopes to get it checked before it becomes serious. Distance traveled, twenty-five miles.

June 8. – Mr. Sawyer is better to-day. We met Mormons from Salt Lake, and they told us there was no sickness ahead of us. This gives us brighter hopes and encourages us greatly. We passed Castle Ruins to-day. They are large stones on the top of a hill, and they resemble old ruins very much, though it was the hand of nature that placed them there. Distance traveled, twenty-five miles.

June 9. – It is now one month since we left St. Joseph, and we have traveled a little more than 500 miles, making an average of about seventeen miles a day. We still have a long, rugged, and weary road before us that will take us many weeks to go over. The health of the emigrants is so much better, that we don't hear of any deaths now. We passed Chimney Rock and Courthouse Rock to-day. They were both on the opposite side of the Platte from us, but we could see them very distinctly. Distance traveled, thirty-one miles.

June 10. – We "nooned" to-day opposite Scott's Bluffs. These bluffs were named for a man by the name of Scott, who perished under them for the want of food.[3] The story of his death is a pitiful one. The view of the bluffs was grand and beautiful from our position. A Mr. Fix and his son, of Louisville, Ky., caught up with us to-day, and they will travel with us a while. Mr. Sawyer had a slight acquaintance with him in Louisville. Distance traveled, twenty-four miles.

June 11. – We are in sight of Laramie Peak now, though it will be several days before we are opposite

---

[3] Merrill J. Mattes in *The Great Platte River Road* (Lincoln, 1979), discusses the great variety of versions of Scott's death. He writes, "Most agree that there was a fur trader named Scott who died tragically at an early date in this neighborhood after being abandoned by companions and that his remains were later found here." From there on out Mattes says that these are the "few points of agreement on the happenings to Scott, adding that "there is every variation imaginable, with no two versions the same." p. 426ff.

it. We have driven fast to-day and passed a great many ox teams, though the dust is so heavy that it almost blinds us. Distance traveled, thirty miles.

June 12. – We arrived opposite Fort Laramie in time to camp for the night. The Fort is on the south side of the Platte. We will lay over here to-morrow as Mr. Sawyer wishes to get a mule shod and make some purchases of a few things that we need. They keep supplies here, but sell at high prices.

June 13. – Sabbath day, and my birthday too – just twenty one. I have been in bed most all day, taking a good rest and trying to sleep. Mr. Sawyer got one shoe put on his mule and the others tightened. Cost him five dollars. We had to leave camp late this afternoon and come out where we could get grass of the mules. Distance traveled, six miles.

June 14. – We are now in the Black Hills. The scenery is very beautiful. Pines and cedars are scattered over the hills and beautiful flowers are abundant. I gather tulips and larkspurs and many other lovely kinds that I cannot name. Distance traveled, twenty-two miles.

June 15. – We passed an Indian camp to-day. A Frenchman living there, keeps a trading post in a wagon. He has a squaw for a wife, who has borne him several children. They seem playful and happy. Distance traveled, twenty-five miles.

June 16. – Nothing has occurred or been seen worthy of note to-day. Same old weary road to travel. Distance traveled, thirty miles.

June 17. – We have a heavy sand road to travel now. It is very hard on the mules. Mr. Sawyer killed a fine antelope this morning, whose fragrant flesh was quite a luxury for us. Grass is not good here and mosquitoes are very bad. Distance traveled, twenty-three miles.

June 18. – We heard to-day that a murdered man had been found in a deep hollow a short distance from the road. The men who found him had seen him before and knew him. They think that he was murdered for his money, as he was known to have a considerable amount, and it is thought that his murderers are in the company with which he was traveling. He had a wife and one child. Great must be their sorrow to be thus so cruelly deprived of a dear friend and protector, and left alone in this wild and friendless country. Some men have gone in pursuit of the murderers. Just ahead of us a wagon ran over a little boy and broke both his legs. Distance traveled, twenty miles.

June 19. – We heard of another murdered man to-day. In this case, as in yesterday's, the man was murdered by a man in his own company, but the proof in this instance was positive, and the murderer was hung to a tree, by the indignant emigrants. We passed opposite the ferry on the North Fork of the Platte. Numbers of emigrants were there waiting to get over, but we were saved the trouble and expense of ferrying now by having forded the main Platte several days ago. We camped at the Willow Spring where the water is cold and good. Distance traveled, thirty-one miles.

June 20. – Sabbath day. We left the Platte for good to-day. Passed the famous Independence rock, and went into camp one mile from it near the first crossing of the Sweetwater river. This rock is a great curiosity, standing, as it does, here on the level plain, single and alone, hundreds of miles from any companion. It is a huge granite pile 600 feet long, 200

feet wide and 75 feet high. It should have been named
Emigrant's Register, as it contains thousands of names
on its surface, some being carved, some being placed
there with paint, and others with tar. The Sweetwater
runs along within a few hundred yards of the rock.
We have had a long and tiresome march to-day, without much water or grass for our mules. The grass is
not good to-night, and the only fuel we have is wild
sage. Distance traveled, twenty-two miles.

June 21. – We have laid by to-day as we found good
grass for the mules, not more than a mile from our
camp. Dr. Barkwell from Troy, Indiana, caught up
with us to-day. We would not have known of his presence, had not one of our boys seen him when he was
watering his oxen near us, and called to him. He
informed us that his youngest child had died on the
plains, which I was very sorry to hear. The trials and
trouble of this long-wearisome trip are enough to bear
without having our hearts torn by the loss of dear ones.
We went to the big rock this afternoon, and placed our
names on it. A rain caught us while there, and we
had to shelter under the projecting shelves of the rock.
We can see a burning volcano on mountains near us
to-night.

June 22. – We forded Sweetwater river this morning,
and passed near the Devil's Gate. This is a pass where
the river has washed a channel through the mountains.
While we were nooning to-day there came up the
hardest hail storm that it had ever been my lot to
witness. The stones came down thick and fast, and
they were as large as walnuts – none smaller than
bullets. The wind blew so hard and furiously that
all the animals within our hearing stampeded. All

hands had a hard time getting them together again. Some escaped entirely, but we had the good fortune to recover all of ours. Some of our men got bruised heads and hands by the heavy hailstones striking them. I was badly frightened and thought the wind would surely blow us away. We are still at our nooning place. Distance traveled, ten miles.

June 23. – We have concluded to go to California instead of Oregon, as was our first intention. I was greatly pleased by this change of intentions, as I had much rather go to California. My brother B. B. Lamar, is there, and to see him is a greater inducement for me than the whole of Oregon can offer. Distance traveled, twenty-two miles.

June 24. – We are in sight of the Rocky Mountains now, and we see the glistening snow on the tops of the high peaks. We camp with Dr. Barkwell, wife and little daughter to-night. I am so glad to meet them, and I enjoy their company so much, as they are the only persons that I have met on the broad plains that I ever knew before. Forded Sweetwater river twice to-day. Distance traveled, twenty seven miles.

June 25. – We passed a trading post to-day. The keeper is a Frenchman. Mr. Sawyer exchanged his wagon for a lighter one, as ours was too heavy for four mules to pull over the mountains. The wagon he got in the trade is not as good as the one we had, but when you trade for anything on this trip, you usually give double value for what you got in return. He, also exchanged the wild mule, that he bought at St. Joseph, for an Indian pony. The pony is not half as valuable as the mule, but we never could break the mule to work or ride well. We are ascending the Rocky Mountains,

but the ascent is so gradual that one would hardly
know that he is going up a mountain. We pass plenty
of snow and had all the ice water that we could use.
Distance traveled, fifteen miles.

June 26. – Passed through the South Pass to-day, and
commenced descending the mountains on the western
side. We soon came to the Pacific Springs and went
into camp a few miles from them. Mr. Sawyer started
out from the springs to hunt a good place to pitch our
camp, and we got lost from him. We got on a wrong
road and did not get back to the emigrant road until
dark, and Mr. Sawyer did not find us 'till ten o'clock
at night. I was so worried about him, and for fear
that he could not find us otherwise, I got all the men
near us to fire off all their guns and pistols. He heard
the firing and came directly to us. Distance traveled,
twenty-eight miles.

June 27. – We crossed Dry Sandy creek this morning.
There are some pools of brackish water in it, though
it is not fit to use. We came to the forks of the road,
the left being the road to Salt Lake and the other the
Fort Hall route. We took the Salt Lake road, though
we did not know yet whether we will go by there or
take some of the cutoffs. We are all anxious to see the
Mormon City, but that route is 90 miles longer than
the other, and we don't much like to travel that far
out of our way just to see it. We forded the Little
Sandy. Distance traveled, twenty miles.

June 28. – We forded the Big Sandy to-day, and
camp twelve miles from Green river on a beautiful
meadow. The grass is so good that our mules are feasting to-night. Distance traveled, twenty-five miles.

June 29. – Soon came to Green river and got ferried over it and camped one mile from the ferry. There is a trading post at the ferry and some Indians are in camp around it. We have taken the McKinney cut-off, as we thought it better to take all the advantages of the trip we could, than to satisfy our desires to see Salt Lake. I saw some beautiful bloom of cactus to-day. They were of many different colors. Distance traveled thirteen miles.

June 30. – Mr. Sawyer went off the road this morning on his pony and killed two sage hens. We ate them for dinner, and they were delicious. He was in sight of us all the time, though I drove along for several miles before he got back to the road. I drive a great deal now, and I am very fond of handling the lines. Our road has not all been good to-day. We passed one good spring of water, and went in camp near another one on the top of a Shoshone hill. Distance traveled, thirty miles.

July 1. – We traveled over some very steep mountains to-day, and again came into the main road. We are now in the Bear River Mountains. Passed through a pine grove and a quaking aspen grove. To-night we visited an adjoining camp to see a lady and her little daughter, who had been turned over in a carriage to-day while coming down a steep mountain-side. When the husband and father got to them, he thought that they were killed, but now it is thought that they are only painfully and not seriously hurt. We saw some very beautiful landscapes to-day. The principal stream crossed was Ham's fork of the Bear river. Distance traveled, thirty miles.

July 2. – Came to the main Bear River to-day, and forded Smith's Fork. It was a very rocky and dangerous ford. We went into camp on the bank of the river and thought we would fish some, but the mosquitoes were so thick, so brave and resolute, that all our time was occupied in fighting them off. I never saw the like before, and we thought that they would surely eat us up. The grass is good here, but our mules could not eat any until 8 o'clock, or after, when the mosquitoes left us. Distance traveled, thirty miles.

July 3. – Crossed Thomas' Fork of Bear river on a toll bridge. Cost us one dollar per wagon. There is a ford eight miles out [of] our way, but it is not very good, so we concluded to toll. We went over some very steep mountains to-day too. Ben Sampson is real sick this afternoon, with high fever and a headache. He has taken cold, but the mountain air is so bracing that I think he will soon feel better. He has stood the trip so well this far that I have hopes of his health being greatly benefited. The mosquitoes are nearly as bad to-night, as they were last night. Distance traveled, thirty miles.

July 4. – Sabbath day. We arrived at the noted Soda Springs this afternoon. Stopped, and went out to see them. I made some soda drinks and cream tartar with the water, and they were very nice and cool. I brought some to Ben and he enjoyed it very much. Said it made him feel much better. The Soda Springs is one of the natural curiosities of our country that is worth seeing. The water is so beautiful, foaming up out of the crevice of the rock. It is quite cool here this evening and it snowed on the mountain and rained in the valley where we were. We camped three miles beyond the Soda Springs under a mountain. We have plenty of good pine wood and lots of grass. I traded a string of beads to an Indian boy for some fish, and we ate them for supper. Distance traveled, twenty seven miles.

July 5. – Lying by to-day to celebrate the Fourth, as we had to travel yesterday. We went fishing this morning, then came back and cooked a good dinner. We had canned vegetables, fish, rice cakes and other little dishes. We see lots of Indians now, and some are at our camp most of the time. They usually want to trade fish for fish hooks and something to eat. We found ice on the water in camp this morning, so you can see how cold it sometimes is here on the glorious Fourth. We were glad to get the ice water to drink.

July 6. – We took Sublett's cut-off at six miles from Soda Springs but we had some very bad roads to-day. Distance traveled, twenty miles.

July 7. – Mr. Sawyer traded our Indian pony for a two year old colt to-day. The colt is not worth much, but we were glad to get that much for the pony as it was nearly given out. So you see that we lost money on that plaguy wild mule that we bought at St. Joseph. Traveled over two large mountains and camp in valley. Distance traveled, seventeen miles.

July 8. – Went over two more mountains to-day, and pitched our camp on Grand creek about 1 o'clock P.M. It is twenty-five miles to the next water, so we concluded to remain here 'till morning and take a fresh start for the long, dry march. We went fishing this afternoon, but did not get a nibble, so we had to give it up as a bad job. Distance traveled, fifteen miles.

July 9. – It is very warm and dusty to-day, but the nights are always cool and pleasant in this country. We are out of the mosquitoes for the present, and hope we will not catch up with any more of them soon. We went over two more large mountains again to-day, and one of them was very hard to descend. These mountains are very tiresome to travel over, as we walk up most of them, and I never ride down one. Distance traveled, twenty-five miles.

July 10. – We commenced descending one of the Bear River mountains this morning and we are not out of it yet to-night. Most of our road lay in a ravine, with frequent small branches to cross. We camp on one of these branches, where we have splendid bluegrass for our mules. Distance traveled, twenty-one miles.

July 11. – Sabbath day. We are lying by to-day, as there is such good grazing here for our animals. We have been traveling slow for the last week, and we will continue to take our time 'till we get to Mary's river. We want to get our mules in good condition for that river valley. As there is so much alkali water and grass in it, we will have to make quick time over it. After that comes the Great Dessert, so you see our road will soon be a difficult and weary one indeed. We picked some currants and gooseberries to-day, and had some tarts for dinner.

July 12. – We came on to the old Fort Hall road to-day, and passed the carcasses of a great many dead cattle. We crossed several bad branches of Raft river, and had to make a bridge for one before we could get over. Distance traveled, twenty-four miles.

July 13. – Had a nice shower of rain to-day, which, greatly to our liking, settled the dust, and it has cleared off cool and pleasant. We are in camp to-night at Steeple Rock. There are a great many names on the rocks. Distance traveled, eighteen miles.

July 14. – The Salt Lake Road meets us again, and all the California emigrants are now on this road. The Oregon emigrants have all turned off on the Oregon route. The Digger Indians stole thirteen mules and one ox last night, from a company just ahead of us. We camp with some company every night now and keep a strong guard out all the time, for the Indians will steal the animals if they get half a chance. We traveled over the Goose-Creek mountains to-day, and had a very steep one to descend. We are in camp on Goose creek. Distance traveled, twenty-four miles.

July 15. – Our four mule team got mired in a bad slough this morning, but we got them out without much trouble. We have had to make a long march to-day to get to water, and we find the grass very scarce. Camped in Thousand Springs Valley. Distance traveled, thirty-five miles.

July 16. – The Digger Indians killed a white man a few days ago, at the place where we camped last night. We saw his grave, but did not know he had been killed by Indians 'till to-day, when some emigrants informed my husband that such was the case. We camped in Hot Springs Valley to-night. Grass is good. Distance traveled, twenty-eight miles.

July 17. – We came to the Hot Springs this morning, and stopped to see them. The water comes boiling out of the earth and it is so hot that I could not more than touch it without burning myself. We camp near Canyon Creek, where we found splendid grass and clover. Distance traveled, twenty-three miles.

July 18. – Sabbath day. I have not been feeling well for several days. I have taken cold. My chest is sore and it pains me very much. I am taking medicine for it, and think that I will soon be better. We came to Mary's river, or Humbolt, as some call it, to-day. All the emigrants dread this river, but we found some grass, which is more than we expected, as Mr. Sawyer says there was very little here when he came by in '49. Distance traveled, thirty miles.

July 19. – The digger Indians came to camp near us last night and stole two horses. The man on guard went to sleep and let the Indians slip past him. These are the most thieving Indians on this route, and I will be glad when we are out of their range. We forded the North fork of Mary's river this afternoon. Distance traveled, twenty-nine miles.

July 20. – A company of men went out yesterday in pursuit of those Indians who stole the horses. Neither the water or the weather is good on this river, and the dust is very bad. We forded the river four times to-day, within a distance of ten miles, to avoid going over hills. Distance traveled, thirty miles.

July 21. – We had a hard march of seventeen miles to-day over the hills without stopping except to water our mules at an excellent cold spring which we found in the hills; had to keep traveling till we came to grass. We forded to the North side of the river and went into camp. We will travel on this side for some distance now, as we were informed by some "packers" to-day that the best grass was on this side. Distance traveled, twenty-five miles.

July 22. – Mr. Sawyer killed another antelope to-day

and we are feasting. Game of all kinds is very scarce this year on the road and I have been wishing for some fresh meat for some time. My husband took some of the meat over to another camp near us and made the people a present of it. In return for his kindness the men came over to our camp with a bottle of old whiskey and treated our men. These men keep whiskey for sale and they retail it at two dollars a drink. That seems like a high price for liquor, but these men have to haul it from the States or from California, over the mountains, across the Great desert and up this river for two hundred miles, so you see it is bound to be a costly drink. We had more mosquitoes to-night than we had ever caught up with before. We drove off the road to the river, Intending to camp there, but the pesky insects were so bad that we were compelled to give up the idea of camping. I thought that they would surely eat us and the animals up before we got back to the road. We traveled 'till ten o'clock at night before they left us. It turned cool at that time and we pitched our camp. Distance traveled, thirty-five miles.

July 23. – The mosquitoes were so bad this morning that we had to leave camp at daylight without our breakfast. They are not quite so bad to-night. Mr. Sawyer is not feeling well to-night. Distance traveled, twenty-five miles.

July 24. – We have laid by this afternoon because Mr. Sawyer is too sick to travel. He has a high fever and a bad headache. His bones all ache and he thinks he has a touch of mountain fever. He is doctoring himself to-day and hopes to be better soon. This river is the worst place on the trip to be sick. The weather is bad, the water is not good and the mosquitoes annoy you to death of nights. Distance traveled, twelve miles.

July 25. – Sabbath day. My husband is better to-day, though he don't feel any to good yet. We had the good fortune to get a camp to-night where there are no mosquitoes. Distance traveled, twenty-three miles.

July 26. – They changed my carriage mule into the wagon today and put one of the wagon mules into the carriage. I did not admire the change, but submitted, and sure enough, bad luck came of it. While crossing a slough the mule I was driving mired down, and before they could unharness him, he began jumping and kicking and broke one of the shafts to the carriage. I was so sorry that I felt like crying, for I thought that we would have to leave my carriage behind. However, Mr. Sawyer went to work and mended it, so that now it is almost as stout as it ever was. Distance traveled, twenty-two miles.

July 27. – We passed a trading post to-day and were informed that it was one hundred miles from there to the sink of this river – and won't I be glad to see the end sink out of sight! I am getting a little tired of this wearisome trip and am very anxious to get through, but I intend to take it patiently as it comes, for I know that it will not be very long now till we reach California. My husband has a very bad sore mouth and throat and he suffered with them very much last night. Burk Hall is the only one of our party who has not been sick on this trip, nor have I ever seen him mad or out of humor. When others get angry and fretted, the soothing balm of his good humor and ready jokes always quiets the troubled waters. Distance traveled, twenty miles.

July 28. – We are not bothered much by mosquitoes now. Mr. Sawyer shot some sage chickens this afternoon and we had them for supper. Mr. Sawyer ate heartily and says he thinks they will cure him. Distance traveled, twenty-three miles.

July 29. – We had a march of eighteen miles this morning without water or grass. Forded the river for the last time to the North side and we will travel on this side of the sink. Distance traveled, twenty miles.

July 30. – Our road is better on this side of the river than it was on the other. We had a nice shower of rain this afternoon, which is a very uncommon occurrence here at this season of the year. It settled the dust and was very refreshing. Distance traveled. twenty-two miles.

July 31. – Arrived at the noted Meadows this afternoon and will remain here until tomorrow. Then our men will cut enough grass to take the mules over the desert. It is sixty miles across the desert and we will have to take all the food and water we can from here. Distance traveled, seventeen miles.

August 1. – Sabbath day. We went down into the Meadows this morning and the men cut some splendid grass, then went on down below the sink of the Mary's, or humbolt river, and camped near the Sulphur Springs; but the water is not good this year. Had plenty of mosquitoes last night. Distance traveled, twenty miles.

August 2. – We made a start across the great desert this morning a little after sunup and took, as Mr. Sawyer thought, the old Truckee route, but in about six miles we came to an alkali pond, which it was impossible to cross. We then went over to the Carson route. This mistake tired our mules that much more than they ought to have been, but we traveled slowly, to save them all we could. We stopped at noon and fed them, then we went on until sundown, when we stopped again and fed and cooked some supper with the remains of an old wagon for fuel. We stopped at a trading post in the afternoon and bought some water for the mules, paying seventy-five cents a gallon for it. The gentleman who keeps the post, sent me a glass of port wine, and I drank it with good grace, for I was tired too. Distance traveled up to tonight, twenty-two miles.

We started again at dark and traveled till midnight when our mules commenced failing fast. Stopped and fed them and bought six buckets more of water, paying one dollar a bucket for it. I thought for sure that we would [not] get our teams through, for the last twelve miles was a heavy sand road. Ben got in the carriage with me, while Mr. Sawyer and Burk Hall walked on each side of the four-mule team, driving and whipping them up, but resting them often. Ben and I were in front, and as I heard the whips popping and cracking, I sincerely pittied the poor beasts with all my heart. But when we came in sight of Carson river, my mule stuck up his head and started off in a fast walk, and the other mules followed suit. I was afraid my mule would run right into the river, as he was so hard mouthed and resolute that Ben could hardly hold him. We arrived at Ragtown, on the Carson river, about sunrise this morning, August 3. Distance traveled, forty miles since dark yesterday evening. This desert and lower part of Mary's river have been the worst sections of our trip and I am truly glad that

we are over them safe. Though the desert is easier
to cross this year than it has ever been before. There
are seven or eight trading posts on it now, where re-
freshments and supplies of all kinds are kept for sale.
There are also some trading posts here on Carson
river.

August 3. – We went up the Carson river five miles
from Ragtown and camped for the remainder of the
day. We bought some fresh beef, and have been feasting on beefsteak to-day. Grass is scarce. Distance traveled, five miles.

August 4. – We all slept well last night and didn't have
a guard out. None of us slept much the night before,
as we were crossing the desert. However, I laid on
my bed in the carriage and slept some in the fore
part of the night and the boys did the same thing in
the wagon, one at a time. But when the mules began
to tire, we all became two anxious for a safe passage
across the sandy waste to be visited by the angel of
slumbers or the god of dreams. We had a weary march
of fifteen miles to-day without water or grass, but we
had splendid grass to-night. Distance traveled, fifteen
miles.

August 5. – We had another hard march of ten miles
over heavy sand this morning. This river, however,
is a pretty little stream of clear, cold and good water.
There are some cottonwood trees, willow and black-
berry bushes growing on its banks, and good camping
and nooning places are easily found. Distance traveled,
twenty miles.

August 6. – I saw a lady where we nooned to-day,
who had a fine son three days old. The arrival of the
little stranger made it necessary for his friends to go

into camp for a week or more, and they had settled down to make themselves at home, quietly and patiently awaiting the time that they might resume their march. The lady was comforably situated and in good spirits. I have heard of several children being born on the plains, though it is not a very pleasant place for the little fellows to first see the light of day. Distance traveled, thirteen miles.

August 7. – Mr. Sawyer sold our four-horse wagon and harness this morning for $25.00. He thought it was not worth taking over the Sierra Nevada mountains, besides it would be very hard on the mules. The men have been getting ready all day for "packing." They will put some light things into my carriage, and drive it as far as it will hold out. Mr. Sawyer will walk and drive over the bad places. I will ride a mule, and the boys will ride another. The remainder of our things will be packed on the backs of the other animals, and we will thus be converted into a pack train. We camp at Gold Canyon. There are fiftey or sixty miners at work here, and there are three families living in log cabins. Distance traveled, three miles.

August 8. – Sabbath day. Mr. Sawyer went out prospecting this morning up the canyon. He obtained about twenty-five cents worth of gold dust, but he concluded that, that would not pay, so we left camp in the afternoon. I bought some turnips to-day, at ten cents each, and I was inclined to think that they were pretty dear vegetables. Distance traveled, ten miles.

August 9. – We came to Carson valley to-day. It is a beautiful valley, and some emigrants are settling here. The Mormon station has been built one or two years. It is a boarding house and store together, in a pretty location at the edge of the mounains, with tall pine trees all around it. There are some gardens here, and I bought some more turnips, at five cents each. We have at last arrived into civilization, though things are still very high. Mr. Sawyer got one shoe put on a mule at a blacksmith shop, and it cost him one dollar. Distance traveled, eighteen miles.

August 10. – We traveled up the Carson valley to-day, to the foot of Humboldt canyon and went into camp. Distance traveled, nineteen miles.

August 11. – Started into the mountains this morning through Humboldt canyon. Crossed three toll bridges. Our road is very rough, rocky, and difficult to travel over. Some stones, right round and large as hogsheads, lie right in the middle of the road. Our carriage broke down, and we have abandoned it. One wheel got fastened between two rocks and broke all to pieces. We packed everything on to the mules and went four miles further, where we are in camp on the bank of a beautiful mountain stream of pure, good water. Our men are making more pack saddles. Distance traveled, fourteen miles.

August 12. – We traveled fast to-day and crossed the first summit of the Sierra Nevada mountains before noon and stopped at a beautiful lake (Tahoe) to noon. I have had a toothache so bad to-day that I could not enjoy the beautiful landscapes and scenery. In the afternoon we crossed the second summit of the Sierra Nevada. It is 9,000 feet high and we went over snow six feet deep. We had to travel 'till ten o'clock at night before we could find a place level enough on which to pitch our camp. After it got dark, Mr. Sawyer walked in front and led the first mule and the others followed with Ben and me in the rear. The road was difficult and nothing but rocks. I could not see the path in the dark, so I just gave my mule the rein and let it follow the others. Distance traveled, twenty-five miles.

August 13. – Our road has been better to-day. We met up with, and have been traveling with, another party of emigrants to-day. This party consists of two men, two ladies, and several children. They, like us, have left their wagon behind, and are "packing." We camp at Lake Springs where there is good water and good grass. Distance traveled, nineteen miles.

August 14. – I had a toothache so bad again to-day that I could take no interest in anything. We passed some very large and tall pine and spruce trees, and are in camp in heavy timber. Distance traveled, twenty-eight miles.

August 15. – We are over now to where there are some settlers. We stopped at an eating place, and the boys took the mules off the road to get water. One of them got mixed and the packs got turned on the others. We came to Placerville to-day about noon. On our arrival it was discovered that our dog had been left behind somewhere, and Mr. Sawyer had to go back twelve miles before he found him. We had a very dusty road to-day, and I tell you I was glad to be in California at last. This is quite a lively place. There are numbers of miners here, and gold mines are near the town; some families have settled here, too. I am stopping all night at a boarding house with a very nice lady. The boys are camping out in our tent, which we all have been sleeping in since we have been "packing," and the mules were taken to a hay yard. Distance traveled, twenty miles.

August 16. – This morning Ben Lamar and Burk Hall concluded that they would stop here and see the mines. Ben is not stout enough to work in the mines, though his health has improved during the trip. However, he is ambitious and wants to dig gold. I hated to leave him very much, but I thought he could do as well here as any place. Mr. Sawyer and I left Placerville at 8 o'clock A.M., intending to go to Sacramento City, and we are in camp near a ranch house on the prairie. Distance traveled, thirty miles.

August 17. – We reached Sacramento City at noon to-day. I went in with the pack mules in a cloud of dust, Mr. Sawyer having to whip my mule up with the others. We have been out three months and eight days from St. Joseph. We are stopping at the American House, and glad we are, that we are at last at the end of our journey safe and well, though we are tired and need rest.

Mr. Sawyer made three trips, in all, to California. He went overland in '49, and came back in the fall of 1850. He could not content himself to stay in Kentucky, however, and concluded to go back again. So in the spring of 1851 he, in company with my brother, B. B. Lamar and George Bruner, all of Hancock County, went out by water, by the way of New Orleans and the Isthmus. He soon got homesick again and came back in the fall of '51, thinking that he would either settle here in Kentucky, or move with his wife to California. He chose the latter course, hence our overland trip in 1852.

A Trip Across the Continent

§ Mariett Foster Cummings

INTRODUCTION

There was published in Santa Barbara, California, in 1925, a very special book for the family involved. It was *The Foster Family, California Pioneers*. It was edited by Lucy Ann (Foster) Sexton, niece of Mariett Foster Cummings, author of the diary here published. The book is now a rare one and is found in only a few libraries. It is a frustrating book to deal with because, although the intent is to tell the Foster family story, there is a great dearth of such positive things as dates, including those dealing with births, marriages, and deaths. Although it is never said explicitly, evidently Mariett had no children of her own, but there were lots of nieces and nephews who all loved her a great deal.

The beginning of their journey was Plainfield, Illinois, where she had lived for sixteen years, according to her diary entry of April 23, 1852.

We get the date of her birth in a round-about way. In a birthday letter to Mariett written on January 11, 1858, her father, Isaac Foster, remembered her original birthday 31 years before.[1] This means she was born on January 11, 1827. It also means that she was 25 years old in 1852, when she and her husband, William Cummings, crossed the Plains to California.

We will clarify the spelling of her name: It is spelled by different persons in three different ways: Marriet, Maryette, and Mariett. The last is the correct rendition. That is how she signed it herself.

---

[1] *Foster Family*, p. 153.

Mariett is listed as a single 23-year-old woman in the Illinois census of 1850. She also was unmarried, the daughter of Isaac and Grace Foster. Her birth place is given as New York. William Cumings [*sic*] is listed in the same census as a 31-year-old fisherman, also a New Yorker by birth. They were married between the date when this census was taken and April 13, 1852, when the first entry in her diary was made.

Other members of the family listed in the 1850 census and their dates at that time were as follows: Isaac G. Foster, the oldest son, age 30, a farmer; Roxanna C. Foster, Isaac Jr.'s wife, age 32; Eugene, age two, their child; Vincent, 27 years of age, a farmer; Arthur T., age fourteen, who was attending school.

Her father, Isaac Foster, was evidently a very vigorous man, one who pushed others to hard work. There is a family story in the Foster book that characterizes this man of "driving energy": [2]

> It seems that a small grandchild said: "Mama, will Grandpa go to Heaven when he dies?"
>
> "Why, I certainly hope and expect so." And then she added curiously: "But what makes you ask?"
>
> "Because if he's going. I don't want to!"
>
> "Why?" queried the surprised mother.
>
> "Because he'll say when he sees us: Well, well, boys, let's be moving. Step around now. There's a lot to be done here. And we have to do it!"

Isaac Foster even liked to tell this story on himself. He was a minister in his younger years, but he was often criticized by the church officials for "reading his sermons." He also informed them on at least one occasion that he did not believe in the literal interpretation of the Bible. He was arraigned for heresy. He began his ministry as a Methodist, then moved over to Presbyterianism, but then he took an-

---

[2] *Ibid.*, p. 102.

other step and became a Unitarian. His wife was a Universalist.[3] He finally left the ministry and took on the profession of a lawyer.

We have not been able to discover the location of the original Mariett Cummings diary and republish here the version that appeared in the family history.

We have also included as an "Epilogue" a biography, somewhat romantic, that Lucy Foster Sexton wrote of Aunt Mariett. By reading both the diary and Epilogue one gets insight into the life of a truly remarkable American woman.[4]

THE JOURNAL OF
MARIETT FOSTER CUMMINGS

[Tuesday] April 13th, 1852   Started for California amidst the tears and sighs of our friends which is indeed a comforting depression upon our spirits.[1] We find the roads very bad. Went fourteen miles and stopped at a little place called Pavilion [Illinois], rather a romantic name for a few miserable huts. I stayed at a public house and ate fried pudding. This I expect is the beginning of trouble.

14th – Started early and passed through the pretty village of Newark. Found the roads about as bad. Stayed at a sick farmer's where we were well accomodated about five miles from Ottawa. Went 23 miles.

15th – Got to Ottawa about one o'clock; stopped at a miserable hotel until noon when a Californian was robbed here. The night before his valise was cut open, $20 in cash and a quantity of specimens taken from it

---

3 *Ibid.*, p. 110.
4 *Ibid.*, pp. 143-147.
1 They started their journey at Plainfield, Will County, Illinois.

and was left on the bank of the creek. Came to La Salle and stayed at Hardy's Hotel, where we saw Mrs. Cutting, an old acquaintance of sister's.

16th – Commenced raining early but we started and found the roads bad and traveling in the rain unpleasant. Passed through Peru, two miles below LaSalle, and a much prettier place than the latter. Some beautiful residences in it. Went seven miles and stopped at a farmer's where we stayed over night. Came off pleasant.

17th – Got up and put on a suit of short clothes [bloomers] to avoid the mud. Got out and walked and in passing one house the women came out and laughed at me or my dress, I did not ask which, but find it much more convenient for traveling than a long one.

After going fifteen miles we came to the pleasant village of Princeton, by far the prettiest inland town I remember having seen, in all the country, on high and rolling ground. I noticed a great many pleasant country seats. Princeton itself is situated on a commanding eminence and contained two churches and a fine courthouse and the dwellings were in fine state, some of them really beautiful. A few miles below Princeton crossed Beaver River, quite a pretty little stream running through a romantic little valley in which we found a village of a few houses called Indiantown.

The road out of the valley led up between two very high, steep hills, one of which I climbed with difficulty. Upon its summit I found seven graves, some of them enclosed by a little paling. The prospect from this hill was beautiful indeed. We passed on and stopped at a little town of nine or ten houses called Providence. Made 26 miles.

[April] 18th – This morning was very cold and foggy, almost as chilly as yesterday in the hailstorm. We did not start until eleven; made fifteen miles and stopped at a wealthy farmer's, but his wife was unwell, so we were obliged to get our own suppers. Our first trial at camp life, or rather Hoosier life.[2] It is Sunday, but circumstances compelled us to travel. However, I do not think we are quite so bad as some that stopped just before us that were playing ball for a Sunday pastime.

19th – Started very early, hungry, for we could not be tempted to make anything but a slight breakfast from the disgusting material set before us. After going ten miles through the rolling, well watered and timbered country, we came to the village of Lafayette.

The place was small and well enough, I presume, but I was prejudiced by what I saw before I came to it. The road was somewhat muddy and so it had been turned through the unfenced resting place of the dead. All along by the road were sunken graves covered with the footprints of animals that had roamed over them at will.

It looked so unfeeling, inhuman in the inhabitants, to live in plain sight of such things, that I could not even think the village pleasant. In a few more miles we came to another village called Victoria. How would England's queen feel herself honored did she know she had such a wonderful namesake in the far west! I

---

[2] In this case the reference is not to a native of Indiana, but to a kind of easy going tramp, or outdoorsman. The best discussion of "hoosier" is in *Indiana: A Guide to the Hoosier State* (New York, 1945), pp. 3-5.

noticed two or three decent looking dwellings and a blacksmith's shop. Made 28 miles and stopped at a country inn.

20th. – Went eleven miles and stopped with Pa's old friend Ferris at Galesburg, a very pleasant town with an Academy of Knowledge located in it.[3] I noticed five churches and many other fine buildings.

21st – Found the roads very slippery from the rain the previous day. Passed over the flattest prairie I ever saw, several miles in extent, and came to the pretty village of Monmouth, county seat of Warren County.[4] I felt interested in it from a tragedy that occurred there two weeks since. A young lady residing in the family of Doctor Young had an anonymous letter not long since, purporting to be from a gentleman she had rejected, saying that four years ago he had knelt to her and she should kneel to him.

The young lady with true spirit warned herself for an emergency with a pistol which she kept near her bed. One night about two weeks since she was awaked from sleep by someone raising her window, which was in the second floor. She sprang and caught the pistol and snapped but it missed fire.

By this time the man was half inside the room with his hand on her bed and exclaimed: "Don't shoot me, Matilda!" But nothing daunted she fired and wounded or killed him, she did not know which. Her bed and the floor bore traces of blood, but he had accomplices

---

[3] Galesburg is the locale of Knox College.

[4] It was persons from Monmouth, Illinois, who founded Monmouth, Oregon, and the Disciples of Christ college, "Monmouth University," later to become a state school, Oregon College of Education, now Western Oregon State College. Ellis A. Stebbins, *The OCE Story* (Monmouth, Oregon, 1973), especially pp. 1-6.

who took care to remove him so that no trace can be obtained of his whereabouts.

What his object could have been no one can divine unless it were, he had so many with him, to abduct her, to which proceeding she gave a tragic terminus. We stopped two and a half miles from Monmouth at a farmer's.

[April] 22nd – Arose early and passed over two of the most beautiful prairies I ever saw, entirely destitute of inhabitants. On one of them we were for a long time out of sight of timber or dwellings. Came to La Harpe, a distance of thirty miles from Monmouth.

23rd – Left La Harpe early and came sixteen miles to the county seat of Hancock county. Carthage [Illinois] is quite a town, a fine courthouse of brick, I noticed. I believe this is where Jo Smith was killed.[5] Came seventeen miles more to Warsaw on the banks of the Mississippi. But I am disappointed in the river. I expected it would be four miles wide but here at the junction of the Des Moines it is but three quarters wide. I have a great many reflections upon leaving Illinois, where I have spent the most of my life, for the first time since I came here sixteen years since.

24th – Crossed the Mississippi on a steam ferry this morning. The prospect was delightful. The eye took in at one broad sweep the magnificent river with its lofty wooded shores and its fine steamers ploughing up the smooth expanse of water. One has such feelings but once (in regard to any one particular thing)

---

[5] A balanced treatment of the violent death of Joseph and Hyrum Smith is to be found in Leonard J. Arrington and Davis Bitton, *The Mormon Experience* (New York, 1979), pp. 77-82.

in their lives, as I had in crossing the Father of Waters. The ferry is just below where the Des Moines empties in by three distinct mouths.

We landed in Alexandria [Missouri], a little town on the flats. I was surprised to see dwellings on those bottoms, which are some eight miles in extent, and in high water are inundated to the depth of five or six feet. The houses and outbuildings were constructed upon piles driven into the ground so as to raise them above the high-water mark, but which they did not all succeed in accomplishing. for the traces of water were distinctly visible upon their sides.

In one house where the door was set open I could see just how it had risen inside, which was about a foot. The fences and trees were similarly marked. I suppose that there is no land in the United States capable of producing such crops as these same flats. I should think from appearances that they were overflowed last year, for it had remained uncultivated through the past season. It is very dry now and I observed Negroes plowing.

I should think that none but Negroes could live as it must of necessity be very sickly and inundation. Father met in Warsaw one of his old California friends, Mr. Warner. I got considerably acquainted with him and liked him much. He is a gentleman. He returns in May with his family. We came thirteen miles and stopped at a farmer's, very fine, hospitable people.

25th, Sunday – Stayed at the farmer's. Rained quite hard.

26th – Started early and passed through the most desolate country I ever saw. Over one tract of 7880 acres owned by Daniel Webster, which I would scarcely take as a gracious gift, perfectly uninhabited. On it we saw six deer. Arthur started in hot haste after them. We kept on our way for two hours, but he did not come up and Vincent turned back in search. He was gone so long that William and Father went back and told Mother, Billie, and I to drive on. We did so and mistook our road and met Arthur. Was obliged to turn back and send Billie after our folks. I sent Ma and Arthur on and stayed at the forks of the road to prevent a mistake on their part.

I was making preparations to camp for the night when they came up. We drove until ten o'clock when we stopped at a log cabin. The old woman looked precisely like the picture of Mother Long in "The Banditti of the Prairies," [6] an old torn, short linsey dress, awful old shoes and an old factory cap with a ruffle three inches wide all around it composed her dress. I was so afraid I could not sleep.

[April] 27th – Passed through the most God forsaken country that ever lay out doors, the fag-end of all creation. We did not see but two or three log huts in the whole day's travel. Those looked more like hogpens than human habitations. The people have no visible means of support. We could not get even an egg of one of them. At the door of each hut might be seen two or three folks and seven or eight young ones, all dressed in butternut-colored cloth. This seems to be the universal color. William says that the people

---

[6] Edward Bonney's *The Banditti of the Prairies or, The Murderer's Doom!! A Tale of the Mississippi Valley,* was first published in Chicago in 1849. There is a modern version of it reprinted by the University of Oklahoma Press, Norman in 1963. The picture of Mother Long is on page 119. It fits Mariett Cummings' description very well.

are all butternut color with a stripe across the shoulders and down the back like our off-mule.

Stopped at folks that lived in a log house with a fireplace as big as a common bedroom. Bacon is the food and butternut the color and linsey the dress. Plenty of wild turkeys here; saw one this morning.

28th – Went through nine miles of the same stumpy, boggy country and came to Kirksville, the county seat of Adair county. But one decent house, the first I have seen in Missouri, in the place, and I should very much doubt there being so many decent men as that. Twenty-five or thirty gathered around us. A great portion of them drank. Almost the best looking man I saw was a negro (quite a compliment to the rest of the Pokes).[7]

Went four and a half miles further and camped in a beautiful grove near a spring of the finest water I have even seen in the state. We pitched our tent and got out our stove for the first time. Found it worked admirably; fried ham and eggs, baked biscuits, made coffee and sat down on Mother Earth and ate with an extra appetite. Made thirteen miles.

29th – Ferried across the Chariton this morning in an old scow, one team at a time. Took us (with our people hunting mules) until noon. I attempted to fish but was so unfortunate as not to get a nibble. The Chariton is not above six or seven rods wide, but deep and muddy-looking like all the streams in this state that I have seen. Camped on the banks of Yellow Creek in an old camping ground. Good feed for the horses, and the creek was fine, soft water. Had a fine bath and caught some fish out of it. Made about fifteen miles.

---

[7] One did not have to be a Slowpoke to be a lazy, dawdling person – any kind of a Poke would fit that description.

30th – Started early. The country that I saw looked pretty. No houses, scarcely, and those of the most hovel-like description. I slept most all day but I rather doubt having lost much in sightseeing, for there is the most sameness for so much variety I ever saw. There is a hill and vale and grove and flat all day long, each a perfect counterpart of the other. Made about 28 miles and camped in a little hollow; horses in a pasture.

There was a camp on the hill of some Ca'linas just starting. which we called upon this evening. They knew about as much as so many Arabs. They were eating their suppers. The women sat flat on the ground and turned their backs to us, peering occasionally from under their awful, old dirty bonnets at us as though they had never seen a civilized person before, which I presume was the case.

May 1st, 1852 – Did not start very early. Were hindered by the men, who traded a horse for a mule and bought a span there. There were two span in our company that had not been broken and they had a great time breaking mules. Came to a few houses called Stringtown, a very appropriate name. Broke a wagon and were obliged to stop two or three hours. We went into a little log hut, destitute of a window, the light they had being admitted through holes between the logs, and found a family living in it from Southern Illinois. Very homesick; thought they were even fools for coming out of the pale of civilization.

The woman said the country was settling very fast, mostly slave-holders from the south; that there was 75,180 acres of land entered at a little land office last fall. Came on and camped on the west side of New Creek. Made 18 miles.

2nd, Sunday – This morning had a severe thunderstorm which lasted until about 10 a. m. About noon eight or nine teams loaded with Pokes for California crossed New Creek close by our camp. I never saw such human beings as they were. We stayed in our camp all night and it rained almost as hard as it could pour down. We slept in our wagons and the rain fell with such force that it misted through constantly.

I did not venture my head out of bed but once or twice and then the vivid flashes of lightning drove me back quickly.

3rd, Monday – Went about seven miles over a very fine country. Crossed Honey and Big Muddy Creeks and came to Trenton [Missouri], the county seat of Grundy county, the only group of houses that might with the least propriety be called a village. We waited three or four hours to get some repairing done and took dinner at a public house, where I saw the first Negro babe that I had seen since childhood.

We see plenty of slaves. Every family has one or more at Trenton. We crossed on a long bridge Grand River, came on seven or eight miles and stopped at an old Illinoisan's. Made about fifteen miles.

4th, Tuesday – Did not get a very early start. Went seven miles and forded Little Muddy Creek; the water came into the carriage box. Stopped about noon at Craven and bought some corn. Here is the very center of the old Mormon war. Two or three houses had been burned off this very place by them. Went about three miles to Cravensville and crossed the De Armee, a branch of Grand River, but much larger in its swollen state. The ferry boat was a very good one and was rowed across. We passed in sight of but did not see

Adam's grave, where Jo Smith says the father of all
mankind, reposes.

The grave, we were afterwards told, is very curious.
There are five trees, two at the head, one at each shoulder, and one at the foot, enclosing beneath the surface
five strata of stone, precisely in the form of a coffin.
Jo Smith in his day had a revelation that Adam was
buried here.

8th – About noon came to St. Jo, but were obliged to
go back two miles to camp which we did on a romantic
little place on the slope of a hill. St. Jo is rather a
pretty city of 4,000 inhabitants and is situated between
high bluffs on the Missouri river. We were obliged
to stay here until the 12th. We did not receive but one
letter. That was from A. E. G. informing me of the
marriage of my best friend, M. E. Goddard to C. F.
Ballard of Georgetown, Madison county, New York.
God bless her; may she be very happy.

12th – Went to St. Jo early, but was detained trading
for mules until afternoon. Went seventeen miles and
camped on the road to Savannah [Missouri].

13th – Passed through Savannah, a small town, but
were advised to go to Old Fort Kearney [Kearny, on
the Nebraska side of the Missouri, site of present
Nebraska City] to cross. Passed through one of the
worst mud-holes I ever saw in sight of the town. Went
six miles and camped on a hill near a herd of cattle.

14th – Started early and crossed the Nodaway in a
rope ferry. Camped by the lone tree.

[May] 15th – Camped on the banks of the Great Tara.
Caught a silver fish.

16th – Traveled through a very romantic country, high

bluffs that looked like a miniature range of mountains. Camped near a little stream in a little valley.

17th, Sunday – We did not intend traveling today, but it was rather unpleasant where we were, so about noon we broke up camp and passed through a valley that had undoubtedly once been the bed of the river. Crossed the Nishnetottemah [Nishnebotna] and about midnight stopped one mile from the ferry, but instead of finding a village as we supposed we should find at Fort Kearny, we only found a miserable log hut and pack house, occupied by the most swinish specimen I ever saw in the shape of a ferryman.

18th – Moved our camp a mile from our old camping ground and dug a hole to get some water fit to drink. Washed.

19th – Went down to the ferry to see Mrs. Thomas Burrell. Saw H. Kaufman.

20th – Went fishing and burned my face but did not have a single bite. Some of the party caught two fish of a new species but which we did not eat.

21st – Came down to the old ferry but was obliged to wait until evening before we could cross. In the meantime we found my old beau Lamb who had with his family started for California. We went two and a half miles and camped on a hill near the little stream of soft water, and our people commenced standing guard. Heard plenty of prairie wolves.

St. Joseph, May 22nd – Saturday – It was foggy and cold this morning but we started early in company with the people who camped with us. As we passed over miles of beautiful prairie entirely destitute of timber, and entirely out of sight of it, occasionally we would pass near a little stream with a slight border of cottonwoods. We crossed Weeping Water and Saline River. The last was slightly salt, but certainly the most beautiful stream I ever saw.

We forded easily and camped on the banks and went fishing. We set our hooks, lost two of them and caught one fish, a white or silver fish. We made about 25 miles.

Raining hard when I awoke. Harnessed the animals early but did not break up camp until eleven o'clock. For the first two miles we saw some timber but after that none, but without doubt through the most beautiful prairie country in the west, just rolling enough to be beautiful and good. Did not see a house or a fence in our whole day's travel.

Camped about three miles from a half-dozen trees, and sent Billie on the pony after some wood. Our animals had a stampede and it took an hour to secure them, as their throwing Billie and pony and Byron all in a stack. It has rained hard all day. Three teams joined company at dusk. Made 18 miles.

23rd, Sunday – Started early and traveled all day over the same boundless prairie. Camped about 25 miles from Salt River.

24th, Monday – Pleasant; traveled on, on, on over the same kind of country, one flat prairie as smooth as a house floor. A mail stage passed us. Saw an abundance of prairie wolves. Just at night came down into the valley of the Platte river, one hundred miles from old Ft. Kearney. Camped on the bottoms. The wolves began to yell before night and were in sight from every direction.

25th, Tuesday – The road lay along the bottom, some

distance from the Platte. About noon we overtook the
Burrell and Kaufman company. Went down to the
river just at the head of Grand Island, which is 80
miles in length. Kaufman's company joined ours, six
men, two wagons, and some pack animals. In the afternoon we saw some Indians, six in number, the first
we had seen. They were mounted and one of them on
a fine American horse, undoubtedly stolen.

They passed rapidly, but not before I saw the dress
of one, which was a breech cloth, and over his naked
shoulders was thrown a round piece of skin two feet
across, ornamented with feathers, as were the horses'
tails. Made 25 miles.

26th, Wednesday – Before we started this morning
we were visited by quantities of Indians that followed
us all the forenoon and camped for their dinner near
us. They cut willows and stuck then into the ground
and spread their buffalo robes over them so as to form
quite a primitive tent.

Their fires were kindled in a thrice and a single
crotch stuck into the ground obliquely supported their
kettles over it. We broke up our noon camp before
them to avoid them if possible, but we had not gone
out of sight of their encampment before we met five
of their number returning driving a mule, and screaming in the most terrific manner and screaming to us
to "Hold on."

We caught sight of their pursuers who followed
them almost into camp, rode around awhile and then
slowly retreated to the hills. There were but 11.

The returning Pawnees created a great sensation in
the camp. There was stripping and mounting in hot
haste, and as they got ready they came singly and in

groups, screaming in the most devilish, unearthly style imaginable. We were between the contending parties.

As the Pawnees came running their horses by us each one would point at the Sioux and at us, and motion us to stop and join them and whip their enemies. They were very angry that we did not, and we were apprehensive of an attack, but they were too cowardly.

A portion of the foremost scoured the hills for their enemies, while the rest as they came screaming and yelling, singing their war songs, running their old ponies, gathered in a group on a slight eminence on the east side. Directly they discovered the Sioux and squaws, 13, in the north, and them commenced a running fight.

We heard three guns and arrows in abundance. The Pawnees had not courage to join the fight, many of them, but the Sioux killed one of them, and then the Pawnees fled, 150 of them, before 13 Sioux and left their dead man on the field of battle. They came back stiller but full as fast as they went out.

In the meantime we had stopped and driven into a huddle, and the men had got their guns and ammunition ready for instant use. When the old chiefs returned they were perfectly beside themselves with rage and fear. One in his impetuous gesticulations struck at one of our company with his bow. He showed him his gun and the chief left suddenly. There were two guns among the Pawnees and my brother gave one of them some ammunition but he had not courage enough to use it.

The Sioux and squaws got two scalps, one on the battlefield and one in the hills. We thought there were none of them injured but an emigrant train that over-

took us said that they met the Pawnees in full retreat
driving before them on foot a Sioux that had been shot
through the body and otherwise badly wounded. He
was bound and weak with loss of blood but they drove
him on with whips. A brave nation, truly! One hundred and fifty of them vanquished by 13.

We passed on and by an Indian village that was
deserted near which was a square of perhaps twenty
feet formed of ponies' skulls with the large part cut
out that presened quite a unique appearance. We
camped on a little flat where the mosquitoes beat
everything I ever dreamed of. However, despite them
we took a bath in a slough nearby. Made over 20 miles.

27th, Thursday – Rose early amidst clouds of mosquitoes and passed over sand hills that came close to
the river's brink. The river presents a most beautiful
prospect, varying from three quarters to a mile and
perhaps more, in width, and thickly studded with em-
erald islands, the largest of which were thickly wooded.
Passed an emigrant train of 10 or 12 ox wagons, bound
for Oregon.

Camped at six o'clock on a flat. Fine feed, and one
of the company dug a well that afforded excellent
water which we were glad enough of after the intense
head of today. After we had camped we were joined
by 16 or 18 mule teams, which made our company
appear quite formidable. Made about 25 miles.

[May] 28th, Friday – Started early, before most of
the camp. Much cooler than yesterday, there being a
strong west wind. Traveled most of the morning over
sandhills that came to the river's brink, but made our
noon camp on a vast flat. Plenty of grass and Platte
water. Passed forty or fifty wagons camped on a great

prairie. Poor feed; dug a hole for water, but it was so strongly impregnated with sulphur that we could not use it. Made 28 miles.

29th, Saturday – After traveling for seven or eight miles struck the junction of the St. Jo and Ft. Kearny roads and a few miles farther on came in sight of Fort Charles, or new Fort Kearny. Camped for noon in sight of the fort; stopped for some time there. There are two or three fine buildings, one for the captains, another for the teacher and doctor, and one for the inferior officers. The soldiers' barracks are turf, sod and all, most miserable looking holes.

Passed on eight miles and camped a short distance from the ferry.

30th, Sunday – Broke up camp late to ferry the Platte, which is one and a half miles. I never dreamed of anything like this river. It is impossible to see an eighth of an inch into it and the bottom is quicksand so that an animal can gain no sure footing and a wagon runs as though it were the roughest stones, one constant jar; and the moment it stops settles very deep.

It took us two hours to cross with one wagon, the box of which was raised a foot, and then we got into one hole where the water ran into the box. I drove the wheel mules and was very much frightened for fear of their drowning. I surely never was so glad to gain "terra firma" before. After we all crossed we went two miles and camped. Found a very heavy watchcase of silver in the road.

31st, Monday – Got an early start and went eight or nine miles and crossed Elm Creek; saw a cow left; saw the first buffalo chips and plenty of skeletons and horns. Passed on seven miles further and came to Buffalo creek which they were obliged to bridge with brush before crossing; a bad place. The feed poor; the prairie has been burned over, and a great want of rain, it must of necessity be poor.

Camped on the prairie; dug for water but without success. Used the river water; and buffalo chips for fuel and they make a very good fire when dry. Two men died in an ox train which we passed of cholera morbus. Passed 96 teams today, all ox but two. Made 28 miles.

June first, Tuesday – Broke up early, and after traveling seven miles came to Willow lake, a kind of mud puddle or series of them honored by that name. Passed one of them where a man was just taken sick of the cholera morbus, very sick, too. Saw quantities of prickly pear and for several days spots covered with saline and alkali deposits.

The flat on this side is quite extensive, the sand bluffs in some places out of sight. The heat today is almost unbearable and has been for some days from eleven to three in the afternoon. No rain for almost a fortnight and no dews of consequence, sometimes so slight as to be almost imperceptible.

Passed several graves, I should think twenty since entering the Indian territory. We passed this afternoon a colony of prairie dogs and saw plenty of them as they came out and barked at us. Their dens covered a good many acres. Made 28 miles and camped near the river.

June 2nd, Wednesday – Passed over a fine low portion of the flat; good grass. Saw three new made graves, one of them made yesterday, a man from Illinois and a lady from Peru, Illinois. Crossed some quicksand bluffs that came to the river's bank. I walked over them and sank into the sand nearly over my shoes every step. Saw several little gray lizards, quicker than lightning. Met the Mormon trail from Salt Lake City. Very sickly.

(Neglect) – Awful sick with the earache and headache last night.

June 8 – Today passed Castle Ruins, a series of curious rocks resembling a ruined city, some of them looking like solid masonry. One could easily fancy they had been inhabited. Saw "Chimney Rock" a distance of forty miles. Came on four miles and camped near the river. Made thirty miles.

June 9th – Started early and passed a grave just finished, an old man from Illinois. Came to a high sand ridge white as snow. Passed Courthouse Rock, square in front, with a smaller one near by looking like a sentinel post. The upper part of Chimney Rock is becoming plainly visible. An antelope came almost into our noon camp. They shot at it but it went bounding off to the hills unharmed. Camped opposite Chimney Rock, said to be 700 feet above the level of the Platte.

It is rock or rather petrified clay in form like this. It did not look so high as it stood in front of a higher bluff. Made 28 miles.

10th – Passed Bluff Ruins, most beautiful, too. I made a rough draft then I was so charmed that I could not gaze enough. Made our noon halt opposite Scott's Bluff, altogether the most symmetrical in form and the most stupendous in size of any we have yet seen. One of them is close in its resemblance to the dome of the Capitol at Washington.

There is a pass through that is guarded on one side by Sugar Loaf Rock, on the other by one that resembles a square house with an observatory. There is one (nearest the river) I will not attempt to describe, certainly the most magnificent thing I ever saw. Away up on the top is a green spot of earth and cedar trees are clinging to its rocky sides and covering its lofty crest.

Camped above Scott's Bluffs near the river. Father took a shovel and dug up some pitch wood, probably deposited by water.

11th, Friday – Drove all day through a desolate looking country, some parts of it literally covered with prickly pears and alkaline deposits. Towards night struck the river, which was absolutely bordered with roses. Camped on some sandhills covered with oats in sight of the river. It has been exceedingly unpleasant today on account of high winds. It seemed as though the wagon would upset some of the time. Made 28 miles.

12th, Saturday – Took an early start and after traveling a few miles struck the river which was bordered with trees, the first we have seen on this side for over 200 miles. In a group of trees near the road was a trader's tent pitched, and several skin wigwams near for the manufacture of moccasins. Saw an Indian village on the opposite side of the river.

Came opposite Fort Laramie about ten o'clock. There is a ferry across the north branch here. The north and south branches unite just below, in sight. There were several Indian lodges and a Frenchman, a trader, living in one of them with a squaw and lots of halfbreed children. There are two fine two-story buildings at the fort, one of them officer's quarters and the other a trading post. We found dried fruits and hams and bacon as cheap as at St. Jo.

We stayed opposite the ferry nearly all day as Father was busy selecting a span of mules from a drove across the river. Went out half a mile and camped. Grass poor. A Sioux visited our camp this evening and he was a fine specimen of an Indian. The Sioux are a tall, athletic, symmetrical tribe. The squaws are quite pretty, some of them, and the babies really so. They seem too proud to beg as their brother redskins the Pawnees, do.

13th, Sunday – Started at five o'clock to find good grass and traveled over a hilly country for ten miles and camped until twelve o'clock. Saw a new flower, the Lily of the Black Hills. Then we passed over the most precipitous hills and the most beautiful gorges I ever dreamed of. The hills were almost mountains and the sides covered with cedar and pine trees in the most fantastical shape imaginable, giving them from a distance a black appearance. Hence the name Black Hills. Just before night we struck the river and camped in a very pleasant spot. Made 28 miles.

14th, Monday – Traveled on, on, through the same gorges and over the same hills until noon when the country became less broken, and the trees less frequent. Have passed but one or two little brooks today. Made thirty miles and camped near some stagnant water. Have not seen the river since we left it this morning. Rained this afternoon; cold, very.

[June] 15th, Tuesday – Did not start early; cold and unpleasant. Went down some steep hills and in about three miles came to a trader's tent with Indian wigwams around it. Did not succeed in getting any moccasins. The country is assuming a curious aspect, high hills of bare rock, some of them closely resembling an ancient citadel and again others conical with a cap of rock of square form. Passed through a gorge a hundred feet deep with pyramids in the bottom and walls of rock around it. The bottom is of white clay rock. A wild and strange place, one that gave a person curious emotions.

Greasewood and sage have been abundant for a few days. About noon came to the river, which looked refreshing after the clouds of dust we have passed through. Made a noon halt late near the river. Found a curious arrow, the blade sharp at the point, and the part joining the wood notched so that it could not be drawn out. Saw two species of cactus in bloom and a new flower a little resembling the pink, but without its fragrance. A man is sick with the cholera within a few rods of us.

Passed on over desert sandhills until about seven o'clock and after going down a perpendicular, rocky hill came into a valley and camped. Grass not very good. Near the river for more than 80 rods were crotches and poles stuck into the ground thick where there had been Indian lodges. Probably winter quarters from the quantities of old moccasins and buffalo skin strewed over the ground.

16th, Wednesday – Traveled nearly all the morning to get a few miles on our direct course for we went over several (to me) high mountains and crooked around to avoid deep ravines. Made our noon halt on a miserable place but did not travel more than two miles in the afternoon when in getting to the river for

water we came directly into a beautiful little valley
of good feed, where we immediately camped for the
remainder of the day, which I improved by having
a thorough wash.

17th, Thursday – Before we left camp this morning
Mr. Sawyer's [8] wagon drove into the valley. The road
today has lain over deep sandhills and we made our
noon camp on one of the highest, from which we had
a glimpse of a buffalo hunt.

The buffalo was coming down to the river very
leisurely when some men encamped near saw him
and gave chase. He ran down across a little plain,
swam a deep creek and plunged for the shore and
effected a landing amids a perfect shower of bullets,
several of which took effect, one of them fracturing
a foreleg.

He ran up the road for nearly half a mile, but there
were a hundred men after him and he turned and ran
for the river and jumped twenty feet off a bluff into
the water swam down a mile and landed on a little
island, when he was so disabled that a man went over
and dispatched him with a pistol.

Came on over heavy hills until five and camped
in a miserable place almost overgrown with cactus.
Made 15 miles. Arthur killed our first rabbit tonight.

18th, Friday – Started a little after four o'clock this
morning in order to pass a large oxtrain before it
got in motion, which we effected. The roads were
mostly sand. Passed over the worst hills we have seen;
came at noon to the south ferry and went up on the

---

[8] See the diary of Francis Sawyer, immediately preceding Mariett Cummings' journal in this volume, for the Sawyer family. The husband's name
was Thomas Sawyer.

side of the worst sandhill for 200 miles to come and
made a noon camp.

Grass good; wild oats. Got a piece of antelope of
a man and saw my first buffalo steak. The trains went
over the mountain but I went across it on the brink
of the river which was at times nearly 100 feet almost
directly down beneath. I did not dare look at the
water for fear of falling. It was nearly a mile across
and intensely warm. I was tired and heated but I
bathed my face and hands in the river nearby a beautiful cottonwood grove and went on over a bottom
covered with alkali to the road which I reached before
the trains.

After going four miles we came to the upper ferry
and left the river and traveled over the hardest road
over hills and through barren vales, for ten miles to
Sulphur Springs. The water is considered poison and
it may be in some of them but we drank some and
gave it to the animals without injury. Made I suppose
35 miles; did not arrive at our camp until after dark.

19th, Saturday – Started early to cross a desert of from
17 to 18 miles in extent. It was hot and no water. We
passed large droves of cattle and sheep that seemed to
suffer much. Our animals had water in the morning,
which I presume they did not, for they went the river
road which was farther, and no water after the first
eight miles.

A little after noon we came to Willow Springs, but
the willows from which they derived their name are
cut down for fuel. They are in a gorge of the mountains and afford delicious cool water which was exceedingly refreshing to the thirsty traveler. Upon leaving the Springs we ascended Prospect Hill, a long and

tedious one, too, passed on eight miles, and camped on a hill by the side of the road about one half mile from a little brook in a ravine. Poor grass. Made 26 miles.

[June] 20th, Sunday – Were obliged to drive until we found grass, which we did by taking a by-road that led down into a flat of some extent and excellent grass that had been uncropped. A rapid little stream four or five feet wide ran through it. We immediately decided to spend the day there and a day of rest was not at all unwelcome to man or beast. Toward evening the boys went out and killed a fine antelope.

21, Monday – Passed through valleys and by alkali lakes where the dust looked like, and produced the same pungent sensation in the nostrils that ashes would do. There were several lakes near the road and one of them was for the distance of six or seven yards encrusted with saleratus in a crystalized form. I noticed a little stick near the center around which a little island of saleratus had formed.

A few miles on we struck the Sweetwater and a little farther on Independence Rock of which we have heard so much. It is an immense pile of rock resembling granite entirely isolated in position and of stupendous proportions. The side near the road is perfectly covered with names. Some have evinced a good deal of ambition in inscribing them on almost inaccessible points.

Six miles farther on we pass Devil's Gate, where the Sweetwater has cut a channel through the mountains of rock. It is 500 feet deep. The rocks are smooth and perpendicular. Certainly this is the greatest curiosity I have ever seen. We went up a little mountain stream for noon camp, caught a trout and had a most delicious bath. Passed on several miles and camped near the river in sight of another and smaller gate that the river passes through. Made 28 miles.

22nd, Tuesday – Did not go the old route but took the river road past magnificent mountains of rock of the most complicated forms and very high, with an occasional cedar tree on their bare and rugged sides. Eight miles, and we struck the old road as it comes down to the river. Here we saw a man that had been left by some company taking his duds up to the rocks. I rode on horseback all the morning, met a Bear River Indian and traded ponies, with William's fireman's dress coat to boot, which the Indian put on over an old blanket, his bare legs protruding beneath.

Passed Bitter Cottonwood Creek, on the banks of which they were burying a woman. The little children were sitting in the wagon, and the husband at the head of the grave, weeping bitterly over the uncoffined burial. Just after noon we came to a ford of the Sweetwater where we encountered a severe hail and rainstorm. We did not ford but kept up the river over a heavy sand road near Rocky Mountains for several miles. The dead cattle are growing numerous over these dry deserts. Went 12 or 13 miles and came to the river where we camped. Poor feed; made thirty miles.

24th, Thursday – Drove for several miles down the Valley to a point where it looked as though the road terminated, but the road made an abrupt turn up through a deep ravine and up a high mountain. Found a French trader's post in one of the ravines, and quite a grocery store, an old squaw and some halfbreed children.

We have gone up rapidly today and it is cold enough to make one's fingers ache. Very showery, and not so fickle as the yesterday, for one moment I would be burned by the sun and the next frozen. Saw snow at a distance on a mountain and some near the road. Have seen snow at the distance for several days. Passed two cold springs, cold enough to make one's teeth ache. Went up a little ravine by a mountain stream for noon halt, – Strawberry Creek, wrongly named; no strawberries there.

Passed over high hills in the afternoon with strata of rock standing out edgeways. Looked like a porcupine's back. Crossed Willow Creek; 12 miles farther on Aspen Creek, its banks covered wih snow. A blacksmith shop on the creek. Crossed and went down a mile to Aspen Grove, behind which was a bank of snow 30 feet deep. Very cold; could not keep warm with double shawl and mittens. Twenty-eight miles.

25th, Friday – Went eight miles and crossed the Sweetwater. In a ravine close by the road I walked over a snowbank several feet deep and supplied myself with a snowball. Made our noon halt on the hill and the men prospected for gold in the ravines without success, though they thought there was gold there if they had time to look for it. No water near the road for many miles but we procured some by going a mile off it, striking a bend of the Sweetwater. This is the last sream we shall see this side of the Rocky Mountains.

Table Rock, the dividing point, has been in sight since yesterday. Went from the watering place four miles over the summit and camped on the slope of a

hill. Good feed. We are on the western slope. Twenty-
nine miles.

26th, Saturday – Four miles to Pacific Springs, the
little stream which we followed for several miles.
Then struck off and for over 20 miles no water. Struck
Little Sandy River, crossed and went down two miles
and camped. Made 29 miles.

[June] 27th, Sunday – Went eight miles and struck
Big Sandy; crossed and went 15 miles and struck the
same river; I think, and camped without crossing.
Took Salt Lake City road.

28th, Monday – Started before sunrise in order to get
to the ferry of Green River, which we did by eight
o'clock. Green River is a deep, swift stream 200 feet
wide. A rope ferry, and the moderate charge of $3
per wagon, 25 cents per head of horses. Went down
the river five miles and then left and struck off fifteen
miles without water over a rolling prairie. First rate
roads. Struck Ham's Fork and camped among clouds
of mosquitoes. Made 30 miles.

29, Tuesday – Went four miles and crossed Silver
Creek, a beautiful little stream. Went on several miles
and struck Black's Fork and crossed on the old Mormon road. Went on and struck the river and camped.
Passed the most magnificent curiosity I have ever
seen on the road. It was a stupendous rock of petrified
clay and sandstone of blue and light and dark brown
color. There were spires and domes, grottoes and caves
of every form and size. It was immensely high and
colonnaded. One's voice would reverbrate several times.
We called it "Echo Rock." Made a small drive.
Mosquitoes awful thick. I went out before night to one

of those curious rocks. I found them composed of clay and gray sandstone. Found pretty stones.

30, Wednesday – Went a mile and forded the stream, a few miles and crossed back. Raised wagon beds. Went on several miles and camped in sight of Fort Bridger, and made a noon halt in a perfect garden in Bridger's beautiful bottom land. Black's Fork divides into four or five branches on this bottom. Found strawberries, the first we have seen, and roses and shrubbery. After dinner crossed another branch to the fort, which is nothing but a trading post.

Major Bridger [9] is a man considerably advanced in years. Has had several squaws of the different tribes for wives. Is now living with a Root Digger which he brought from California. Has in all six halfbreed children by three different wives. He lives in the fort in one room in the most Indian-like manner, but is immensely rich. Has a Mexican grant of ten miles square around the fort, stock in abundance, and gold without end, and yet is much of a gentleman but lives like a hog. Camped near the fort on the other side of another fork. One hundred thirteen miles to the city.

July first, 1852, Thursday – Started early and crossed the last fork of Black's Fork, a very rapid, narrow, deep stream. Raised the wagon beds and then got wet by one of the wagons becoming unblocked and broken. Came to the hills, the sides of which were covered with cedars. Are ascending rapidly today, but passed

---

[9] Jim Bridger, of course, was one of the most eminent of mountain men. Cornelius M. Ismert, "James Bridger," in LeRoy R. Hafen, Editor, *The Mountain Men and the Fur Trade of the Far West,* VI (Glendale, California, 1968), pp. 85-104; also a picture of the fort on page 102 and one of Bridger himself on page [15].

down the steepest hill we have ever seen, stony and bad, into the Valley of Jehosophat. Rather fine.

Near the middle crossed Muddy Fork and through several valleys and then climbed the Utah Mountains, the highest that the road passes over. The descent was very difficult and to make it worse the mules ran halfway down. On the slope was a very fine spring. We passed on over mountains and through vales for several miles to Spring Brook, which we went down a mile. We camped in a little valley where we found the rest of our company. Made 32 miles. The watch tonight saw four Indians near the camp.

2nd, Friday – Went about a mile and crossed Bear River in several channels. One mule got badly hurt. Climbed some bad hills and went down some bad ones until we struck Echo Creek in Echo Canyon, a beautiful, fertile valley, varying from 300 yards to just wide enough for the little stream and road, which kept constantly crossing.

The mountains on the south side were a mile high, with cedars and cottonwoods ornamenting their sides. On the north the most stupendous cliffs of red rock, of gravel cemented together and sandstone, some of them of indescribable beauty and magnificence.

At noon we camped opposite the entrance to a cave high up in the rocks, which we explored. The entrance was an arch, the cavern 30 by 25 feet and high enough for a person to stand erect in. The rock in which it is is of very soft gray sandstone. Striking anything forcibly on the floor, it sounded hollow underneath, and in fact in the corner was an opening but not large enough to admit of entrance. It led down undoubtedly into another underneath. The rocks at the side towered hundreds of feet above. The sides were full of holes and looked almost like honeycomb.

Three Utahs came down out of the hills to beg, which they understood well enough. They were only half clothed. They talked English intelligently and begged for pistols, breeches, biscuits (big ones), powder, shot, caps, jackets, tobacco, cups, et cetera. One of them had got the legs off two pairs of pants and with the waistbands hanging down and what had been a woman's white nightdress, but no one would have thought so from the color.

In the afternoon we passed whole families, men, squaws and pappooses, some of them more than half naked and catching crickets, all begging. Passed down several miles and camped where the mountains and rocks were a mile high, and where it was twilight in the valley when the sun shone on the mountain peaks. Splendid feed, never better, and quantities of wild gooseberries without thorns. Made 25 miles.

3rd, Saturday – Went fifteen miles through this canyon, the wildest and most magnificent scenery, surpassing anything I ever dreamed of, constantly crossing and recrossing the stream, in some places the rocks hanging over our heads in every form, and the valley constantly narrowing until finally we came to Weber river. It runs directly across the foot of the canyon. Went down it a mile and made a noon halt and went fishing. Caught one speckled trout. Went one mile farther down and forded; good crossing. One mile farther down camped. Made 18 miles. Caught some more fish.

[July] 4th, Sunday – The anniversary of America's Independence. Tomorrow it will be celebrated at home with great ceremony while we are away out in the wilds of Deseret,[10] toiling on, on. Left the river and struck up a canyon with a little stream which we have kept constantly crossing. A great many springs coming out of the mountainside but bad water.

Ran this canyon out and struck another with a fine stream of water, the valley so narrow that we cross the stream once in two rods, some of the times, the bottoms some of the way a perfect chapparel, some very steep, stony hills. In the afternoon climbed a long, stony mountain six or seven miles to the top and the canyon in some places so narrow that it would hardly admit the passage of a wagon.

Saw several mules tired out on reaching the top. We saw through a gorge in the mountains the Valley of Great Salt Lake spread out before us. The descent of this mountain was very difficult, almost perpendicular in places and four or five miles before we reached the bottom the road ran in a gorge and the mountains towered high above on either side, covered with small, dead cottonwoods that looked on the top and sides like a network of hoar frost.

Did not arrive at the foot of the mountain until dark and camped near a temporary blacksmith's, barber and baker shop that some enterprising Mormons had erected. Made 30 miles.

July 5th – This morning we were awakened by the firing of cannon in the city, which is 12 miles distant. Did not get started for the city until 10 a. m., and had an exceedingly bad mountain to climb and de-

---

10 Deseret was the name given by the Mormons to their provisional secular state in 1849. The term means "Beehive." It preceded the term "Utah" for the designation of a large area of the Great Basin. Arrington and Bitton, *op. cit.*, pp. 162-163.

scend. Then the road led through a very narrow canyon in one place resembling a gate, for the rocks jutted into the stream high on each side and we were obliged to pass down the bed of the creek, which was just high enough to admit the passage of the wagon.

The city, when we first came in sight of it, presented the appearance of a herd of white castles. We drove to the last ward, next the church farm, to the house of an old acquaintance, and stopped. In the afternoon we drove up to the Tabernacle to the latter part of the celebration, which consisted of a ranting Mormon oration, music by a superb brass band, and a comic song, "The Potato War" by a gentleman, and a very long benediction.

The Tabernacle is the most superb building of the kind I ever saw. It is built of adobe, 160 by 60 feet in length, one story in height and arched, with Gothic windows in the ends. The altar is in the middle of one side and is an elegant affair. The seats at the end and side are elevated from the altar to the doors one above the other, so that a person has a perfect view from any part of the house.

There are no posts or columns to obstruct the sight. On the front of the building is an elegantly carved cornice and a gilded design of the rising sun. They are at present laying the foundation of a wall that will enclose 10 acres, including the Tabernacle, inside of which they intend erecting a more costly and superb temple than they have ever before attempted. The city is laid out in good taste, the streets all running at right angles, and around each square they have made the water to run for the purpose of irrigation. The city is four miles square and contains (I should think) 5000 inhabitants. I saw Brigham Young, the governor of Utah Territory, and several of his brothers. He is 51 years of age but does not look more than 30. He has 30 or 40 wives and 12 children under one year of age. His family numbers over 100. His harem, where most of his wives live, is a poor, miserable log adobe affair, directly in front of his elegant, Gothic-windowed barn!

His house is rather pretty. Next year he intends building a large establishment for the Mrs. Youngs, some of which are living at their fathers' yet. It is not at all uncommon for a man to marry three or four sisters and their mother. One lady that brother was some acquainted with and her mother married an old man that had already two or three wives.

They marry and unmarry at pleasure several times a year if they choose. The state of society corresponds well with the Age of Barbarism in the east. The crops are fine, particularly the wheat, which they are harvesting.

July 6th – Today we had the severest hailstorm I ever saw. The hail was of the size of a walnut, and so thick that a person could not see three rods. It damaged the crops very much, threshing the ripe wheat and breaking down the corn. The Salt Lake Basin is covered by mountains whose peaks are covered with eternal snows.

July 7th – Rested and went up town. Gave $2.50 for a pair of bootees.

July 8th – Did not get out of the city much before noon. At the outskirts of the city passed the tepid sulphur spring, and bath house. The scent was very disagreeable to me. A short distance above the bath is a spring. The water was very clear but deposited a bright green substance, and was almost too warm to bear the hand in. A few miles farther on we passed Copperas Spring, almost boiling temperature, steam constantly floating over its surface.

The smell was particularly disagreeable to me. Near it they had made an opening in the mountain where they procured their copperas. Came on 10 miles from the city and camped.

July 9th, Friday – The finest farming country we have seen, pretty thickly settled all along, and every little distance mountain streams running across the road, of the purest soft water. We are in plain sight of Great Salt Lake and two mountain islands. They are sixty miles north. I saw some of the salt, which is of the purest, whitest quality. The lake is said to be 300 miles in length and to contain lakes of the freshest water. There are several large rivers emptying into it and no outlet whatever. We passed on several miles and camped near the mountains on a little stream of cold, snow water.

10th – Started for the Weber River in the carriage, fishing. Fished all day faithfully and caught 17 fine speckled trout. But as we were doing up our fishing tackle preparatory to a start home they floated off into deep water and sank past recovery and we went home crestfallen indeed – fishless.

[Sunday] 11th – Moved our camp to within two miles of Weber and went fishing again with better success. Caught fifteen large trout and gathered a fine lot of ripe service berries.

12th – Started early; went two miles down the river and forded; passed over a mountain and in five miles came to Ogden river which we forded, and passed on to Ogden City, a few old log houses and a blacksmith's shop where we stopped to get some repairing done.

13th, Tuesday – Did not leave until afternoon. Got some wheat of an old farmer Mormon. Drove to Willow Springs fifteen miles and camped on a side hill after dark.

14th, Wednesday – Are getting out of log houses and Mormons fast. Passed the last house this afternoon. Our course since leaving Salt Lake City has been north along the rim of the basin. Towards night came to a ravine full of springs. Some of them were cold water, tolerable good, warm springs, and boiling salt springs around which the ground was encrusted with crystallized salt. A short distance away was a lake of alternate cold and hot water. I went down to it but the mosquitoes drove me quickly away. Camped within three miles of Bear River. Excessively hot.

15th, Thursday – Ferried the river on a boat made of two skiffs lashed together, at the small price of $3.50 per wagon, the river not more than four rods wide and still. Three miles from the river crossed Miladd [Malad], a miry stream but a poor apology for a bridge across it. Went eleven miles farther and camped near a spring of brackish water about noon. Very warm.

16th, Friday – Rained all night and showery all day. Drove thirteen miles over hill and dale and came to Blue Spring. Poor water. Fourteen miles farther to a spring of tolerable water, and camped. The longest 27 miles I ever traveled. How often have I thought of my dear friend Mary E. Ballard. She has been married three months today. How earnestly do I pray that she may be happy and that she may never know sorrow or care. How I would like to see her and hers.

17th, Saturday, – Started early and in six miles came to a very pretty stream in quite an extensive valley that looked very fine, but in traveling over it we found it covered with sagebrush. Met a large company of California packers who have been one month on the road. Went 6 miles farther and stopped at a kind of marsh. Ten miles farther in a large valley came to Pilot Springs, small but affording the thirsty wayfarer good water. Six miles farther struck the mountain and ascended the first bench and camped near a large ox-train composed of the most verdant of Missourians.

18th July, Sunday – It is the holy Sabbath time but rest is denied the worn traveler. This is like all other days on this road and the weary pilgrim to the shrine of gold plods on his tiresome way. Started early, went six miles, crossed Stony Creek, a fine stream of snow water. Saw an Indian close by, tolerably dressed, begging, as usual. Long, low ranges of mountains in sight, covered with perpetual snows. Passed over the head of a valley of some extent and came to Trout Creek. Passed up it four or five miles and camped. Made 28 miles.

19th, Monday – Made an early start and went four miles and crossed Raft River, a little brook, nothing more. The other road is in sight. Went up the stream some distance and up through a canyon opposite Steeple Rocks, magnificent, conical rocks as white as marble, glossy and bright, several hundred feet in height.

They are three in number. In the canyon below we saw a group of similar ones.

A mile from here we came to the junction of the two roads, down a long hill and through a valley of some extent. We came to a small spring of water. A short distance farther on made a short noon halt. In the afternoon passed over a series of the steepest hills I ever went over, one nearly perpendicular. Late in the afternoon struck Goose Creek. Passed up it two miles and camped. Made over thirty miles.

20th, Tuesday – Very cold this morning, uncomfortably so. Drove hard; did not stop for noon. Passed up through a long, narrow canyon crossing the creek. Here saw four Root Diggers and found quantities of ripe yellow currants, very fine flavored. Some magnificent rocks lay by or above the road, the fronts of which were covered with lichen of a bright yellow and brown. Camped a little after noon opposite Rock Spring, where the road leaves Goose Creek. Made 24 miles.

21st, Wednesday – Started just as the sun gilded the mountain peaks. Cold so early. I was barely able to hold up my head it pained me so, and a high fever. Drove over a very stony mountain 13 miles and found a spring but neglected taking in water. Found no more drinkable water for 20 miles, the roads very dusty and the day very hot. Two mules failed, and even obliged to take them out of the team. Found some poor water, gave the animals some, drove on into Thousand Springs Valley and camped near water and good feed. Thirty-four miles.

22nd, Thursday – Laid by today to recruit our animals.

The valley is full of springs of great depth and very near together. There is a marsh that seems to me to be made soil over a large lake. It is springy and more or less covered by water and all over it are these holes, some of which are filled with fish of a variety I am unacquainted with.

23rd, Friday – Passed oxteams incessantly through dust so thick that we could not see the wagon before us and much of the time not our own leaders.[11] Our road has been mostly over a plain, excellent roads but very warm. Made 28 miles, camped near a patch of splendid clover off the road.

24th, Saturday – In a camp near us a little child was buried this morning. Over hill and dale and down into a saleratus valley where there was a spring of indifferent water. The ground, wherever there was water, was like the strongest lye. At noon struck the head branch of Humboldt river, passed down it for eight or ten miles and camped in a splendid place; clover and fine grass. Made 25 miles.

[July] 25th, Sunday – In camp today with a large mule train. Very warm. Got out my instrument and had some fine music.[12]

---

[11] "No matter what route was taken by an overland party the going was difficult beyond the Continental Divide. Rocks mangled the feet of the animals and alkali-laden dust burned faces and throats. Moreover this high dry country was nearly always traversed at its driest and hottest period, and as the trains increased in number the ground, even on the lush prairies eastward, was churned to fine dust that enveloped the route in a perpetual crowd. By 1852, when 100,000 people had already crossed the country, the dust-cloud never had a chance to settle, watering and camping places were perpetually fouled, and within a month after it sprouted all forage was gone for a long distance on both sides of the trail." *Nevada, A Guide to the Silver State* (Portland, Oregon, 1940), p. 114.

[12] Her "instrument" was a melodeon.

26th, Monday – On down the stream [Humboldt]. After noon crossed the Lantine [Lahontan?] fork.[13]

27th – Overtook Coburn and family and heard from Dr. Spencer's family. Our road today led over high mountains for 24 miles; no water but two or three muddy springs, little which did not afford any water for the stock. The road was very, very dusty in places, cut down so that the side of the road would be even with the top of the wagon wheels. Animals and people suffered much today.

[July] 28th, 29th, 30th, 31st, and until the sixth of August we were traveling on, on down the Humboldt, which every day became more muddy and unwholesome. No feed of consequence and for seventy miles before reaching the meadows one constant desert without feed or water, 23, 22, 14 miles. Mostly deep sand. The meadows are godsends to the weary, way worn traveler and animals. They cover thousands of acres; tolerable grass very plenty. The river spreads out over a great extent. The day we arrived at the meadows I was attacked with the mountain fever, a violent pain in my limbs, back and head with a high fever.

[August] 7th, Saturday – Cut grass, cooked, and so forth, preparatory to crossing the desert and in the afternoon drove twenty miles without water to the sink. The river here is a large lake dotted with islands and as we were on the dividing ridge between the lake and the old sink, the last rays of the setting sun were gilding the crests of the surrounding mountains,

---

13 Probably the North Fork of the Humboldt.

imparting to the scenery a magnificence which I, as sick as I was, could not but admire.

It seemed to me I must die, and that same evening William was attacked with the same disease. We were a sick pair in that close wagon, burned up with fever, racked with pain. How often one thinks of home and its comforts!

8th, Sunday – Laid at the sink, sick and weak, until noon, then started into the desert. About twelve at night came to Boiling Springs, halfway. Their roar is to be heard at a great distance. The ground for a large space sounds perfectly hollow and is perforated with holes, away down in which we could hear the water boiling. The largest must be many feet in circumference.

The column of steam was larger than from a steamer and the water splashed away out. It had a strong sulphur smell. We could not see it to any advantage in the night, and William and I were so sick as to be hardly able to hold up our heads. I have no language to describe our sufferings through that long, tedious night. They fed the animals some feed and between seven and eight o'clock in the morning we struck Truckee river, beautiful, clear water and quite a large stream, a perfect godsend after the destitution and miserably unhealthy water we have had for hundreds of miles, back.

Went down the river half a mile, and at a ranch Pa found some of his California friends, real fine fellows who treated us to everything in their power and took our animals to a good pasture with theirs, good clover feed.

There are great numbers of Indians about here.
They call themselves Piutes. Their country extends
from Pyramid Lake to the Sink of Truckee. They are
very friendly and more intelligent than the Root Diggers. They procured for me great numbers of little
fish resembling a sardine which they caught with
ingenious little hooks made of a little stick one fourth
of an inch in length to which was fastened nearly at
right angle a little thorn.

These they baited with the outside of an insect. The
line was simply a linen thread with six of these little
hooks attached. They gathered also quantities of bear
berries, a small red fruit growing on quite large bushes,
said to be very wholesome.

We stayed at this trading post the 9th and 10th.
During both days I was very unwell, as well as my
husband, but we were still and would not complain.
This incessant traveling kills sick people.

[August] 11th, Wednesday – We deemed our animals
sufficiently recruited to recommence the long journey,
so with many regrets we bade adieu to "Old Ned"
and started on.

The roads we found exceedingly rough and in many
places over high mountains, some of the most picturesque scenery we have yet seen. Once we found ourselves on a high, rocky mountain, while hundreds of
feet above us towered great masses of rock and on our
left was a gorge of thousand feet in depth. At its foot
was the beautiful river with its softly-waving border
of willows and lofty cottonwoods and behind it as far
as the eye could reach mountain rising above mountain.
In places our road led so near the river's bank that

there was danger of upsetting into it. We made fifteen miles and camped near the river. Plenty of clover.

12th, Thursday – Our road today has been less rough than yesterday, though we passed down some steep hills and on the side of mountains where I was in constant fear of upsetting. Crossed the river, a very good ford, about noon. Came to the meadows, and also to a marsh which took us nearly all afternoon hard driving to get around and at night we were just about as far ahead as at noon. Camped near the river. Drove near 30 but made fifteen miles.

13th, Friday – We have been four long months today on this journey. I am sick and oh how weak! I am constantly losing instead of gaining. This constant traveling hurts me. Crossed the river and struck into the hills. Over some rough ones sixteen miles. Struck Peavine Springs on the side of a mountain commanding a splendid prospect to the north. Here was an extensive valley containing a large alkali lake and the blue outlines of the mountains in the dim background gave it an interesting appearance.

Near one of the springs was a man from Indiana exhumed by the Indians for his blankets. He died the 7th, but was in too putrid a state to be reburied. The willow withes were round his ankles where they had drawn him out of his grave. The feed here is fine, water excellent. We made a long noon halt and commenced climbing hills again.

A few miles farther on we came to another valley and lake. The road led where the lake had recently been but the water receded and left the ground hard, smooth and white and it had the resemblance to ice when the sun shone upon it.

Two miles on we struck Springbrook, passed on a mile and encamped. Made 24 miles.

14th, Saturday – I am yet sick. Sometimes think I shall not live long. It is hard to die so young and William, my William, who will console him? Passed up the creek nine miles and crossed and two miles brought us to the summit of the Sierra Nevada mountains. I walked a few rods and feebly did my feet press California soil for the first time. The goal of my ambition, and I said to myself: "Will my bones rest here in this strange land?" Six miles across a beautiful valley came to one of the head branches of the Feather River near a ranch, and camped for the rest of the day.

[Eleven years later]

Columbia, January 1st, 1863 – Mary is with us and I am learning to love the gentle hearted girl as if she was my own. My home seems more cheerful with her young face and pleasant ways.

January 1st, 1864 – Ah, last year was a sad one, indeed! Death has taken Mary, gentle, loving, truehearted Mary. I have watched her sweet life to its close. The waxen lids have forever shut out all the beautiful works of His hand and the faces of those she loved so tenderly.

The future seems so desolate, so unsunned by one ray of comfort or hope. Was I sick, her tender sympathy alleviated half the pain. Unselfish to the last degree her life, though numbering less than sixteen years, was filled with all the graces of mature, perfect womanhood.

Words can not tell how I loved her and how I miss her everywhere.

EPILOGUE

MARIETT FOSTER CUMMINGS
(Memoirs by Her Niece)
LUCY FOSTER SEXTON

The first home of the Foster family and their friends coming across the plains was San Jose, California. Mariett Foster Cummings and her husband had come with her father on his second trip.

Her new home was at the junction of Alviso and Almaden Roads, about a mile from San Jose. It was a low, six-room cottage with porch across the front and six French windows and two doors upening out upon the porch.

The three front rooms were furnished in mahogany which had come around the Horn as had also the windows, doors and hardware. The bedroom was furnished with a rolled end bed, an oval dresser and a highboy. The curtains in the three front rooms were pale blue and gray damask with lace behind them, the carpets with large pink roses and pale greens.

The parlor was furnished with lounge sofa, chairs, card table and folding tea table. The upholstery was black hair-cloth. The dining room contained a folding dropleaf mahogany table with small side table and writing desk. In this desk the old letters and her diary were found, years after she had willed it to her nieces.

At the rear of the house was a back bedroom, kitchen and workroom and back porch. They had planted an orchard and flower garden. A large sycamore tree, over which climbing "Seven Sisters" roses grew, shaded one end. Each porch support had other varieties of roses and many shrubs and flowering annuals grew vigorously, as only California shrubs can grow in a short time.

This home Mariett Cummings' brother, Isaac G. Foster, bought furnished when he crossed the plains; also the several acres of land that went with it, as Mr. and Mrs. Cummings wished to go to Columbia [Tuolumne County] to the mines. Mrs. Cummings took her melodeon and secretary with her.

The town was built over a gold mine and eventually they mined it off, or others did who came later. Here she felt the love of a mother for her niece, Mary, of the loss of whom she writes in her diary. They were very prosperous there and next came to San Francisco, where her husband was in the furniture business at the corner of Montgomery and Pine in a large basement.

Their home in San Francisco was on Mason Street Hill, another large cottage where she entertained for many years. Her wide hospitality made a sweet influence in San Francisco.

They went with a party of artists into the Yosemite Valley from Columbia when it was scarcely known. They camped and made the first sketches which revealed the beauties of Yosemite to the wondering public.

It was on this trip that she made an oil painting from the floor of the valley. Two sketches by another artist, George Terell, one of Nevada Falls, the other of Vernal Falls, dated 1858, were presented by Mr. Terell to Mrs. Cummings. When they returned, they exhibited their work in Columbia City and San Francisco.

This was a delightful trip to the Valley. The route,

with their pack train of mules was by way of Indian Canyon trail. They camped in the meadows of Royal Arches, Mrs. Cummings told me, "because of better grass and fewer mosquitoes, and to avoid the Digger Indians, staying there a week."

In her will she gave Lucy Foster Sexton the oil painting which she made on this trip, and her paint box. To another niece, Stella Olmsted Foster, she gave the two sketches of Terell dated 1858, and the daguerreotype of Mrs. Cummings. These articles were presented in June, 1925, by the nieces to the Museum in Yosemite.

Her home was filled with beautiful furniture, a grand piano, and China was sending her wonderful things. Her cabinets had many treasures. Her help was Chinese; these she had to train. Her collections of paintings, silver, china, cut glass and linens were the treasured gifts she left her nieces.

To the writer were left her oil paints and paintbox of California make and wood; her Caucasian shawl; hand made and tucked linen ball dress; gold nugget gold pin; cut glass; painting of Yosemite by herself; pictures and many other treasures. Her parrot had died and its painted portrait was among the things treasured.

At one time on Shotwell street besides her garden and plants there were three parrots, a mocking bird, goldfinch, many cages of canaries, a dog, a cat and goldfish. These took an hour's care, then another for the garden and house plants, another with the cook. She loved fancy dishes, always doing them herself. Then she had the afternoon to herself, with the evening open for other things.

She said one must have a time for each duty, and some for the improvement of one's self. The care of her father was one of these, and she classed it as a loving duty. His last days were in her constant care in this beautiful home overlooking San Francisco Bay and the Berkeley hills. Her brother Isaac, sister-in-law Roxanna, and the writer were often with her there.

She was a lover of old lace and an expert in its value. These were the fullest years of her life. She often visited her brother Isaac G. Foster, and his family, on the coast back of Stanford, bringing her gray and scarlet parrot.

When the parrot was having its bath one day, a woodpecker was placed in the cage. When the parrot saw it she screamed and flew out the door for half a mile into a hillside of blackberries but was recovered. Mrs. Cummings was a great help to her sister-in-law in her shopping, as they went to San Francisco twice a year for supplies and again to San Jose for fruit, and for visits to old friends. It was only a day's trip of thirty miles to each place.

She had been allowed to dance herself, so planned her niece Lucy's party dresses and hats. When her little namesake came she did many charming things for her. She felt deeply her sister Juliet's not having advantages out on the stock ranch at San Luis Obispo. The wild flowers of the coast were a perpetual joy to her and our first lessons in botany.

The home was filled with specimens, the table never without its adornment, nor the rooms. All were to her things to admire and she could hardly find words with which to express herself.

She sometimes brought her friend, Miss Emerson,

with her, and both were good horsewomen. The beach and the mountains and the redwoods made time pass quickly on these outings. She entertained many noted people at her home in those early days at dinners and receptions. Her beautiful voice and her recitations added to many charming gatherings in that City of Gold with its wealth of the world being sent it in exchange.

She always kept her friendship for Doctor Spencer and his family and many times they were together. At that time a young man from the Bank of California made his home with them. She delighted to show her niece the theatre and art galleries and to treat her to that great luxury, ice cream.

One of her friends, a banker, lost his wife, leaving a child two years old. He wished Mrs. Cummings to take care of his little son. She did so, and gave her love to it, as did her husband. She loved it as a mother, as though it were her own.

The boy was beautiful in face. He took several years of constant care as he was delicate. He grew up to be the sorrow of their lives, one of those so called sandlot hoodlums of San Francisco's early days.

The building of the Nob Hill palaces was a delight to her and the Park, she said, was her own planning. She had much to do with its planting and growth from a ranch of sandhills; also the Woodward Gardens with museums and greenhouses in their time, like her, transplanted from the east to the west, an education and training, a leaven to lighten California's young life and bring to it a love of the beautiful things only dreamed of, yet to be realized in her lifetime.

Mr. and Mrs. Cummings moved to Piedmont Springs

as the husband's health had faded. There another daughter of her sister Juliet, Stella Olmsted, came to stay with her, her brother's son Fred, visiting there week-ends while he went to business college in San Francisco. Stella lived with her for awhile. Those were jolly days for the young people.

The family came back to Shotwell street, San Francisco, where they lived until the husband and the child they reared died. There, after her father had left her some money her brother Isaac tried to get her to invest it in a home, but she thought the Comstock mines were so rich they were a better investment.

She put all her money in them and lost it all, even her diamonds going to pay assessments. After closing her house she was companion to two elderly people, reading and being with them daytimes. Her object was attained. She received enough to put her in the Crocker Home for Old People where she had her lifelong friend, Miss Emerson.

She came south to visit her niece Lucy and nephew Eugene. They both urged her to make her home with them, and almost she said "Yes," their gardens so appealed to her. She was taken very sick and had to go to the Bard hospital, Ventura, to be treated. Her niece Lucy with two daughters and the granddaughter went to visit her there. The four generations were grouped, two of them named for her Mariett the second and Mariett the third, in the room, and she was a happy woman to have lived to see her name carried on.

The Daily Notes of
℘ Sarah Pratt

INTRODUCTION

One of the convictions that has come home to this editor of *Covered Wagon Women* is that there are still many, many such documents in private hands. They may be family treasures kept in some dark drawer or covert closet. These added to those in libraries and in museums make up a treasure of American historical records.

In giving speeches and lectures on the subject of overland diaries and letters of women, several times some person has come up to say, "My neighbor upstairs has one," or "My friend down the street knows of one."

In our introduction to the "Letter to Mother" of Lucia Loraine Williams in Volume III, 1851, we told of phoning Radio Station KGO, the massive talk station in San Francisco, and of the exciting responses that have resulted from such calls.

It was in the autumn of 1979 that the first KGO call was made in the wee small hours of the night. The announcer allowed us time to tell about the project. We had hardly hung up the telephone when it rang. The caller was William Briggs of Sacramento. He said, "We have the 1852 diary of my great grandmother, Sarah Pratt."

The upshot has been that he and his sister, Barbra Briggs, have given us full access to the precious record which follows.

The ancestor who wrote the diary was Sarah Pratt. She was listed in the 1850 Federal Census of Liberty, Jackson County, Michigan, as being 18 years old, birthplace, New

York. Her parents were Silas and Sally Pratt. Silas was a farmer. The four other children listed were as follows: An older brother, Cavanne (spelling not certain), age 22, a school teacher; sister, Eliza, 20; brother, Edgar, 16; a brother, Darwin, eight years old.

In the diary "Pa" is mentioned countless times, with never an appearance by the mother, Sally. Darwin is not mentioned at all. Eliza was along, as was Edgar, who is referred to as "Ned" many times.

The overland journey of the Pratts differed from most in that it was later in the year. They crossed the Missouri River at Kanesville (Council Bluffs) on June 7 and started with some Mormon and other associates to Salt Lake City, where they arrived on Tuesday, August 10. They did not go on farther west until Saturday, August 21. The remainder of their journey was via the so-called "Mormon Corridor" south and west of Great Salt Lake over hot deserts and through the Cajon Pass to the newly-founded community of San Bernardino.

Sarah was evidently a young woman with an active, probing mind, but she was not, nor did she become, a Mormon. She did hear Mormon sermons and observe baptizings. However, her comments are those of an independent thinker observing other persons' religious practices.

She was in favor of resting from their journey to observe the Sabbath, however. Family tradition has it that they and their ancestors have been "variously Protestant."

There is one tantalizing allusion in her entry for Sunday, November 14, after arriving at San Bernardino on the ninth: "some of the co[mpany] attended church, I read A. J. Davis works." The author of the book she read was Andrew Jackson Davis, one of the leading spiritualist writers of that day. She could have been reading his *Principles of Nature, Her Divine Revelations,* which had been published in 1847.

It was on Friday, December 10, 1852, that she wrote
another interesting entry in her diary: "Mr Miner starts
for Pueblo [Los Angeles]." There is a family tradition that
her romance with her future husband, Morris Miner, a
native of Austria, went on during the covered wagon journey; however this is her only mention of him in the diary.
They were married in San Francisco in 1853.[1]

Morris Miner (often mis-spelled "Minor") is mentioned
in the published *Journal History of the Church* as being a
Mormon elder, a single man, both on April 7 and on June
18, 1851. He was a member of a mission directed by Parley
Parker Pratt (no relation to Sarah) from Salt Lake City
to San Bernardino, also in 1851. It is our own good fortune
that Parley Pratt's own diary for that journey has been
published. The entry of special interest is that of May 21,
1851: Pratt told how on Tuesday, May 20, Miner said he
was dissatisfied with the leadership and the other members
of the "Pacific Mission." He "had a falt finding Spirit,
and requested to be released from the Mission and remain
a member of the Church." A council was called, and, after
hearing Morris Miner's case, they reproved him and "gave
him Leave to Resign his papers of Recommendation and
appointment to the Mission and remain at the settlement."
So it was that Miner left the company with some packers
who were "mostly profane and wicked unprincipled men." [2]

Parley Pratt's own biographer, Reva Stanley, in *The
Archer of Paradise*,[3] wrote of this episode, "The truth
of the whole matter was that Miner didn't want to be a
missionary. He wanted to go to California to hunt for gold."

So Sarah Pratt, a young woman with a probing mind,
became the wife of a man who was from Austria, spoke

[1] "Obituary," Alida Miner Fogg, *Sacramento Bee,* March 20 ,1946.

[2] Reva Holdaway Stanley and Charles L. Camp, "A Mormon Mission To
California in 1851," *Calif. Hist. Soc. Qtly.,* XIV, No. 1, (March, 1935), pp.
59-73. This reference is on page 67, entry for May 21, 1851.

[3] (Caldwell, Idaho, 1937), p. 249.

with a German accent, and was in revolt against the Mormon connection. After the San Francisco marriage in 1853, they lived for awhile in Martinez and then moved to the beautiful Napa Valley just a few miles north of San Francisco Bay.

The censuses of the following decades are revealing about the growth of the Miner family. They were in their Napa Valley home on July 12, 1860, when the Census taker visited their farm — listed Morris Miner as a "Farmer," 34 years old with a financial value of $4800. There were three children: Edward P., five years old; Nancy, four, and Edney, one year old.

During the next decade Morris Miner died, as it was reported in the San Francisco *Evening Bulletin,* in its issue of October 29, 1866, "In the Rodeo Valley, Contra Costa county, Oct. 26th, Morris Miner, formerly of this city."

Sarah was now a widow and would live on with her family around her for many years in Napa. The 1870 census told of two more children, Alida, age 9, and Esiah, age 7. The mother, Sarah, at age 41, was "Keeping House," had real estate valued at $6,000 and personal property worth $2,145.

Alida,[4] the nine-year-old daughter listed in the 1870 census, grew up in Napa, and in 1883 she became the wife of Edmund Wilson Fogg in San Pablo, California. They became prominent citizens of Oroville, California, where Fogg was a banker. It was their daughter, Edleda, who became the wife of William A. Briggs of Sacramento, who's children, William A. Jr., and Barbra, were the persons who supplied the little three by five inch book that was the diary

---

4 Alida is pronounced a-LYE-dah. There are several references to the Foggs: "Obituary," Alida Miner Fogg, *Sacramento Bee,* March 20, 1946; George C. Mansfield, *History of Butte County, California, With Biographical Sketches* (Los Angeles, 1918), pp. 683-84, 687; J. W. Wooldridge, *History of the Sacramento Valley, California,* 3 vols., (Chicago, 1931), vol. III, pp. 254-56.

of their great grandmother. It is with their kind permission that it is printed here.

THE DAILY NOTES OF SARAH PRATT, 1852

Wednesday Apr. 21st 1852   After the usual ceremony attendant upon such occasions we left *cherished homes*[1] and started for the "far west," that land of *golden* hopes & yellow fancies. Our hearts beat high with expectation but suddenly our prospects seemed darkened for a while by the *smashing* of a globe lantern, suspended from the top of the frames   Arrived at Concord [Michigan] 1 oclock P.M. had a social chat with Mr Collins & Dwight Crittenden. Left my bonnet in the care of Collins to be sent back home – after stopping about an hour took up our line of march for Homer, where we arrived 6 oclock, nothing of importance occurring on the way, except a rent in my dress caused by a too hasty exit from the wagon, supper at the Dorsey house – – – we had been there near half an hour when we were cheered by the arrival of Messrs Mow. Aldrich. Rice. Snow Gordon and family. The roads were very bad, weather warm and pleasant   distance to day 14 miles

Thursday 22nd   Cloudy, and cool, started at 8 oclock, roads continue bad, halt at Tekonsha 12 oclock, arrived at Union City [Michigan] 5 oclock P.M. Stop at Mr Buell's. In the evening have a pleasant visit with Mrs. Isaih Bennet. Our luck appears to have followed us for on halting at noon we discovered that our Camphor

---

[1] The beginning point of their journey was Liberty, Michigan. They are so listed in the United States Census, 1850, Jackson County, Michigan.

was spilled and the glass of our new lantern broken
A bad beginning makes a good ending – distance this
day 22 *m*

Friday, 23rd   After bidding adieu to our friends at
Union City we proceeded on our route through heavy
timbered country for several miles. thence several more
over beautiful rolling ground, the pleasantest I have
ever seen   At noon we took our company who stayed
8 *m* beyond the City   stopped in the shade of a dry
oak tree to take our *lunch.* after resting half an hour
started on   after traveling I am come to a beautiful
little prairie 7 *m* wide where we crossed   the weather
to day is fine, not a cloud dimmed the horizan until
after noon when light clouds began to gather in the west
& before night showed indication of a *spell* of *weather*
Arrived at the Centerville [Michigan] exchange half
past five – distance 26 m

Saturday 24th   Our route to day lay through Burr
Oak plains across one or two small prairies   passed
through Constantine, Mottville & arrived at Adams-
ville just before dark. Commenced raining just after
we stopped for the night   distance 31 miles   *Road
good*

Sunday 25th [April]   Rained most of the time to day

Monday 26th   Cloud in the morning, some rain
started 8 oclock, roads very bad on account of the rain,
passed through Edwardsburg, Bertrant, & arrived at
Hamilton 6 oclock, about 1 oclock came to a deep
slough or *mud hole,* where some poor fellow had probably met with hard luck, having to drag his horses
out of the mire   we got along without much trouble
Takosen Prairie lay on our route this afternoon dis-

tance 26 mils   met with a gentleman & lady who had been to Cal.   obtain information   *cleared of a little after noon.*

Tuesday 27th   Left the Prairie about 10 oclock   our route the rest of the way lay through heavy timbered country for a few miles then over large Burr Oak plains and toward night sandy hilly to the right Prairies to the left   Arrived at Michigan City [Indiana] 7 oclock P.M. & at Wards tavern 4 miles beyond about an hour and a half later. Clouds in the morning clear in the afternoon   distance 26 m

Wednesday 28th   Rainy in the morning, started 8 o cl   about noon cleared off, sun shone out very hot, traveled all day over sandy plains & bluffs. crossed the Central & Northern Rail Road several times   arrived at widow Gibsons tavern quarter before 9 P.M.   distance 27 m

Thursday 29.   Rainy in the morning   roads very sandy   clear in the afternoon with chilling wind traveled several miles near the lake Michigan   forded a stream where the bridge was washed away, arrived at Chicago 6 o clock P.M.   had the best kind of accommodation, ladies sociable & pleasant, heavy thunder shower after we stopped   rainy all night   30 miles

Friday 30th   Rainy in the morn, went down to the lake shore, Started 11 o clock A.M.   When we had got about a mile from where we stayed Pa found that he had left his overcoat, so nothing remained to be done but go back for it   after wait with intense anxiety for an hour and a half he returned, & as John [Simpson] & I suspected had been lost – All aboard we started again about 1 o clock. The other teams

having gone on   Thunder showers & sunshine alter-
nately. Our route lay across the great prairie west of
Chicago   stopped for the night 10½ miles west of
Chicago, distance 10½ m

Sat May 1st   started 7½ o clock   plank road 18 miles
then came the 'tug of war' mud, mud thick and sticky
like putty   about 2 o clock came to a place that was
impassible, wheeled round, & marched back as far as
the first corners ½ m   went across on to another road,
after a great deal of hard labor arrived at Aurora
[Illinois] 5½ o clock almost tired to death, got supper for the men & went to bed   Thanks to God for
his mercies   pleasant   distance 30 m

Sunday 2nd   spent the sabbath in reading & cooking,
rainy all day, retired early almost sick with hard cold
eat nothing since yesterday morning

Monday 3rd   Pleasant   started 8 o clock   very muddy   Prairie   stopped for the night 5 miles west of
Little Rock   distance 20 miles   –

Tuesday 4th   Clear, off at 8 o cl   roads muddy,
prairie interspersed with groves, rolling, broken with
sloos 24 miles   passed through [space] stopped at
Gilmores 5 m west of Paw Paw [Illinois]

Wednesday 5th   Clear, roads better   soil much like
yesterday   weather warm with refreshing breeze
sandy swells in the afternoon, sheet of water to the
right which proved to be Rock river   A.M. some of
the party duck hunting. Take a by road on account
of bad road   arrive at Dixon 4½ o clock   supper at
the stage house   indications of rain Distance 22 miles

Thursday 6th   Bought a horse & saddle in the morning before starting   shower in the morning   crossed

the Rock river pleasant in the afternoon passed
through Sterling [Illinois] & stopped for the night ¼
mile west of the little ville of Lyndon at the house
of a farmer   thunder shower immediately after stopping, man came home drunk, mince pies, the rest of
the company stay the next house beyond   24 m

Fri 7th   Pleasant   follow the course of the Mendosa
[Mendota?] river   cross on a ferry in the afternoon
arrive at Port Byron [Illinois] on the Mississippi the
sun about an hour high, crossed the Missippi in a horse
ferry – stayed all night at La Clair [Le Claire, Iowa],
22

Sat 8 – route lay over Prairies, Snow shot at ducks &
missed the figure. ride on horse back race with the
forward trains, prairie squirrel, stopped to get a staying   no hay, stopped at a private house Mr. Lathrop.
He had been to Cal – woman sick with the scurvy.
Hungarian physician set Mr Gordons boys arm   20
miles

Sunday 9th [May]   stayed at Mr Lat[hrop]   baked
pies, washed, ironed, sewed, stung by bee

Monday 10th   Got an early start   we had not pro-
ceded far however before I missed my neck ribbon
John [Simpson] went back after it, about   half mile
farther on found my scarf was among the missing, &
John turned the team around and went for that. this
left us about 4 miles in the rear. Pa went on with the
rest of the company on horse back, we took the wrong
road and did not arrive at the place of destination
until the rest of the company had been in nearly an
hour & a half,   when we arrived John was obliged
to treat all round to prevent being laughed at   very
pleasant all day, cool breeze, part of the way over

prairie high bluffs, groves of timber, followed the
course of the creek   arrived at Tipton sun half an hour
high, ate in the wagon, I did not eat any supper, been
suffering all day with diarhaea, took *some brandy* and
sugar   Circus expected here tomorrow   gives rise to
conversation   distance 25 miles

Tuesday 11th   rainy in the morning   route across
the prairie passed through several groves & some bad
sloos, rode horseback in the afternoon   other two wagons went round a bad sloo, got ahead of them. our road
for the last 8 miles lay through timbered country, good
road. forded a little creek about 3 oclock, arrived at
Iowa City a little before sundown, stopped at the stage
hotel, in about 20 minutes after the other teams arrived
in town but at another house. in the evening took a
stroll around the city. called where the rest of the company were staying   music in the evening, description
of the state-house at noon crossed Cedar river   log
ferry propelled by the current by means of ropes and
pulleys   got ahead of the rest of the company in the
afternoon. in the evening had conversation with a lady
who is Cousin to Mrs Bennet of Union City [Michi-
gan]. She was very glad to obtain information con-
cerning her – distance 25 mi

Wednesday 12th.   Clear. left Iowa City 10 o clock A.M.
crossed the Iowa river on a rope ferry. over prairie
and through groves   stopped for the night 18 miles
from the City in a little log cabin   15 m

Thursday 13th   very warm in the morning but cloudy,
heavy thunder shower in the afternoon. Gordon's &
Snow's train got *ahead*   roads very bad after the
shower, arrived at Snooks grove a little before dark
distance this day 26 miles

Friday 14th started 10 o clock   roads very bad for
6 miles through the woods then across the 20 mile
prairie. arrived at Sugar grove an hour after dark,
camped out for the first time   french horse lame to
day 23 m   saw Sam Inm[an] & *wife in the evening*

Saturday 15th found pleasant myself some what
lame in the morning from sleeping on a board – after
I had arranged my affairs ready for a start went where
Inmans folks were camped. last evening we found
Mr. Bransoms & Hargrove. our route lay over roll-
ing Prairies – camped a little way from Newton
[Iowa] – 19 m

Sunday 16th [May] lay in camp all day – cold and
windy – good company – livelly times. lame horse no
better

Monday 17th got up about 2 o clock. As in consequence of having such a hard place to sleep made a
fire & took a nap by it. weather pleasant but cold
enough for overcoat & mittens route nearly the same,
through groves & over prairies. Scotch people camped
for the night in Apple Grove on the bank of a little
creek. went fishing after tea. 22 m

Tuesday 18th Pleasant – prairies a few miles of
timbered land   arrived at fort Des Moines 4 o clock
P.M. crossed the Des Moines river on a rope ferry –
stopped to buy corn 5 m east of the fort lost my
company rode with the Scotchman. shower in the
afternoon – distance 13 m

Wednesday 19th staid at Des Moines Description
of the fort of Horseshoe Lake Fishing excursion
Washing – Butter Bread Eggs

Thursday 20th Pleasant Crossed the Coon [Rac-

coon] river by ferry – route across prairie, at noon
halted at Lanes grove – encamped for the night on
the prairie where there were a few scattering trees
found good water by digging – lame horse mud
better 25 miles

Friday 21st   started from our encampment 7½ o clock.
25 miles

Friday 21st   Cloudy. off early in the morning, 6 miles
through grove & scattering timber when we arrived
at Winterset, a little village situated on the prairie,
deep ravines or ledge hills   commenced raining about
10 o clock   Indian Rubber coat missing   with difficulty find a place to encamp near dark. continued raining all night   I went to the tavern. 31 m

Saturday 22nd   Continue in camp, raining in the
morning   cleared off about 2 o clock, find we are near
Sam Inman again. also our Scotch neighbors, all in
good spirits, fishing in the afternoon. visit to the Scotch
tent in the evening —

Sunday 23rd [May]   after the usual labor of the
Sabbath such as overhauling drying, fixing, & cooking, we retired into the grove on the opposite side of
the creek and listened to a sermon from a Mr Brown
who was encamped near, sermon again at 4 o clock by
Mr Kennedy our Scotch friends —

Monday 24th   Pleasant, very warm in the morning.
cool breaze after we got fairly out on the prairie, in
20 miles arrived at a creek very bad to cross, no dwellings   encamped for the night at Marvin Bandells[?]
35 miles

Tuesday 25th   Cloudy but very warm   passed three
newly made graves. suppos to be emigrants. passed a

number of carcasses, cattle & horses. heavy hills bad
sloughs. sprinkling of rain in the afternoon – dined
at Indian town which consists of 2 houses & dwellings
one grocery horseback ride in the afternoon, meet a
gentleman from the bluffs. story of the robbery – 3
o [clock] meet a return team had been in company
with Spencers from Mich. inquire for Deacon Mow.
arrive at [space] just before sundown no settlements
on Prairie 30 m

W 26th fair, very warm. several bad *slous,* part of
the company detained by accident. Cornelia getting
her head hurt by accident. wait for them to come up
8 miles from encampment cross a stream at Myers
Hill. stoped noon for horses to feed. cross Silver Creek
bridge, arrive at encampment on the prairie early,
stoped at the Creek to obtain wood and water – horses
pull the wagon by being hitched to the hind end 15
miles

Thursday 27th Cloudy in the morning, very warm.
men lost their pony's. came in sight of the Bluffs, meet
a number of Indians. arrive at Kanesville 3 o clock
P.M. encamped 1 mile from the village – 16 miles

Friday June 5 [should be 4] Left our encampment
about 10 o clock A.M. expecting to arrive at the upper
ferry 10 miles distant but were detained by Mr. Mow
& company waiting for their wagon to be repaired
halted in Kanesville until 4 P.M. while there was
introduced to some – two – ladies from Ann Arbor on
their way to Cal. Our route from Kanesville lay
through a very romantic region, road good but wind-
ing, pleasant. rode horseback. arrived at a good place
to encamp on the flat of the Missouri, good spring
water, high bluff 6 miles from Kanesville —

Saturday 5th   rainy in the morning. clear off at 10
but windy, lay in camp – Mr Gordon returned to get
wagon tires set   took a walk on the bluffs —

Sunday 6th   Cloudy & windy with appearance of
rain   pleasant in the afternoon

Monday 7th   Cloudy in the morning with sprinkles
of rain. took up our line of march for the *ferry* across
the Misouri which 3 miles distant   good success in
crossing   two wagons detained until afternoon account
of wind, crossed two more wagons in the afternoon,
hailstorm I accompanied Mr Hardgrove to a part of
their company about 2 miles from the river to camp
the rest of the company being on the other side of the
river

Tuesday 8th   The rest of the company crossed early
in the morning arrived in camp & made preparations
to start   three teams started ahead   halted 6 miles
from camp for the rest to come up – strawberries,
after the rest of the company overtook us came 3
miles & camped for the night – Pleasant   cool breeze
9 miles

[The following entry for June 8 was written on a
page much farther on in the blank part of the little
book:]

Wednesday June 8 [should be Tuesday]   Last night
we had an unusual gale of wind & although the sun
arose clear & bright the air was chilling but we heeded it not – the Rubicon was passed & every one seemed
to feel that the exertion was necessary – as for me I
felt unusually gayetus & happy. the cool bracing air
seemed to impart new vigor to my frame   my vision
was stretched to its full extent gazing on the beautiful

rolling prairie spread out on either side with nothing to break the unvaried greenery except here and there a clump of trees looking like far off islands in the sea –

Wednesday 9th   heavy wind in the night. cold (in the morning) enough for overcoat & mittens. Clear, rolling prairie,   crossed Papea [Papillon] Creek on bridge, paid 50 cents toll to the Indians   arrived at Elk Horn river 2 o clock P.M.   crossed by ferry, Indians, cattle swim the creek   take in wood and water at the creek. camp on the prairie 6 miles from the creek   24 m

Thursday 10th   Pleasant   not much timber   encamped on the Plat river   met teams from Salt Lake [?]three more trains join

Fri 11th   A little past midnight we were aroused by the cry of "turn out all hands there's a horse missing" & sure enough our gray horse was gone taken by the Indians *without doubt.* search was made but no trace could be found except tracks where a horse had been pushed into the river – at the usual hour the company started. P went back to our noon camp for fear she might have strayed. overtook us at noon. encamped on Long lake near the Platt, crossed Shell creek in the forenoon   pleasant   very warm – 22 miles

Saturday 12th   Clear. heat excessive   arrived at the ferry of the Loup Fork[2] about noon, return teams at the ferry   sent a letter home, after crossing the ferry, heavy sandy road for a half mile. passed Looking Glass fork after traveling a mile or more   were obliged to return to the Creek to encamp   saw several graves – 20 miles

---

[2] This means that they were traveling on the north bank of the Platte River.

Sunday 13 [June]   Clear but windy. had to take our tent down in consequence, bathed in the river.

Monday 14   started 8 o clock– High wind   route lay over sandy Plains & bluffs   camped on open plain, saw many graves. sheep. distance 80 miles

Tuesday 15th   Lay in camp all day in consequence of rain, arrival of Mr P [J?] Perrine. —

Wednesday 16th   Off at 7 A.M.   fair, route over sandy plains & barren hills. camped among the bluffs without wood or water. passed springs at the right. 25 m.

Thursday 17th   Clear, very warm – sick   forded Prairie Creek about noon   Wood Creek at 3 P. M. elevated wagon boxes – streams not *wide* or *deep*. many graves   elk

Fri 18th   Clear & warm. staid at our encampment till 11 A. M. in order to prepare food as we did not expect to find wood & water   saw many graves today, route lay about 2 miles from Platt river, came to a stream on our left about 4 P. M.   camped 2 m beyond, new moon, beautiful encampment   moskitoes, traveled 16 miles

Sat 19   very warm. crossed two steep ravines   camped near the Platt.

Sunday 20th [June].   sermon in the afternoon by an emigrant encamped near   20 m

Monday 21st   Route near the Platt, Many graves. prairie wolves – crossed Elm & Buffalo Creek   slight shower about noon, alkali, Mr Mow was attacked very violently with the Cholera

Monday 28   Left our encampment at 7 A. M. reflections on passing the grave of Mr Mow – route lay near the Platt, being sandy road in the P. M. very warm, cloudy in the afternoon with indications of rain. we found the other company meet in new night camp on the flat – 21

Tuesday 29th terrible thunderstorm last night. started up past 7 o clock kept heat excessive 10 o clock overtake the other company who lay encamped by 2 beautiful springs of water route most of the way very near the Platt river. roads heavy sand, & muddy 23

Wednesday 30 roads good in the A. M. crossed North Bluff fork, from here over sandy bluffs to Bluff Creek pleasant ride on horseback – many graves 24

Thursday July 1st 1852 – Warm with cool & refreshing breeze route over muddy *flat* & sandy bluffs crossed several small streams engraving on the bank slight shower in the A. M. many graves – prairie wolves, camped on Rattlesnake creek 21

Friday 2nd Started 7 o clock cool & windy, rainy early in the morning. route near the P river heavy sandy bluffs in the afternoon. crossed a number of small creeks. Cedar Bluffs to the right on the opposite side of the river stork in river push from one of the bluffs slight hail storm in the afternoon, camped past 5 three miles from the lone tree. terrible hail storm, heavy wind. chase for the horses, adventure with the hailstones, saw many graves. —

Saturday 3rd – Clear, heat excessive roads most of the way heavy & sandy passed a number of graves. encamped late at night on a sand bluff – heavy thunder shower in the evening

Sunday 4th [July]

Monday 5th   Windy. very disagreeable riding on
account of sand & dust, route near the Platt, saw a
few graves, route part of the way sandy, encamped
on the flat about ½ mile from the river – thunderstorm in the evening   tents pitched in the ring, wolves,
description of the ruins on the north of the Platt.
get a view of Castle & Chimney Rocks   visit from a
gentleman from the other side of the river

Tuesday 6th   2 miles east of C. rock. Clear & weather
comfortable, roads rough, sandy part of the way
passed Castle Rock   description of the rock   camp
late near 2 miles from the river   thunderstorm shortly
after camping, excursion to the river. evening scene
wild Sage, several graves.

Wednesday 7   Started up past 6 o clock   route some
distance from the river. discription of the Court house
also Scotts Bluffs   Cloudy windy, cool   go to the
river to water teams   roads good   passed but few
graves to-day, ride with Mr Gilkey, view of Laramie
peak about 60 miles distant

Thursday 8th   started 8 o clock   Pleasant road some
of the way sandy romantic scenery on the opposite
side of the river, Alkali & Sage   ride on the bluff
with Ned   ride in waggon with Ezra – encamp on
the valley of the Platt 26 miles east of fort L[aramie].

Friday 9th   start early, romantic bluffs on the left,
singular appearance of the bluffs on the right, about
5 o clock get a view of the fort, trading house   encampments near the fort. description of the fort, saw
but few graves   pleasant   roads part of the way very
sandy. cloudy in the afternoon indications of rain.

encamp after sun set 1 mile west of the ferry the walking scene

Saturday 10th
Sunday 11th [July]

Monday 12 Started alone 9 o clock leaving the remnant of the company on the ground, get in the mud. remnant of the company overtake us at noon. tug of war over the black hills. spring of water at the right, drive till sunset, do not find the rest of our company encampments near, pleasant with cool breezes, no water near encampment walk most of the way. poor feed come to river P[latte].

Tuesday 13th Clear, very warm. hilly horses suffer with thirst walk most of the way. ride on the pony in the afternoon papers on trees, a number of graves overtake that part of our company that left us at the fort an encampment near a small creek, wild sage for fuel. captain elected during our absence. price of horse shoeing raised to $1 dollar per shoe for setting. feet blistered

Wednesday 14th Clear, not very warm on account of cool breeze, roads good except hills, walk, romantic scenery, encamp on a hill, good feed, dried beef

Thursday 15th Clear heat excessive roads sandy. very hilly very romantic scenery. singular appearance of the hills, climb to the top of one. ride on the mule, Neds adventure with the trunk, discoveries of the footmen appearance of the rocks, arrive at the Platt and encamp after sunset. swim the horses for feed, Mr Beveds adventure, remarks lifepreserver, ride astride, buffalo on opposite side of the river

Friday 16th drove till noon. two teams stopped for

the purpose of recruiting until Monday. the rest go on 2 miles and halt, difficulty in the company, arrange to start the next morning, rain in the afternoon, rainbow, french horse sick

Saturday 17th   start 8 o clock   leave Beveds & Hardgrove to finish their business, they overtake us at noon, heavy hills in the afternoon   camp on the flat close by the P river. Milwaukie company near – division in Mr Browns company. medicine for horse. bathe in the evening warm

Sunday 18th [July]   Clear. very warm. windy in the afternoon

Monday 19th   Clear but windy, start early   roads very sandy. horse no better   get one of Mr Snows to work in the team   come to P river several times, see a buffalo on the opposite side of river,   men get deceived by cattle in grove   camp near a high bluff names on bluff[3] rocks, romantic scenery

Tuesday 20th   very warm, hilly & sandy   arrived at the upper ferry about 5 o clock   leave the road & go about 3 miles for feed, buffalo on opposite side of river   Mr Beirley purchased 2 pair of oxen

Wednesday 21st   came to the road where we left in order to get water from Platt river   account of deaths at the ford. said to be 40 drowned   dead bodies below the ford   at noon a train pass from the south side of the river   steep hill to descend   commenced raining about 11 o clock. smoke on the mountain, Indians.

---

[3] The one name of a member of their party to appear to later observers of Independence Rock was J. F. Simpson. He dated his inscription July 18. Sarah's note here indicates they were at the rock on July 19; however, she is sometimes confused with her dating, and also John Simpson was quite a wanderer. Robert Spurrier Ellison, *Independence Rock, The Great Record of the Desert* (Casper, Wyoming, 1930), p. 37.

company returning lost their mules, meet a part of
them just at night with their animals. having found
them about 27 miles most of them in a train taken up
for strays   had Mr Bierleys oxen on before our horses.
camp on the open wild flat   had no water

Thursday 22   start early, heat excessive   cross several
small steams, willow springs   many campers. G. shot
a cow at noon, ascend a high hill. several graves, difference among the company in regard to stopping   officers resign   camp near a small stream   good feed

Friday 23rd   part of the company go on, Gilkey Hardgrove, Bronsons & Pratt lay over, very warm   good
feed

Saturday 24th   Clear, warm, noon at Independence
rock   alone   description of the rock, adventure coming down   ford Sweet water river. trading post at
the ford. camp 1 mile west of Devil's Gate. trading
post near the gate   spring of water, adventure of Gil-
keys cow   beautiful moonlight scenery

Sunday 25th [July]   return in the morning   lost book
for the return accompanied by H. T. Bronson to
risk the passage of the Sweet water through the rocky
mountain   description of the passage, birds nests,
thoughts elicited at the place, clear very warm, roads
good with the exception of sand in places. overtake
the rest of the company about noon, found part of them
packing, came 2 miles and camp on Sweet water, beautiful place, good feed. pass junction of [?]

Monday 26th   start 6 oclock, cloudless. roads good.
ford river   2^{00} camp by river. first of company that
were behind go past, packers stop at the ford, division
of the company arises from a difference of opinion in

regard to driving route near a high range of rocks
many names, carcasses, bathe in the evening camp on
opposite side of the river conversation with sheep
drover, thunder with high wind but no rain –

Tuesday 27th off at ½ past 6. Clear very warm,
roads good, ford river 2 in morn, sight of snow capped
mountains, packers overtake us ford river again and
halt for noon. singular marsh, ice, alkali, Hardgrove &
Gilkey stop on the bluffs 4 miles from the river the
rest drive to river, meet one man returning. cloudy in
the afternoon sprinkling of rain drive until after
sunset delightful evenings chilly nights very warm
days. disension in regard to the company breaking up
– camp on sweet water

Wednesday 28th start early clear road good except
a little sandy, ford the [space] alone except Bronsons
team, bathe in the river

Wednesday 28 wait until 9 oclock for the rest of the
company they do not come, ford river I find some
berries at noon heavy wind, some rain. Gilkey & H
noon in sight of us. many carcassas. few graves roads
good

Thursday 29th fair follow the river 10 miles, then
up hill & down over mountain bluffs grave on the
mount marshy lake, springs, cross several small
creeks camp late near a spring poor feed L & K
½ miles back of us. after dark when we arrive in camp
(if it can be so called consisting of but two teams)
starlight & serene induce a corresponding state of
mind

Friday 30th start *4 oclock* in order to find feed for
teams, cross two streams trading camp find Burly &

co about 4 miles from our encampment   leave the
road & strike a branch of the S water   return the
oxen to G. B   carry flour   start again at 10 oclock
arrive at a large stream a little after noon   find Mr
Burley there, request to travel with us, catch a fish,
lose hook, walk with G. B.

Tuesday [August] 3rd   pleasant   start early   road
[?   ] bluffs to the right   rather cloudy. morning
arrive at Green river about noon   find Gilkey & Hardgrove camped [?   ] arrive night   F. out [?   ]
traders   Kentucky   company   pass   [indecipherable
line]

Wednesday 4th   start early   arrive at the ford of
Green river bare 2 miles distant   ford rapid stream
camp 3 miles from ford   trading post near   Indians
cross river in afternoon   part [?   ] camp with us
rainbow in morning

Thursday 5th   start early   travel 2 miles & stop to
get breakfast & feed for horses   road good. ford Black
Fork   pocket book adventures   Ned finds a worn old
bill left   H. returns for Pocketbook   E. & John do
not arrive until the evening

Friday 6th   pleasant roads   good   very warm   romantic scenery   ford Black fork & [?   ] get left,
frenchmen names on rocks   pretty flowers [?   ]
light shower in P. M.   camped at a bend of Blacks
fork

Saturday 7   fair   very warm   road uneven most of
the way   ford

Tuesday 10th   sky cloudless   cool wind   scorching
sun, roads very hilly, rocky   Indians, beautiful scenery   ascend the mountain, Indians baiting ponies

beautiful springs of water   hole through the rock,
leave a note cache cave   cross fellow Creek also Echo
creek, singular of

Saturday 21st   Leave the City of the Great Salt Lake
about 2 oclock on our way to Carson valley   stop to
see the boiling Sulphur springs   the Jew is with us
we are to board him forty per week – meet Mr. White-
side just at dark & he informs us that he cannot find
the cattle we were to get 15 miles from the city – packs
the horses again, give up the cattle   go on to woods
tavern 8 miles from the city, & stop for the night

Sun 22nd [August]   Start on the back track – the Jew
goes on to overtake the horse wagons & get his clothes
having put his carpet sack in one of them   we came
to where John & the widow were camped   stop a
while & then vamose for the city. John & the widow
stay until the next day   Stop for the night at Mr
Gannot[?]

Mon. 23   John arrives just at night   have a very pleasant visit with a Mr. Tripp in the evening – pa endeav-
ors to make another trade

Tuesday 24   Succeeds in trading his horses for two
pair of cattle   Mrs Hitchens agrees with Mr Tripp
for him to return to search for her horse   we are to
go on & wait

Wednesday 25th   Left the city once more & went our
way for the land of gold but this time with very different feelings & on a very different route [4]   good road,
pleasant camp in about 10 miles from the city   now
wait the news of the horse

---

[4] They were traveling the so-called "Mormon Corridor," which was the
southwest way to the Pacific Coast from the Salt Lake Valley to the San

Thursday 26   pleasant – Tripp & Ned arrive in the
P. M. & no traces of the horse   conclude she must have
been stolen

Friday 27th   start early & arrive at the hot springs
or wells 4 P. M.   two wagons came soon after   a young
man arrives just at dark & wishes to be carried through
makes a bargain with Mr. Sutherland

Saturday 28th   wash in the forenoon   start 11 A. M.
road over the ridge   beautiful appearance of the valley & Jordon river   pass several small teams (farm
for sale)   nice farms   drive till after dark   Mr [?]
is back of us   camp on Pleasant Grove [?] creek
three wagons near – 20 miles

Sunday 29th [August]   cattle gone in the morning,
Pa looks for them until 2 oclock P. M.   about 12 oclock
John comes with them having strayed back to their
camp   rose bushes on the creek   cover tent floor with
bushes   arrange a shelf   thought while left alone
old man visits us, story of his indian battle   belief of
the Mormons in regard to their strength   buy chicken
melons –

Monday 30   wait for John   start half past 9. John
stops to bait cattle at noon, cross a large creek   find
no feed till we get 8 miles from the creek. camp about
8 P. M.   John camp ½ mile beyond us. go to their
camp in the evening. Indian. get lost returning to
camp in buggy

Tuesday 31st   do not start early   many Indians at

Bernardino area of Southern California. Part of the way it followed the
much older "Spanish Trail." Jefferson Hunt and a Mormon company had
explored the alternatives of a "southern route" in 1847. It had been used
often between then and 1852. Milton R. Hunter, "The Mormon Corridor,"
Pac. Hist. Rev., VIII, No. 2, (June, 1939), pp. 179-200, especially pp. 184ff.

camp in the morning while Pa gone after oxen   cross
several small creeks   two more teams ahead of us
Utah lake to the right   camp near Hobble creek

September 1st Wednesday   very dusty (all the way
from Salt Lake valley) pleasant company, Mr Van
informs us of the marriage of one of their company,
that in the evening   baptizing, inquiry for the [?   ]

Thursday 2   cross Petteskirt creek   roads dusty, very
warm, camp by a ditch some distance from the creek.
meet 8 indians just before camping, plenty of them
around

Friday 3rd   nothing of importance   arrive at the
city of Nephi[5] about 2 oclock   many Indians   more
teams arrive at night   the city is on Salt Lake, County
of Joab [Juab]

Saturday 4th   lay in camp waiting for more company
more arriving in the afternoon, go to get berries in the
Kanion   cave to the left   climb mountain   Mount
Nebo on the right   Stephen McGee goes to San Peet
[Sanpete, Utah] to engage in a sawsmith   pleasant
many Indians

Sunday 5th [September]   more teams arrive today at
the school house   expecting to hear preaching   get
disappointed   Stephen returns [?   ]

Monday 6th   wait for one of the company to visit a
sister   go to the mountain again for service berries
blacktailed deer

Tuesday 7   leave Nephi the company consisting of
three wagons with horse teams & 7 with oxen & 1
packer with mules   roads good. shower, ride mule

---

[5] Nephi was also called Salt Creek at this time. It had only been settled
in 1851 by enterprising Mormons. Rufus Wood Leigh, *Five Hundred Utah
Place Names* (Salt Lake City, 1961), pp. 65-66.

in afternoon. cross [?] creek & camp narrow
streams very deep   said to be 100 loads of stones at
ford   rainy all night   *John* [Simpson] *speaks up*

Wednesday 8th   start very early   camp for noon on
Sevier river   Kinkades team cross and camp on the
opposite   river where we ford about 4 rods wide
camp at night near a small creek at the foot of the
mountain   Indians visit camp – two Spaniards in the
company   other company camp near, lost can water,
singular appearance of the mountain on the side towards the sun, roads good some hilly   20   Lath[rop?]
baby sick

Thursday 9th   Spaniard & John play game in morning   Mr Hickert[?] ax him [?] take off shoe
find the lameness to be occasioned by being pricked,
roads hilly & some stony. pleasant, cross a large plain,
camp at Cedar Creek. 2 oclock   13½ m

Friday 10th   pleasant   very warm   roads good. arrive at Filmore [Fillmore, Utah] 2 oclock   camp on
poor place 2 miles from the settlement. building state
house, small farms mostly Spanish

Saturday 11th   pleasant   arrive at a creek about noon

Sunday 12 [September]   lay by in camp all day
wash

Monday 13   roads good, arrive at willow flats   many
Indians   stop until 2 oclock & travel all night   roads
very hilly. Indians follow us. said they were going to
Salt Lake, Indians stop about 12   arrive at a small
creek about 4 in the morning   cattle & people very
tired   25 from flat   Eliza & the squire rode together – ahem

Tuesday 14th   when it came day light left the place

where we were stopped & go about 1 mile up the creek. lay there that day

Wednesday 15th   rained all night last night. showery until 2 in the afternoon   lay in camp all day   Mrs. H tent blew down   play cards   another team of packers arrive

Thursday 16th   start early   roads good   arrive at good feed & water about 3 miles from camp   stop to bait[6]   part of the company stop for the day   Simpson Bainbridge & Pratt go on   stop and bait again about 3   hilly in the afternoon   arrive at Sage creek after dark   cross & camp   no good feed   22

Friday 17th   start at daylight & travel 5 miles to good feed water, many Indians come while we are getting breakfast   leave about noon, cross another stream Indian Wi-kee-ups. sage plain   cross the mountain camp in flat. no water – cold & rainy   clear in P. M. but cold wind

Saturday 18th   start early   made good most of the way   snow in the morning   search for water   meet an indian, red mountains to the left, arrive at the settlement on the Kanyon creek 4 oclock P. M.   rest of company arrive in the evening   another camp close by

Sunday 19th [September]   pleasant   stay in camp, walk to the mountain cool   visit the ruins in the evening[7]

Monday 20   rest of the company gone   we stay till 4 P. M.   Indians come to our tent   try to frighten me while Pa is after cattle   pa runs against one   gun Indian drew his arrow at Pa   arrive little Salt lake

---

6 "Bait" is a old term for feed, i.e. stopping to graze the animals.

7 Probably the Paragoonah Pueblo, an archaeological site "of no mean importance," according to Leigh, *op. cit.*, p. 73.

at the right   at [blank space] find the gate locked. Indians halloo nearly all night

Tuesday 21   do our trading & get ready to leave the city about 3 P. M.   Mr Simpson got the butter we had   engaged some of the company   arrive in town and informs us of the wedding in the company after they left us — arrived Summit creek where the rest of the company were camped about dark   Hinsford arrives in the evening with some liquor to treat the bride & groom   they both get mad

Wednesday 22   roads good   start early   indecision in regard to the road   finally take the left hand road which led to the iron works 6 miles out of our way arrive at Cedar springs 2 P M   to creek after dark

[8 unreadable lines which she also had crossed out.]

Saturday 24 [25]   roads good   windy   cool winds arrive at Pynta [Pintura] creek   poor feed   20

Sunday 25 [She is off on her days of the week for the rest of September. Sunday was the 26th.]   part of the way very hilly   travel 9 miles to cold springs   warm & pleasant   find the other company there   beautiful place   good feed   spanish book

Monday 26 [27]   roads very hilly   scenery delightful. find many grapes — (mucho uvis)   stop to gather some & get behind the train. arrive at a branch of the Santa Clara & camp for the night   saw mucho parmita the fruit resembling in shape our cucumbers

Tuesday 27 [28]   start early   hilly   stopped to bait on the hillside, went to the brow of the cliff & took a look at the valley below   very beautiful scenery — the other train passed us & stopped at the foot of a very steep hill, ride on the mule   wild vines bearing fruit

resembling a pineapple muskmelon but very bitter,
reach the Santa Clara at the foot of the steep hill
travel down river some ways – leave it just before night
& reach a spring of poor water, good feed   find another
train camped here waiting for more company   Indians follow us most of the P. M.   saw some beautiful
specimens of cactus

Wednesday   Lay in camp to rest & feed the cattle
many Indians   purchase a bow & arrow   the indian
of whom I purchased it stole it & vanished

Thursday 29 [30]   Start about 8 oclock in the morning   rough roads   stopped for breakfast some 6 or
8 miles from the spring, found some excellent berries growing on bushes from 4 to 6 feet high   the
fruit resembles cranberries, but much more pleasant
camped at night on a tributary of the Rio virgin
where were several springs of excellent water   roads
sand in the afternoon, saw mucho pomato or sick plant
rain in the morning   snow on the mountain

October 1st Friday   start about 9 oclock   roads very
sandy – travel down the Rio virgin crossing it 2 times
10 miles   the other trains go on

Sat 2   roads sandy   follow along the river & camp
where the feed is tolerable long –

Sunday 3rd [October]   warm   pleasant   very dusty
cross the Rio Virgin 6 times   very sandy   camp where
the road leaves the river. John finds a calf – our wagon
& Simpsons cross the river. the rest noon on the other
side. Mrs Willoughby with us – sick in the afternoon –

Tuesday [5]   Leave the river & ascend a very high
hill. noon at the top of the hill only 2 miles from we
camped. Indians come from the muddy to meet us.

John sells the calf to them for a bow & eight arrows.
roads very rocky, steep hill to descend   arrive at the
muddy 12 at night   I fell under the wagon   find two
other camps at the M[uddy]

Wednesday [6]   lay in camp. story about the squire
fish, the Muddy is a deep stream with a swift current
from 10 to 15 feet wide   Indians very troublesome
steal many articles from the camp   get a case for my
arrows

Thursday [7]   stay at the same camp   Marion & John
talk of leaving

Friday [8]   start very early for the ford about 5 miles
distant   ride behind Mr [?   ]   stay at the camp
near the ford the rest of the day   many Indians come
to trade. Marion frightens them

Friday 8th   stay at the camp till one oclock   the[y]
leave for the desert or 52 miles without water before
sunset & bait the cattle [?   ] 20 minutes   drive all
night   road hilly & rocky. plenty [?   ] grass &
grease wood

Saturday 9th   stop & bait the cattle   get breakfast
a little after sun rise   road very hilly & rocky part
of the way. ride a mule. arrive at the Las Vegas river
[?   ] one hour   high   The Las Vegas is about 2
feet wide deep rapid [?   ] good water, sinks   a
little below here were [?   ]

Sunday 10th [October]   Lay in camp. gather grapes

Monday 11   John Simpson & a gentleman from the
other train go ahead intend to get through in 8 days
the rest of the companies go 5 miles & camp for the
day –

Tuesday 12th   start early   roads very rocky   the

worst we have had   in the afternoon drive at Cotton wood Spring just before sun down   2 cows missing – Springs near to

Wednesday 13th   lay by in order to look for the lost cows   two men return to the lead wagons, could not find them. Peters cow comes with the other train, who another day or two Las Vagin[?] he had not missed her.

Thursday 14th   started before breakfast & went 2 or 3 miles to get feed, some water & camped till 8 oclock in order to travel through the night, on our right was the most romantic mountain peak we have seen. reached the base of the mountain bluff which we had to ascend after dark. good road after we descended into the canyon   part of the road very rocky & hilly   stopped to get breakfast where was some good bunch grass early

Friday morning 15th   traveled about 5 miles after breakfast over hills   feed tolerable when we arrive at cotton wood   have water but no feed   stop here to rest [several faded words] noche   when we take agua with us & go about 7 miles to good bunchgrass & stop for the noche

Saturday 16th   road very bad   one would hardly think they could be worse   arrive at resting springs after dark. tired almost to death intend to stay a week – Mr Sutherland goes on alone in the afternoon & horse team stop with us   horses gone in the morn

Thursday 21st   It is finally agreed to by the Co to go ahead today – start 9 oclock   drive 5 miles to camp near a small stream of alkali water   roads bad part of the way   in the afternoon some of the men go ahead to look at the road & find we are about 8 m from the spring where we intended to go when we left the springs

Friday 22nd   It was just at the daylight we came to
the spring   immense   high   mountain   quantities of
alkali   cattle [?   ] are sick

Saturday 23rd   start 9 oclock   bad road   beautifully
scenery   heavy sand in the afternoon [3 unreadable
words] arrived Salt Springs 4 oclock

Sunday 24th [October]   Visit the mines in the morning   start 1 oclock to go across the 38 mile desert.
pleasant   good roads   drive all night saw many core-
opsis by the way & arrive at bitter springs about noon on

Monday the 25th   find Mr G.[?] here, he leaves 4
P. M.   finds grass 2 miles from the springs & returns
to tell us   no feed by the springs   ox no better   dark
prospect

Tuesday 26   Stop at springs & drive the 3 cattle to
feed at [?   ] bridge   go on   cattle in a very bad
condition   water bitter   [line obscure]

Wednesday 27th   Start about noon to cross the desert
gradual ascent, heavy sand, beautiful flowers. go on
ahead & kindle fire. meet Mr Bainbridge & broth-
erinton about midnight returning for an ox which they
left. after this descending to the Mohave travel all
night   stop for breakfast

Thursday 28th   Arrive at the Mohave 12 noon   Mr
B & co ie brothers   Storm at 4 p m   the Mohave cannot be called a river as there is no water except at
places

Friday 29 –   Lay in camp, plenty of wild grapes
some footmen arrived in the afternoon   account of the
Indians on the sandy & at Cottonwood Springs Br
Brotherton goes in shoulder packes and dutch billy &
Mary also the [?   ]

Saturday 30th   Go 10 miles. heavy sandy road, not
very good feed – sick ox some better but very weak
water sinks in the sand while watering the cattle.

Sunday 31st [October]   Contention in the morning
about driving   start about 9 A. M.   roads most of the
way very heavy & sandy   walk most of the way – fail
in our search for water till near night. find water over
a mile from the place where we we camped   Lewis
and myself together with the English people & Mr
Sutherland were ahead   I returned, the rest kept on
packer from San Bernardino overtook me before I
reached camp   brings news from the squire & co –
I am almost sick –

Monday Nov 1st   Stay till almost 5 P. M. our cattle
strayed   go to water   had no feed   10 miles   feel
quite sick & tired out. find a note on the big Cottonwood tree from Lewis. Road sandy   heat exception
before we leave camp – Mr Lewis returned very early
in the morning from the cattle that had been left the
day before – then started on to overtake his wagons –
Mr Long & W were obliged to leave theirs again to
day & for good –

Tuesday 2nd   Start before sun up & drive about 3
miles to feed & get our breakfast   stay 2 hours. then
drive till near noon & stop to rest the cattle a little
while again – meet Lewis shortly after coming back –
It was quite cold in the morning   a smart breeze in
the A. M. which increased till it blew almost a gale
before night   suffered considerable with the cold wind
& dust   very deep sand part of the way – camp about
4 miles from the last crossing of the Mohave   this is
the first time the wind has produced that mournful

dirge like sound which we usually hear much earlier
in the states

Wednesday 3rd   Last evening about 10 Mr Brown
arrived at our encampment having left his team with
his wife & Mrs Lord   he is going to the ranch &
then return to meet his co   the wind subsided during
the night & it is a bright & beautiful morning although
quite cool – start 8 oclock for the last crossing of the
Mohave expecting to find it 3 or 4 miles distant
road rocky part of the way & some heavy sand – arrive
at the crossing 2 P. M.   camp near a spring half a mile
from the ford   Mr Long shot three ducks, got one of
them   L reads   The "diamond" in the evening – 10
miles

Thursday 4   Agreed to lay in camp to day which was
spent in washing, baking &c &c &c   Betty & Long
go duck hunting   account of the fir trees

Friday 5   Leave the river & strike off to the right
good road but a little ascending most of the way
beautiful specimens [?   ] plant – drive till 3 P. M.
& camp for the night. no water except what we had
with us – bunch grass – very cold night –

Saturday 6th   Start before day break & drive about
6 miles   stop to feed & breakfast   road good to the
summit of Cahone [Cajon] pass   then down a very
bad hill   sand rocks in the Kanyon – arrive at a place
to camp 3 P. M.   find Mr Brown there, meet Bainbridge & Blackburn – 10 miles

Sunday 7th [November]   Lay in camp   Mr Crabb
goes on – Browns train arrives about noon – Long goes
with crabb & two other fellows from Smiths train who

entertained us with a 'speech' the evening before, opinion of some of the men in regard to the gold mines

Sat & S   camp

Monday 8th   Find Mr Bainbridge & brother in camp having arrived in the night – road down the kanyon very rough, romantic scenery   follow the course of a small stream   arrive at a camp 2 P. M.   two men arrive in the evening, team returning with provisions Mr Long sends some things to W.   fruit of the Prickley Pears

Tuesday 9th   Lane of Browns Co killed a bear in the morning, road good, Pa & John go with Mr Browns train   Mr Miller go to the fort[8]   arrive San Bernardino 3 P. M.   get some grapes for a bit per pound –

Wednesday 10th   Cloudy in the morning. sun shone out about 10 oclock – Lewis made me a visit – Pa & John return from town near night   L. comes with us again

Thursday 11th   Pleasant, moved from our camp into a field about 1 mile. Sold waggon for 100 dollars. Willoughby & Long have sold (all)   Mr Crabb here to day, wild horse – nothing of importance only that I am very weary and about sick

(Friday 12th)   Visit the fort   partly engage a school saw Mr Thompson lady   Billy came for his ring – he & Long leave in the morning   Lewis makes me a visit in the evening

Sat 13th   Lewis comes in the morning   Will Thompson & Sutherland leave   Mr Brown & some of his co

---

[8] The "fort" on the San Bernardino site was a Mormon bastion, one of "a chain of forts from Salt Lake City to the Pacific Ocean," founded in 1851. Leonard J. Arrington and Davis Bitton, *The Mormon Experience* (New York, 1979), p. 118.

go to Los Angeles, visit with Dr. B in the evening. indications of rain   sprinkle in the morning

Sunday 14th [November]   Pleasant   some of the co attended church, I read in A. J. Davis work[9]   visit with Dr B in the evening –

Monday 15th   Sprinkles in the morning   move to the fort – engage to teach school, pass examination   terms $30 per month besides expenses – a load is from my heart

Tuesday 16th   wash & bake – scene in the tent close by

Wednesday 17th   Commence the duties of school. description of the houses and scholars – Pleasant I stayed in the tent for the last time   *settlement*

Thursday 18th   Cloudy – rained through the night cleared off at noon

Friday 19th   Rained very hard all day   pa did not get away as he expected – Mr Kangan [?] came to bid me good bye – *They are to leave in the morning*

Saturday 20th   fair   Pa left this morning   no school – commenced Spanish & Phonography[10] in the evening

Sunday 21st [November]   Pleasant   Mrs Rich here

---

9 This was Andrew Jackson Davis, one of the leading writers at the time on spiritualism. From 1845 to 1847 he delivered in Manhattan, "while in a state of trance," 157 lectures. They were published later under the title, *Principles of Nature, Her Divine Revelation, and a Voice to Mankind,* published in 1847. H. W. Schneider and Ruth Redfield, "Davis, Andrew Jackson," *Dictionary of American Biography,* v (New York, 1930), p. 105. Also Howard Kerr, *Mediums, and Spirit-Rappers, and Roaring Radicals* (Urbana, Ill., 1972).

10 "Phonography" was the term used for "shorthand" at the time. She was probably studying the book by Isaac Pitman of Bath, England, *Phonography, or Writing by Sound, being also a New and Natural System of Short Hand.* This book had gone into eight editions by 1852. Thompson Cooper, "Sir Isaac Pitman," *Dictionary of National Biography,* xxii, *Supplement* (London, 1949-1950), pp. 1138-40.

trials   lesson in the evening – call at Mrs Blackburns just before dark   account of the death of Gen. Bean story of the woman who was shot on the road

Monday 22nd   School as usual. nothing of importance occurred

Tuesday 23   weather quite cool   snow on the mountains

Wednesday 24th   Cold disagreeable wind all day some rain, suffer with much cold

Thurs 25   Pleasant – cool last night – ice this A M of an inch thick

Friday 26th   very much fatigued at night – attend singing school in the evening. my heart is full –

Saturday 27th   No school   finish the ocelot cape – every day seems to mortify my pride more and more

Sunday 28 [November]   Pleasant   sewed all day – took a walk in the evening   visit with El mira

Monday 29th   Pleasant   almost sick with a cold up late on account of fixing floor to house

Tuesday 30   Some rain – cool nights – saw Mr Crabb at noon   receive a letter from Lewis   hear from Pa – oh how slowly time *walks*

Wednesday   Dec 1st   Cloudy – pleasant in the P. M. two gentlemen visit the school & inform that we are to make returns from the school   Mr Stout [?] here in the evening   Dr Burns calls

Thursday 2   Warm & Pleasant, spend most of the day making returns

Fri 3   Warm & Pleasant, two strangers come to the door

Sat 4th   Cloudy, rains some throughout the day, finish the returns & finish my dress also –

Sunday 5 [December]   Cloudy in the morning, rains some, clear in P. M.   attend church in the evening for the first time since I left home   sermons by mormon missionaries who have arrived here on their way to the four quarters of the globe   they arrived here from Salt Lake on last Fri

Monday 6th   Cloudy, indication of rain   every in the usual way

Tuesday 7th   sermon in the even   attend with Mrs Hopkins, obliged to leave with the children   Pleasant.

Wed 8th   sprinkles little –

Thursday 9th   warm & pleasant   cold nights   every morning this week I have taken a walk very early in the morning

Fri 10th   Pleasant   Mr Miner starts for *Pueblo* [11]

Sat 11th   Pleasant   O how lonely this day has been, visit Mr Crabbs in the evening

Sunday 12th   Pleasant   two sermons & 30 baptized

Monday 13th   near a dozen more baptized   I went to the water to witness the ceremony at noon   Mr Clogs came here – Mr & Mrs C spent the evening with me

---

[11] This was Morris Miner, who would become her husband in 1853, starting for Los Angeles. See introduction to this document.

Letters on the Way to California
⸘ Lucy Rutledge Cooke

INTRODUCTION

It was in 1923 that Frank W. Cooke,[1] a creative teacher of printing and journalism in the California city of Modesto, had his students set the type and publish a book that has become a classic: *Crossing the Plains in 1852: Narrative of a Trip from Iowa to "The Land of Gold," as Told in Letters Written During the Journey.* The author of the letters was Lucy Cooke. They were "printed solely for the descendants of the author in memory of the faith and optimism that were hers throughout the perilous journey of those early days 'Across the Plains.' " The letters had been edited by the author many years before and by others after her death and before publication.

The book has since been republished by the Plumas County Historical Society, Quincy, in 1980, and it is still in print. This time it has been produced under the aegis of Robert S. Cooke of Taylorsville, a grandson of William and Lucy Cooke. Robert Cooke has been most helpful in our *Covered Wagon Women* project.

It became our good fortune to learn that most of the letters still exist in the collection of the California Historical Society, San Francisco. It is with their gracious permission that the letters are here published directly from the manuscript collection. Only "Letter Number Four" of the printed version is missing. There is also material written by Lucy Cooke after the overland journey that is here omitted.

---

[1] "Marginalia," *Calif. Hist. Soc. Qtly.*, XVIII, No. 4 (Dec., 1949), pp. 380-81.

The manuscript collection was given to the California Historical Society by Mrs. Viola M. Priest, late granddaughter of Lucy and William Cooke, in 1951.[2]

The American story has always been one of mobility. Recently the United States Census Bureau revealed that each person in this country tends to move some ten times in a lifetime. The saga of Lucy Cooke tells a story of human mobility. Just look at the changing events and moves made by an English girl who emigrated to the United States in 1848:

Lucy and Marianne Rutledge, sisters, sailed from England on August 11, 1848, arriving in New York City on September 16.[3]

They traveled overland and by boat the length of the Erie Canal, then across the Great Lakes to Chicago, then overland again to Davenport, Iowa, where their uncle was a Baptist minister.

Soon afterwards her sister, Marianne, married a Mr. Willis and moved to Rockingham, Scott County, Iowa. They invited Lucy to come and live with them, which she did, giving music lessons to finance her way.

She, in turn, took music lessons from Mrs. Sarah Cooke of nearby Davenport. That is how she met young William Sutton Cooke. They were married on December 26, 1849.[4] They lived in Moline, Illinois, until the spring of 1851, when they joined the senior Cookes [5] in a new move to Dubuque, Iowa. Their first baby, Sarah, was born there on August 16, 1851.

During the spring of 1852 the "California fever," as

---

[2] "News of the Society," *Calif. Hist. Soc. Qtly,* xxx, No. 1 (March, 1951), p. 82. It is Ms. 443.

[3] Much of the material that follows is from two sources. (1) The typewritten "Biography" that accompanies the Lucy Cooke manuscript letter collection; (2) the published version of the letters, hereafter referred to as *Crossing the Plains.* Its source is described in the beginning of this introduction.   [4] *Crossing the Plains,* p. 80.

[5] The Cooke family had also emigrated from England. William had been born in Manchester. The older Cooke's had migrated to North Carolina from Leeds in 1828, when William was one year old. Typewritten "Biography."

Lucy called it, was at a high pitch, and both families of
William Cookes decided to start out for Pacific shores.

Let Lucy Cooke tell in a reminiscence the next part of
the story published in the printed version of 1923:

> Mr. Cooke, my husband's father, secured twelve young men
> as passengers, who paid their fare to be delivered in Sacramento,
> California, so those, with our own family, consisting of ten per-
> sons, including myself and baby, made a goodly company. We
> started from Dubuque with four wagons, one a light spring
> drawn by two horses, the others having oxen with cows for
> "leaders."
>
> Mr. Cooke started his men folks first, to drive across Iowa to
> Council Bluffs on the western side of the state, whilst Mrs.
> Cooke, two young children, myself and baby, were driven by Mr.
> Cooke Sr. down to Davenport in our two-horse wagon with
> covered top and laden to the bows. We wished to bid farewell
> to remaining friends ere we started the "Plains across." I spent
> my brief sojourn with my sister and her husband at Rockingham;
> then Mr. Cooke Sr. took our team and joined the company at
> the Bluffs, leaving Mrs. Cooke, myself and children to come
> down the river on the steamboat plying to St. Louis, and thence
> up the Missouri River to our destination, where our company
> would be awaiting us.

Lucy Cooke's early letters describe this river voyage,
then later ones tell of everyday happenings on the overland journey. A distinctive feature of her story is that they
stopped over the winter in Salt Lake City and went on to
California the following spring.

At the time of the crossing Lucy was 24 years old, and
her husband, William the younger, was 25. The older
Cookes, William and Sarah, had with them the rest of the
children in their family: John Richards, 21 years old;
Thomas, 19; Eve Anna, ten, who went by the nickname,
"Lilly"; Edward, seven; and Richard, five.[6]

---

[6] Two sources have been used to find the vital statistics of the Cooke
family: A family Bible from which Robert S. Cooke, Taylorsville, California,
copied the information and sent it to us; and the Seventh Census of the
United States, 1850, Iowa, p. 108.

While the rest got settled in Salt Lake City, "Pa" Cooke
went on with the caravan to California. Sarah Cooke con-
verted to Mormonism in Salt Lake City, and William Sr.
did the same in California. He later returned to Salt Lake
City, where he became a member of the police force. He
was killed "in line of duty" on October 18, 1858, "shot
by a ruffian named McDonald, alias Cunningham." [7]

Mother Sarah Cooke took up her work as a teacher of
vocal and instrumental music. Her pupils included children
of Brigham Young, the Mormon leader. In later life she
became disillusioned with her adopted faith and in the
early 1870's defected and became a leader in the Women's
National Anti-Polygamy Society.[8]

Lucy, William, and baby Sarah Ann went on from Salt
Lake City in the spring of 1853. The last letter is written
from the Carson Valley on the east side of the Sierra
Nevada range. There they were to await the opening of
the passes with the melting of the mountain snows. In early
July they crossed the mountains, and, she says in remi-
niscing, "coming out by Roopley's ranch, near Hangtown.
We here slept the sleep of the just, under a spreading oak
tree, and thus we passed our first night in California." [9]
They settled in the gold country and spent much of the
rest of their lives in El Dorado County in the Placerville
area. Lucy taught music to generations of children. William
Cooke is listed as a miner in the 1860 Federal Census of
California. They were then living in Iowa Hill in Placer

---

[7] *Deseret News,* October 20, 1858. Information supplied by Walter R.
Jones, Librarian, Special Collections, University of Utah, Salt Lake City.

[8] Irving Wallace, *The Twenty-seventh Wife* (New York, 1961), p. 275;
Ann Eliza Young, *Wife No. 19* (Hartford, Conn., 1875), pp. 570-71. This last
author was one of Brigham Young's wives who left him and was aided
and abetted by Sarah Cooke and the Anti-Polygamy Society.

[9] *Crossing the Plains,* p. 71. There was a Hangtown in El Dorado County.
If this memory of Eliza Cooke's is correct, it contradicts Erwin G. Gudde,
who in *California Gold Camps* (Berkeley, 1975), p. 150, tells of the tradition
that Hangtown became Placerville in 1850. Perhaps it went by both names
for several years.

County.[10] Later he went into public service. In the 1880's they moved to Virginia City, Nevada, where William served as judge and justice of the peace. He died in 1898.[11] Lucy Cooke became blind for the last decade of her life. She moved to San Francisco, where two of her eight children lived.

A reporter for the Healdsburg, California *Tribune*, visited her in 1914, and the following story appeared in its June 4 edition: [12]

> On a recent visit to San Francisco, I spent a short while at the home of a white-haired old lady – blind these many years. But though the light of her eyes has been extinguished, and unending earthly darkness has enveloped her, this old lady shows marvelous interest in the world's activities of today, and her mind is alive with plans and hopes for the future.
>
> "Oh, if I just had my sight. I feel I could set the world on fire!"
>
> And if I could put into type the emphasis and vigor with which this declaration was made. I believe you would agree with me that she holds a marvelous grip on life and its opportunities.
>
> How old, do you ask, is this white haired lady?
>
> Well, she is not sensitive on this score, so it will not wound her feelings. I know, to say that the days of her life run back to the opening of the second quarter of the last century – March 1827, to be specific, and that totals up to eighty-seven years.
>
> And more than sixty years of that long life have been spent here in the West – in the mining camps and towns of California and Nevada.

A year and two months later she died, and the same newspaper, the Healdsburg *Tribune*, published the obituary in its October 28, 1915, edition: [13]

---

[10] Eighth Census of the United States, California, Placer County, Iowa Hill Township, No. 7.

[11] Bob Cooke, "Memories & Comments, Taylorsville & Genesee," Plumas County Hist. Soc., *Plumas Memories,* June 1974, p. 21. The death date is from the Cook family Bible.

[12] *Crossing the Plains,* p. 93.   [13] *Crossing the Plains,* p. 91.

In Memoriam — Mother

At Rest – In San Francisco, October 22, 1915, Lucy Rutledge Cooke, aged 88 years, 7 months and 12 days; a native of London, England; mother of Mrs. A. Lane, of Reno; Mrs. W. G. Thompson, of San Francisco; W. R. Cooke of Orosi, F. W. Cooke of Healdsburg, Genevieve Cooke of San Francisco, J. E. Cooke of Taylorsville, Plumas County. Mrs. G. W. Hatch of Oakland and the late Henry S. Cooke of Virginia City, Nevada.

THE LETTERS OF LUCY R. COOKE

St. Louis   April 15/52
"Pontiac No. 2"

The men are trying their guns
& there is such a noise

Left my sister on April 13th/52

Dearest Marianne

I met with Mr & Mrs Belcher on board the "Golden Era"[1] who informed me that Uncle returned the Sunday before I started   Twas a great pity some of them could not come down on the Monday as I should then have seen them   I wrote a letter to Uncle and gave it to one of the LeClair folks who was on board. We arrived here last evening Wednesday before supper having been only *1* night coming down   We did not see John R[ichards] when we arrived therefore we stayed on board   all night & this morning (Thursday) Ma went to find him & succeeded & have now taken our passage and are come on board the "Pontiac No. 2" but will you not think it enormously high when we

---

[1] Louise Barry, *The Beginning of the West, Annals of the Kansas Gateway to the American West, 1540-1854* (Topeka, 1972) gives the best summary of Missouri River steamboat activity in 1852 on pages 1073-1075.

have to pay $70 for our passage, The usual rate now
is $20 each the Capn deducts $10 for J R helping
onboard however Ma had but $30 to pay down but
the Capn seemed willing to run the risk of getting the
balance when we arrived at the bluffs The boat is
loaded with Californians & indeed so is all St. Louis
& you would be amused could you look down this cabin
& see tables full of young men writing the last letters to
friends but dear I fear we shall have a terrible time
for there seems thousands going, some I hear are returning from the Bluffs giving up the idea of going
I really could wish Wm & I were among the number
poor Ma this morn said "Oh I wish we never had
started" & she looks so dejected & sorrowful, I think
if we had not passengers to take through she would
want Pa to return, not that he would be at all disposed
to do so but returning now is hopeless I fear & indeed
I trust we shall find that all will be well, it has seemed
althrough as if the providence was leading us this way
& if so we shall not be left to perish There are some
very pleasant Ladies onboard who are going to the
Bluffs to meet husbands & friends so I think we shall
have nice company there is also a company of 50
young men on board from Cincinnati The Dr Frank-
lin No 2 did not go up the Missouri as advertised
Ma was talking about it to a gent on the "Golden Era"
& he said she would be sure *not* to run up there as she
was only insured for the Mississippi & when we got
to St Louis she was just starting out again for Dubuque
so that we should have had to change boats if we had
been on her This boat *they say* will start to night
but that may be the talk for some time however its so
pleasant here I don't care when we go There's an

English lady quite busy knitting white cotton stockings
openworked front such a pretty patn so she can show
me all about mine. Tho we've been on board but an
hour or 2 we seem so well acquainted with all Californians they all treat each other with kindness &
seem so agreeable   one lady is now walking up & down
with my sis while I write. The Stewardess is English
is from St *James* St *Oxford* St   she has traveled a
great deal her father was in the Hudson Bay Fur
Co & she went with him. she seems very fond of children & I think I shall be able to wash baby's fixings
comfortably on this boat. the Stewardess on the "Gold-
en Era" was awfully crabby I had such a time with
her, she happened to be washing so I stole her suds
when she went away & then she accused me of taking
the clothes pegs out of her clothes for mine which I
did not I must now finish as I fear the lady will get
tired of holding sis tell Mrs Wright I adopted her
plan of giving her to the lady because she said "Oh
what a sweet little baby" & if they will all hold her
that praise her why I shall scarcely be able to nurse
her all the way for every one says what a sweet healthy
looking child she is Give my kind regards to Mrs
& Sarah Wright & all the Colemans & accept the love
of your own
    We have just dined   had nice lettuce & spring on-
ions, there's lots of rhubarb & asparagus here & it
seems so hot, the waiters are all in their shirt sleeves
the Californians look such a motley group some have
oil cloth coats & hats & near all hickory shirts   I have
dined in my brown gingham dress as I thought I should
then look as well as the rest   The Moline folks were
not on the boat with us, as they did not hail it it passed

without calling at Moline but very likely we may see them yet as we shall not start very soon   How I shall wonder if Uncle came down soon after I left   I guess I shall not hear from you any more till we arrive at California however I shall write from Council Bluffs & as often as there's a chance   You must direct to me to Messrs Gratiot & Childs Sacramento city Cal   My side still troubles me but I think its a little better, my ankle is quite troublesome   baby is well. I think we shall hardly need cloaks again   it seems so like summer   John R seems quite pleased with baby. Dont be surprised if we come back again & now dear, dear Marianne farewell   I cannot only indulge the hope we shall meet again   give my kindest love to your dear husband   I shall always love him for his great kindness to me & your own kindness I shall never forget

good bye my loves
yours ever.   Lucy

[The preceeding letter was postmarked "Saint Louis, Mo.   Apr 16". Addressed to "Mrs. Willis Rockingham, near Davenport Iowa"]

April 19th 1852
Pontiac No 2

My dearest Marianne

Being quite unoccupied I sit me down to write a little account of our journey thus far   This is Monday evening   We came on board last Friday Morn & at present we have come only about 200 miles   Oh what tedious travelling it is on this river   Our boat is a very slow one & then it is so heavily laden   but I feel almost dismayed to think we have not come a fourth of the distance, the river abounds with sand bars on

which we often stick a long time, last night we were
on one most of the night   Methinks its well dear Polly
its not you thus travelling for you'd be scared all the
time for the river is covered with floating timber &
snags   it seems almost a wonder they should attempt
to run at night. Yesterday was the sabbath   Oh how
I should have enjoyed riding with you & your dear
husband to hear that good Mr Adams but thats all
gone as tho' it had never been   We had some hymn
singing on board & it did my heart good to look over
the guards down to the deck of the boat & see a company of men singing from hymn books & then engaged
in reading a portion of scripture   We stopt to wood
about 4 miles from a town so many of the passengers
went off & walked to the town & then came on board
the men poor things rush ashore every time the boat
stops as tho we had been at sea for a month   To day
we passed Jefferson city the capital of Missouri   There
is a splendid State House on the banks of the river.
We have not as yet passed more than 3 or 4 towns.
there seems nothing to interest one   I've seen a few
orchards and the trees were so covered with blossoms
Oh how it makes me think of your *happy home*. Ma is
just as downcast as ever. She thinks she shall never be
happy again   to day she said she would be willing
to teach a large class of piano scholars a year for nothing could she by that means be back in Dubuque as
comfortably fixed as she was before she left   none of
the arguments she used to induce her to come away
have any weight now   I think she would have me to
believe it was entirely on Williams account that they
take this move but I cannot quite think so as of course
it was as much for her other sons. I do long to get to

the Bluffs to see if our husbands are in good spirits about the journey My dear babe was vaccinated from Richard W it was only done in one place but it has taken nicely so I'm glad I only had it once R W had 3 & it made his arm dreadful bad. Tell Mrs Wright Ma is not afraid to use cold water at such a time for R W's arm was in such an inflamation that she had to keep putting wet cloths to it all one night. dear little Sissy is so good she goes to sleep now in the evening without crying at all & takes a sleep of 2 or 3 hours every morn John R is so fond of her he takes care of her every meal time while I go to the first table I bought her a little chair like Mrs Burnells except that mine is wicker work I gave 1.00 for it I have not padded it yet dont know if I shall, sis likes it very much I get along pretty well with my washing tho we have not that English chamber maid she left before we came from St Louis & would you believe the reason she told us in private was that she would not consent to having the steward sleep in her state room so she left & a young black woman has taken her place but she is very accomodating & I have a capital place to dry my clothes We at first had a double state room in the gentlemens cabin which was very uncomfortable as it was quite dark We soon got it exchanged for one in the ladies cabin which is very pleasant so we can go & sit alone there & enjoy our own meditations My side is sometimes very bad I cannot yet sneeze at all I've not had a mustard poultice on I dont seem to have much opportunity to attend to myself. Tuesday Afternoon my dear baby slept all the morning while I sewed awoke just before dinner After dinner I went to washing her

clothes while one of the ladies took care of her   I have
now got through having washed 12 diapers sundry
aprons night gown & petticoat   I've not yet changed
my own under clothes   I feel to dislike putting on
those you last washed   they will bring back past scenes
very vividly   My ankle was very troublesome when I
first came on board   one of the passengers assisted me
to melt some rosin bees wax & tallow & make a plaster
I've obtained the 2 former & applied them & it seems
to have benefitted the sore, for I've felt nothing of it
since. How very much colder it seems as we go up
the river & there is little appearance of summer or
rather spring   how I should like to know how Mr
Willis gets on with his plowing   Oh if I could but be
settled somewhere near you   what joy it would *I think*
give me but I must be silent on this subject   I told
Ma the other day that I had told Mrs Willis we would
come & try to raise money enough to return to Iowa
& purchase a home near you. she did not seem to like
the idea very much but I shall always look back with
regret to your home   you were too good too kind to
me while sojourneying with you. Oh how long the time
seems since I've seen my dear husband   we've written
one letter to them from St Louis, suppose it will reach
there before we do   We are in considerable doubt as
to where this boat will take us, for saying we want to
get to Council Bluffs it seems is very indefinite as the
bluffs so named extend over 200 miles. some say we
shall not go higher than St Jo's if so we shall be rather
awkwardly fixed for boarding is $2½ per day there &
we should have to remain there until we could send to
our folks besides then we should not be able to pay
the ballance of our passage so I hope yet it will all

turn out for the best   Lilly has just been heming 4
silk cuffs for a gent on board who paid her 50 cents
for the job   I wish I could meet with some such sewing for I had to borrow 35 cents of a passenger to finish
paying for my baby's hair   The ladies are quite at
a loss to know how to amuse themselves   I dont know
what we will do before we reach the end of our journey   Ive only dressed baby in her red saque twice as
I dont like her to wear it for fear we shall so soon
spoil the beauty   Ma thinks it very pretty & all admire it

Thursday Afternoon   Dear M   my little babe is so
sick   I was up all night with her   she takes little or
no nourishment & what she does she throws up directly
   poor babe   she moans all the time & is in a high
fever   We think perhaps it proceeds from her vaccina-
tion   at first we thought it was hooping cough coming
on as she coughed very much yesterday. I intend to
mail this at Lexington which place we expect to reach
in about one hour   we shall then have come 50 miles
short of ½ way   Oh how I wish we never had come
I must bid you my dearest & your dear husband adieu
I will write whenever I can

Yours ever affectly [stet]
Lucy

[Written Across the Lines on this Last Sheet]
Why they say this is the 22nd   is it not your birthday
God bless you my beloved sister & fervantly pray we
may both be spared to meet again in this world & if
not may we strive to spend together a blissful eternity
   How surprised you would be if we should return
from the bluffs   wish there was a chance of it

On board the "Robert Campbell"
April 30th 1852

Dearest Sister

My last letter to you was sealed ready for posting before we arrived at Lexington at which place I got a passenger to mail it

When we arrived there we stoped along side of the wreck of a boat which had been blown up about 2 weeks previous name the "Saluda" [2] Oh never never shall I forget the sight it presented even 2 weeks after the dreadful occurrence   there was not the width of 2 planks left in any part of the boat & towards the middle & all around the engine boilers &c   there was nothing left but just the skeleton or outside planks the machinery was a great part laying on land & 2 or 3 houses were blown down by the explosion   Oh what an awful thing it was   doubtless many were on board going to their friends as we are   The boat had just got to the landing   some had gone off her when she blew up   most of the passengers were killed but strange to say not one of the cabin boys were hurt   John Richards knew most of them   Oh how it made me wish I was done with steamboating but such sights are good occasionally as they cannot help but call forth our feeling of gratitude & thankfulness that our lives have been precious in the sight of the Almighty   Such feelings have again been called forth in an accident of which we have been participants   yes even we have not come up this long to be remembered Missouri with-

---

[2] Louise Barry, *The Beginning of the West*, p. 1073, tells of the *Saluda* having "burst her boilers" on April 9. Possibly some 135 persons died. This was the worst wreck of the season under very bad river conditions on the Missouri. The saying about this unpredictable river was, "The crookedness you see ain't half the crookedness they is."

out having our disasters to recount but still we are left among the living and Oh may it be still to praise God

In arriving at Weston on Sunday Afternoon on board the Pontiac No 2 took on a few passengers, proceeded slowly till Monday Morn when about 9 o'clock we saw some men moving about & there was a cry of "A man overboard" but it was presently hushed up & the gents were laughing which soon alayed the fears in the ladies cabin   but about ½ an hour afterwards I saw deck hands & cabin boys all running into the gentlemens state room & fetching out blankets & comforters   we were then informed that we had run on a sand bar [3] across a log & had stove in a plank at the bottom of the boat   they were trying to fill the hole with bedding but without effect so in about 10 or 15 minutes we were passengers on a sunken boat   but fortunately it was shallow water so we were only about 3 feet under water but still we seemed to be getting lower & lower   The clerk who was owner of the boat came into the ladies cabin much agitated & told the ladies to put on their bonnets & shawls with as much haste as possible not to stop to get anything else on any account as they wanted to put us ashore as quick as possible   you may perhaps imagine a little our feelings tho I must say none of us seemed to be very much terrified   still all was confusion & to add to our misery it was a very cold morning the wind very high & just commenced raining   we were about 150 feet from shore   well a colored man took dear sissy & I carried the carpet bag & down to the front of the boat we hurried. When we arrived there the water was up

---

[3] On April 27, the *Pontiac No. 2* was reported sunk 20 miles below St. Joseph at Smith's Bar. Her hull was under water and broken. Although the cargo was a total loss, there were no lives lost. Barry, *op cit.*

over the deck so that we had to walk planks but we were too late to get into the yawl first as it was already full & we were hurried back to the ladies cabin many assuring us we were perfectly safe & more comfortable there than we should be ashore as there was only one little log cabin in sight   we therefore kept pretty contented for about an hour when the boat gave signs of breaking in two   it was therefore again thought advisable to put us ashore so the yawl was again sent & after much struggling managed to get in but we had a good load most of the passengers wanting to be among the first to be on terra firma. the river was very very rough   it took 4 men to row the yawl, however we soon got ashore & would there have a good view of the Pontiac & reflect on our forlorn condition. We landed among timber so the men set fire immediately to a large tree laying on the ground & we soon had a famous fire & as more passengers came ashore more fires were kindled still the ground was very damp & covered with dead leaves   old timber   Ma advised me to go with baby to the cabin so I went there but found their only room almost full. I sat down a while then feeling very hungry it being about noon I went back to the rest & then found that they had all had their dinners as provisions had been sent over from the boat for the cabin passengers. I was a little vexed with our folks for not saving me some as there was none left. I got a reproof from Ma about showing temper at such a time & was told they was a house about ½ a mile off were several had been & had their dinners so off there I posted with baby & found a pretty comfortable dwelling with the dinner table set, so I made quick dispatch of buiscuits butter molasses with 3 or 4 cups of tea after which I

felt considerable better tempered   I sat down to the
fire & expected probably we might have to wait there
a day or 2 before another boat came to pick us up but
after we had been there about an hour we heard a boat
was in sight so I gathered all my traps   a gent took
baby & back to the bank we started.when there we
found that the Captain of our boat would not charter
the other Captn to bring his alongside the sunken boat
without which it was not legal to do so & as we had
not got any of our baggage ashore why it was no use
to think of going on that boat   however she took a
few passengers from us & then went on her way telling
us there were 2 more boats a few hours behind which
greatly cheered us   It was not however till dusk that
we succeeded in getting all our baggage each one striv-
ing to be first in obtaining theirs & there was but one
yawl however we did at last get all but John R had
almost to fight his way through   As it began to get
dusk the cabin boys, cook &c brought ashore aparatus
& materials for preparing supper as just before the
moon arose we seated in front of a large tray full of
meat coffee & hard crackers &c & seemed to eat with
considerable relish   we had some brilliant fires & all
together it looked quite California like. I however felt
the damp from the ground was affecting me as my
knees trembled so that I could not sit still & I was very
fearful baby would take cold as we had no shelter to
go in   Fortunately a boat came up & as we had got
all our baggage with us we obtained a passage in the
"Midas" & about 9 o'clock we went on board. it was a
lovely moonlight night but even the moon seemed dim
compared to our numerous fires. The Midas laid by
till morning when she took on more passengers & bag-

gage few if any being so fortunate in not losing anything on board the Pontiac the "Midas" left the ill
fated boat & many of her passengers who were trying
to get their baggage at least that part of it which was
in the cabins was all on deck & in the hold was a total
loss. the boat was then laying in 9 feet water at her bow
& 4½ at stern she had broken very much across the
middle where she laid over the log The Captn &
clerk are very much assured in their manner of acting
to passengers as they would not refund any money
paid for the whole passage to the Bluffs & would not
allow any person to bring their baggage ashore without
making them pay heavily for it One gent paid $100
for himself, team & several other men & he had to pay
$6 for getting a barrel of things ashore The men were
busy all night and obtaining what they would from the
boat. there were a great many wagons on the hurricane
deck all of which I saw on the bank in the morning &
those of the passengers who got on the Midas with us
set to & wrote an article for a St Louis paper respecting the shameful conduct of the Captn & officers towards the passengers so as to prevent them getting the
Insurance as that is forfeited if any money is extorted
from passengers for getting what they can of their baggage so we left them all to fight it out We had a
good number of mules & horses on the Pontiac & they
poor things stood for hours up to their knees in water
they were then cut loose & a man in the yawl dragd
one, the others all followed & waded to shore But to
return to ourselves we reached St Joseph's about 11
O'clock Tuesday Morn & there had to engage passage
on a boat for the Bluffs as the Midas went no higher
St Joe's looked so lively with Californians (we thought

perhaps some of our folks would be there)　　there
were 4 boats there　a band of music on board one
struck up in front of all the folks "Home sweet Home"
this seemed hardly appropriate as so many if not most
there were leaving their "Homes" but no sooner had
the band played that than they started "Oh Susanna
dont you cry for me I am bound for California" &c
&c　this seemed to set all on the jig as its a very lively
tune. We were fortunate in having paid the Captn of
the Pontiac $36 for he would not have returned any
had we have paid the $70 as agreed　The Midas agreed
to take us to St Joe's for $2 each but on Ma telling the
Capt she had but $5 left & we might have to stay in
St Joe's some little time he charged us $3 for the 5
of us　We met with the boat on which we now are
which left that day for the Bluffs　it is the one that
first passed us after we were sunk　she did not leave
St Louis for 3 days　after we did so you may judge
we were very slow & we seemed every few hours to
stick on sand bars　Well we reckoned to be at the
Bluffs in 3 days but the first night we came on board
this boat we got on a bar & stuck for *18* hours　then
we got on pretty well till yesterday when we got on
another & remained there about 6 hours　the lead was
thrown　I sat & watched them at it a long time, when
it was first heaved the depth was 12½ feet & it soon
got down to "3 feet – scarce" & there we stuck as the
boat draws 3½　Well all of the men passengers &
horses were put ashore to walk about a mile & after
a long time we managed to get over　We often see
Indians one of whom directed us were the channel
was yesterday & we found it where he said. last night
we had to lay by the wind being so high & all night

it blew a hurricane The Captn came in the ladies
cabin in the middle of the night to tell the Chamber
Maid to dress & to see if the ladies were scared I
was sleeping on the cabin floor so it made but little
difference to me as I soon fell asleep however its now
about 3 in the afternoon & we're still chained to the
banks as its too windy to attempt to run. this morning
all the horses were put ashore to go up to the bluffs as
its only about 60 miles from here & they will most
likely get there before we do we sent a letter to our
folks by a man telling them where we were if we could
only get on well we might soon be with them Its 2
weeks to day since we left St Louis I shall now quit
writing till I arrive at the bluffs I do hope there will
be a letter there from you as it would have plenty of
time to get there if you wrote soon after I started
Good bye dearest
M A
Wednesday Morning Here I am seated in our little
wagon with baby stretched out at my feet asleep We
arrived at Kanesville last Saty afternoon we expected
to see our folks as soon as the boat reached the landing
but was much disappointed in not seeing any of them
there & finding that the town was 4 miles back from the
landing we went on the hurricane deck & sat there
wondering what we should do when Ma spied out an
old gent from Dubuque in the crowd. she called to
him & inquired about our folks. He knew all about
them & said they would some of them soon be down
to the boat as they would see from the town when a
boat came up so after waiting an hour or 2 William,
Pa, Thos, & Eddy came along in a 4 horse waggon
they had not till then heard of the fate of the Pontiac

but were suspecting us on it for a long time. You may be sure we had a joyful meeting all seemed quite well & perfectly happy Pa got into a store as soon as they arrived here & is receiving $50 a month which is better than nothing well they drove us *home* in great glee. Ma stoped at the Methodist minister's house with the little ones & William & I went to a cabin which Mr Rickey was occupying we slept on the floor & it was quite laughable to see the big holes all around & above it not being as water tight as Mr Willis's stable. I felt the wind very much but dont seem any the worse for it now On Sunday we all went to church but I had to come home before the sermon was over as Sissy was so fidgetty. In the evening William got the tents ready for me to come to, so I took up my abode there. it is such a fine tent so large. they bought it here for $10 it is a government tent, second hand but very strong. The one we made is used by the men. Wilm & I have slept in the light waggon since Sunday as we came to the tent & we prefered having a place to ourselves, but its very crowded in the waggon & I have to make baby a bed across our heads still I shall try & make it answer You will expect me to say something about California emigration here Well there are not near so many teams camped here as I expected to find but they say more than half that have been are now going out town look like a fair all the time This Kanesville is a poor little mean place I dont think there's a brick house in it. most of them are log cabins We move out to morrow (Thursday) & go to a bottom about 10 miles off where there's a ferry We shall camp there about a week previous to our final start as the

grass is hardly forward enough. All the Dubuque
company [4] will camp there & thus start together
William has just sold that span of horses we came
to your house with as one was not strong enough for
the trip   they were sold at auction yesterday for $165
without harness   William is going to buy 3 more yoke
of oxen   One of the cows calved yesterday   how I
wish you could have the calf as our folks say they
shall knock it in the head or give it to the Indians
We gave a concert last night   borrowed a piano in
town   I had the honor of playing duetts & singing.
the house was crowded it being but small still we
cleared $23 so that will pay some ferrages & is quite
worth having   John R, Thos & another young man
does our cooking   we have 2 little stoves. I would
much rather cook for myself & Wm as the boys keep
every thing so dirty but fortunately I'm always happy
so dont mind the dirt so much & let John & the young
men cook for the men but would not consent to do
part without doing all as he said he wanted to use
both stoves at a time for the men   Friday night –
Well dear Ina here we are at rest again   We left
Kanesville this morning & have come about 8 miles
to day & expect to cross the river sometime as our
ticket will come in turn then   We are now camped
on a large level bottom surrounded by magnificent
bluffs at the base of which we have spread our tents
We got in here in good time to day suppose about 1
o'clock there were not many teams in then so we had
our pick of a camping ground & Oh how lovely is

---

[4] In the printed version, Lucy Rutledge Cooke, *Crossing the Plains in 1852*
(Modesto, California, 1923), there is published after the printed edition of
this letter (pages 18-19) the "Bye-Laws and Resolutions of the Dubuque
Emigration Company to California" and also a list of the male members of
the party.

the view from here. many of the friends went up one of the steepest of the bluffs at the back of our tent & took a drum fife &c &c & what a noise they have been making then they all marched down in procession. There are now I should fancy 70 or 80 waggons just here so you may guess we have plenty of company, indeed the noise seems equal if not exceede any town I've seen of late years In our men's tent they are playing a violin, banjo & bones. The noise has attracted such a crowd that its quite impossible to get in then the frogs are making if possible more noise than they do at Rockingham When we got here this afternoon our folks turned all the cattle lose as that was the way all were doing & now just before dark they collected them together tying them down to stakes ready for morning but 2 cows are missing they have gone back to Kanesville we hear so William has started off after them it is now dark they have been gone a long time so I fear he has had to go all the way one of the missing cows is the one which had a calf I wonder none of us thought she would go back to it if she had a choice. William has disposed of the calf. he offered it to a man for 50 cents but he was a mormon & selling out to go to Salt Lake therefore did not want it. soon after one of our men found a boy driving a calf in the street to take him if he wanted another. the boy said yes so he told him to come to our tent & he should have one well about an hour after a boy came & took the calf away. he had not been gone long before another boy came for it we then found it had been promised to 2 boys therefore the 1st that came got it but the second one went away swearing terrible about it & saying well theyd have a fight about it & the smart-

est man should keep it, so I dont know how they settled
the matter   Wednesday evening we had a storm   the
rain came down in torrents & continued near all night
& what a miserable plight we were in for our folks
had not dug a trench around our tents so as we were
on the side of the bluff the rain soon came in our tent
& there was not a dry spot any where & unfortunately
the little waggon which Will & I sleep in was in town
at the blacksmiths so we had to sleep on the ground
for the first time but we had those 2 heavy bolsters &
several pillows and [among] us. Ma had a straw bed
Richey's folks had moved out of the cabin they rented
which was close by so William went down & made a
large fire in it thinking we might as well occupy it
Ma preferred staying in the tent but I consented to
go so just before I went to it one of our boys went
down to it & found it full of Indians who were apparently pleased with their good quarters   William was
quite mad to think he had been at the trouble of making a fire at night for Indians & scolded me because
I refused to go & sleep there & let him turn them out
so we let them remain in quiet & we got along as
well as we might expect. In the morning near every
thing was wet but William made us pack everything
as he wanted to get here so as to be near the ferry so
all was got in readiness but the rain continued therefore we had to wait that day   towards afternoon the
sun came out & we hung our bedding & clothes to dry
& got all comfortable for an early start this morning
I am pleased to tell you that Mr Gilbert whom we
used to board with in Moline came in to Kanesville
he went into the store where pa is & heard someone
say Mr Cooke so Wednesday went & spoke to him &

inquired if, he was from Dubuque & so soon found
out where we were. he came immediately to our tent
expressed great joy at meeting with us & indeed it
was mutual for he is certainly one of the excellent of
the earth   we soon decided to go in company if possible   Mr. G. invited Will & I over to their tent
We went yesterday afternoon but found they had
started off that morning for the ferry & are gone on
to the river bank. we are now camped 4 miles from
there but suppose we shall meet with them tomorrow
as our turn to cross will come before theirs   We left
pa at the store   He will quit to morrow night (Saty)
I am sorry to find this is the last chance we shall have
to write to you for some time & am much disappointed
that you have not sent any letter to me here but feel
certain you must have sent by the Newby's who have
not yet arrived but doubtless will soon catch up with
us & then if they should bring me a budget what pleasure it will afford   Pa got us a nice pair of waterproof
blankets to put on the ground so I hope we shall do
better now when it rains. Willm complains very much
of the quantity of baggage Ma & I have   I had a cry
about it this morning as I seemed to have parted with
almost every thing   he was very sorry when he saw
me crying & promised never to say anything more
about it   the 3 heavy waggons seem full to the top.
ours carries our bedding my box & few other matters
we rode very comfortably indeed from Kanesville
baby sat in her little chair most of the time while Ma
& I were sewing   yest we were sewing as we rode
along   I have made Sis a little sun bonnet to day
Soon after we got here a farmers waggon came up
with corn, hay, chickens butter & eggs for sale   we

bought 4 chickens at 12½ cents each & had them
for supper to night   they were so nice   Provision in
Kanesville is very reasonable   beautiful potatoes for
40 & 45 pr bushel & great plenty of them   corn 25,
eggs 6 cents each   flour is dear now brings 10 dollars
per barl   Pa has got us 36 lbs prunes 2 boxes figs a lot
of raisins, so we shall have some nice things occasionally   Saty morn   Dear Sister a gent has just come for
the letters so I must hastily conclude   give my warmest
love to Mr Willis; Uncle Aunt & all friends. I wanted
to write more but have not time   shall write again
from Ft Laramie
                    Yours with much love, Lucy Cooke
I mail a paper with this

                 Written early part of May 1852
                    In Waggon on the Plains of Nebraska
Dear Marianne
    I wrote a letter & left it with the Ferryman at Loup
Fork as he stated he would be going to Kanesville
shortly & would then mail it with a bout a bushel more
which had been given him   Ma thought it very doubtful it you ever got it   I have not written since then but
will now try & give you some little account of our
travels up to this time   We had to wait at Loup Fork
ferry from Saty to Tuesy before we could get across &
then had to swim all the oxen which was quite a job
as the river is wide full of sand bars & quick sand
William earned a dollar by swimming a horse over for
a man which he gave me to keep but unfortunately I
had a hole in my pocket so have lost it & some more
We made but about 6 miles that day & then camped at
such a beautiful place   Oh it was lovely   how my

dear sister would have liked to have been with us just then   I went in the river to bathe in the evening   could not get any one to go in with me as there was such a cold wind blowing but I enjoyed it very much   For 2 or 3 days nothing occured of particular interest so you will not lose much by my not keeping a regular journal   We were very anxious to get up with Mr Gilbert who has gone some distance up the Platte river to ford instead of crossing it as we did   Rickey's Cony [Company] also followed their plan   On Thursday night we had come 28 miles from the ferry & just as we were going to bed Mr Perrin found that 4 of his horses & a mule had run off   William offered to go with others to look for them. they started & expected soon to meet with the missing horses but had gone 10 miles & seen nothing of them so they returned   they were in their shirt sleeves & fixed up for a ride back to Loup Fork as all thought that was where the horses had started for   Our train went on in the morning as we lent Mr Perrin oxen to draw his waggons   We here heard of Mr Rickey who was about 11 miles a head but he was alike unfortunate in his horses as 11 of them had got away the same night Mr Perrins did & they succeeded in finding all   William & the 2 men who accompanied him returned having been absent 2 nights & 1 day   they had got all the horses   found them standing waiting to cross the Loup Fork   on their way back some ill disposed person cut the ears off one of the horses in the night   they dont know who it was but was it not a shameful thing to do   On Friday we all started off but it was quite a wet morning & continued to rain fast all day. You may judge therefore that we felt bad on arriving at our company ground with every

thing wet to find that there was no wood to be had for
fires   Oh how miserable I felt   I would have given
anything to be able to have stepped into your house to
supper   Our men cut up one of the horses feed boxes
to make a little fire to fry some meat & boil coffee but
all the clothes had to remain wet till the next day when
we hoped to meet with better luck. Saty noon we passed
a buffalo skull stuck in the ground with writing on
informing us that Rickeys had passed that place at 10
O'clock that morning   We passed 3 graves near here
but all of persons who died in 49 or 50. Saty evening
we camped at a nice place having plenty of grass wood
& water so the waggons were emptied & things put out
to sun & dry   There were 3 other camps in sight so
we had lots of company   here we stayed all Sunday
May 23rd   Some of us went to preaching in another
camp about ½ a mile off we having gone previously
to a creek to bathe   The gent a methodist preached a
good plain sermon from the words "If ye then being
evil know how to give gifts unto your children &c &c"
I enjoyed the service much particularly prayer by a
gent   Oh it calmed my feelings & made me feel as
I used when blessed with religious privileges in days
that have passed   In the evening a prayer meeting was
held at our camp in Pa's tent   it was tolerably well
attended   thus passed my 3d Sabbath on these vast
plains   Well now I've got to give account of last
week's travel which has been all along the plains where
there has been but little variety   we met 3 waggons
one day returning & on inquiring the reason found
that the heads of each of the 2 families had just died &
widows were going back to their friends   poor things
they had our sympathies   Pa has been out hunting

most of this last week but succeeded in killing nothing but birds till yesterday when he shot a buffalo he carried some of the meat to tents in the evening which they all had for supper   I was not able to eat any having got a very very bad mouth & throat   my tongue is so swollen & in such ulcers that I m unable to speak much & can swallow nothing but liquids   I never had my tongue in such a state   To day (Sunday May 30th) we have laid by Pa having resolved not to travel on Sundays unless obliged   We had quite a fuss about it this morn as we were the only ones in our company who did not wish to travel   In consequence of our staying Perrins left us this morning Mr P being determined to a short distance every Sunday & so we have none left of those we first started with but we hope soon get with Rickeys some Sabbath keeping friends & then we shall feel more comfortable   Our folks are very busy airing the things in their waggons There have been many teams past us while laying by here to day & one large flock of sheep for Salt Lake City   This evening a prayer meeting was held close by us. Pa & Ma attended but I was prevented on account of my mouth & throat   A doctor has passed here to day to visit some Cholera patients among the men belonging to the flock of sheep which have stoped a little above us   (Monday June 1st) this morn we started early & have passed over some awfully sandy roads   it seemed almost impossible for the cattle to pull through it   We have met with the doctor above mentioned & learn from him that 2 of the men attacked by Cholera died last night & was dying this morning   he said it was not much to be wondered at for they had nothing with them to eat but bacon, hot bread & coffee as juice, beans, pickles or anything of that kind necessary on such a journey We hear much of the cholera but I think generally speaking people frighten themselves into it for where we have so much pure air I cannot see how folks can catch anything of the kind. this evening we camped rather early by the side of a creek we have a very small party with us. All the other Dubuque folks have left for some cause or other. (Tuesday Morn June 2nd) to day we started very early so as to lay by in the heat of day We had travelled an hour or more before sunrise I felt quite cross at being awoke in the middle of the night. We stoped about 11 O'clock & started at 2 camped about 6 near a creek & the Platte river. the latter Ma, Lill & I went & bathed in but it's a nasty muddy river with a very swift current still its better than nothing close by where we camped some folks came up who had a sick woman along I went to see what was the matter with her & found she had had Cholera but was getting better. (Wednesday June 3rd) We met with the sick woman on the road Pa & Ma went up & spoke to her She seemed much better & had quite a talk with them told them her husband had just died of Cholera We soon passed them & in about an hour heard the woman was almost dead & that those whom she was with were stoping to dig her grave!!! we were astonished at such unaccountable treatment we cannot believe the woman was dead, think she was only under the influence of laudanum which they were giving her pretty freely This evening we came up to the lone tree our guide informs us are not to meet with another [tree] for 200 miles we plucked some to send to friends but so many have done the same that

there is but one branch of it left   I intend sending
you a sprig   To night we camped by the side of a
nice wide stream but very shallow & it being a very
hot evening Ma, Pa the children went & paddled in it
for near an hour   I undressed baby & let her sit in
the water   Oh she did so enjoy it & so did I to see
her   Towards night a wind storm came up which blew
away our tents down but we soon got used to these
trifles   Near us are 5 men camped   They draw a
truck   they 1st came up with us on Sunday & our boys
made considerable sport of them, called to them &
said there was good grass for their cattle where we
were &c &c   the men seemed quite pleased with the
success they met with in traveling   (Thursday June
4th) We have had to drive about 27 miles to day on
account of a camping ground   We are now with in
sight of Rickeys & are a few rods ahead of Perrins so
that we have come as well as they who traveled on
Sunday   I hope now we shall keep near Rickeys. We
passed the 5 men who were with the truck & poor fellows it has broken down and they have now taken
pieces of it for poles to sling over their shoulders &
pack through   I pity them. We have had a very pleasant day for riding as the sun has kept in all day & considerable rain fell last night   There are great numbers
of trains all the way   We go & we hear there are
thousands be hind   Last week the mail carriage passed
us on the way to Fort Laramie. We fear he will leave
before we can get there to mail our letters   We met
a company returning from California   they were the
1st we had passed going in an opposite direction to ourselves   Oh the musquitoes are as thick as sand almost
here   Yesterday for the 1st time we put on the horse

nets   they are of great use but are almost too small for
our horses as they come but little lower than their sides.
Our horses are very aristocratic & these nets seem to
make them feel more so   We have all just been over
to Rickeys camp & had such a meeting. they all seemed
so pleased to meet again   we intend if possible to keep
near enough so as to attend meetings on Sundays in
their camp   (Friday) started this morn as what to
me seemed a ridiculous time viz 3 O'clock   Ma I &
the young ones continued our nights sleep   we rode
till about 10 then staid for 2 or 3 hours by a creek to
let the cattle graze   We nicely played the joke on
Rickeys by starting so early as we afterwards heard,
for they intended to be off before any of us & had taken
the bells off their cattle the previous night so as not
to awaken us in the morning but we were too smart
for them as they knew nothing of our going till we
passed them. (Saty) We stayed by the side of the Platte
river   Ma I & Lill went in bathing which we do very
often, so does dear baby   This time we had poor camping little or no grass so on Sunday we moved further
therefore had no chance to attend preaching   My
throat continues very bad   I used Suger of lead once,
but it had such a curious taste & turned my teeth so
black that I could not endure to use it again   I now
keep sucking alum which seems to cleanse my mouth
but really I dont know if it does further good   (Wednesday June 9th) Here we are opposite Fort Laramie
it being on the other side of the river   Oh what a
treat it does seem to see buildings again   My dear
husband has just been over to the store there to see if
he could get anything for me & bless him he's come
back loaded with good things for which he has had

to buy exorbitantly   he's brought 2 bottles lemon syrup
at $1¼ each a can of preserved quinces 24   Seidlitz
Powders [5] 24   Soda do & packet of candy & a bottle
of ink   the latter is a 10 cent bottle but here it was
30   he says they have a splended store with every thing
& everything that can be called for   Oh it seems as-
tonishing to meet with such a place out here away
from all the world   the store was full of folks & clerks
were as busy as they could be   There are but few
soldiers here now as they are gone up on the Humboldt
to protect the governor who is appointed to Salt Lake
There are some 6 or 8 buildings here at the Fort, Ware-
houses Bakery's &c &c   I am very weak from my sore
tongue & throat so much so that I can scarcely walk
at all   every movement makes my tongue ache so
much   it seems wonderful that dear baby continues
so fat & well as she does   she's a little (tho not very
little) picture of health & gets every day more engag-
ing   William has several times taken her to the river
& bathed her   I think it most probable we shall go
by way of Oregon as so many think that route the most
preferable & there we come to settlements 500 miles
sooner. We have now posted over 200 miles without
timber   its so good to see trees again   I frequently get
very tired of riding & wish it were possible to step
in to your nice home   Oh how pleasant everything
must look around you by this time   We are now in
sight of snow on the tops of Laramie peak, but the
buffalo that we saw in the picture at Mrs. Telfair is
not here   I suppose that Indian killed him   We have
not seen Indians till now for 2 or 3 weeks   These are

---

[5] Seidlitz Powders were made up of a mixture of sodium bicarbonate,
tartaric acid, and Rochelle Salt (potassium sodium tartrate). This combination was a laxative named for springwaters at Seidlitz, Czechoslovakia.

the Sioux & a noble race they seem, not one comes round to beg as all the other tribes did & they are well dressed. We have had very good success hitherto with all our cattle   2 or 3 have had sore feet but have nearly recovered. I hear we are to have another calf soon   one of our camp killed an antelope the other day. They said the meat was very nice. I have so lost my taste that its useless for me to try anything. I just live on chocolate & currant bread   We have a good cook now. John R gave it up some time ago & it goes on much better without him   he now drives the oxen in turn   My baby cries so I cannot fill this sheet as I intended   I shall most likely write again from Fort Hall or Salt Lake   the latter we don't pass if we go to Oregon but if we do go there i e Salt Lake we shall expect to be there to spend the 4th of July   I shall continue writing to you as much as I can but since my throat has been so bad I've not been able to do it regular

William sends his kind love to you & respects to all dear friends. give your dear husband a kiss from me & my love to him & LeClaire friends we have not met with Mr Gilbert again   I hope you are writing long letters to me to Sacramento City   do there's a love

I remain Your ever affectionate sister

Lucy Cooke

[The following was added below Lucy's signature:]

I am obliged to close this abruptly as baby is crying to come to me

Give my kindest regards to Mrs Burnell & Adams's also Mrs Coleman Mrs Wright Sarah Jane   May 9th 1852 [6]

---

[6] Someone has added here "June?".

Last Monday was dear Williams birthday   25 years old

Nebraska Ter   June 10, 1852
we arrived in Salt Lake 8th of July
Dearest Sister
I mailed my last to you from Fort Laramie yesterday & now commence another epistle   The road from the Fort changes considerable   we have now past over the Plains & glad I am for theres so little to interest on them. yesterday we travelled about 18 miles & camped near Rickeys & several other companies on the banks of the Platte. Oh what rough riding it was all day but still the magnificant views made up for it. We were long before we could find water but at last did & the grass is abundant on the hill sides & very rich   (Friday June 11th) Have come to day about 20 miles over plenty of rocks & stones   I have rode the last 3 days in one of the ox waggons as I could better lie down there than in our own as its so crowded & I have been so very poorly   My dear William waits on me hand & foot   What should I do without him   bless him My tongue improves but slowly, the ulcers seem as large & thick as ever   We are coming near the Rocky mountains so suppose shall have nothing but jolt jolt now   the mountains we pass have such splendid pines on [them]   Oh you would enjoy some of the views We are teazed considerably with the "prickly pear" or Cactus   in some places it nearly covers the ground there's plenty of wild sage all around. We are now traveling without a guide [book] as the writer of the one we had went on the South side of the Platte from fort Laramie & we intend keeping on the North side &

so head the river   We met some packers to day on
mules from Oregon   they said the grass was abundant
all the way so thats good news   (Saty 12th) Have had
a very pleasant days travel, magnificent scenery   was
hilly but not so rocky as the 2 previous days   We are
still in sight of Laramie peak & have been for the last
5 days   We have camped to night near Platte river
having traveled about 18 miles   (Sunday) Quite a
cold morning, my dear William had a bad tooth ache
yesterday & to day his face is swelled up quite hide-
ously   he seems very poorly indeed so now its my turn
to be nurse   I let him have his breakfast in bed &
made him starch at noon   We have had quite a long
day in airing all the things in the waggons for Sunday is
the only time we have for such things   The men mostly
do their washing on that day   We have just had supper consisting of fish Tomatoes Rice & ham with hot
bread & tea   I drink chocolate all the time since I've
been sick. I'm thankful to say my mouth seems much
better to day. I have been using a gargle made of sage
tea, alum, borax & sugar & it seems to benefit   We've
all been bathing, Sissy as well, she loves it so much
Oh how much I've thought of you to day & could see
you & dear brother going along side by side to Davenport   Oh shall I ever travel that rode again with you
I dont know what I should do if I thought I should
not return to Iowa to you again. Your home is the dearest place on earth to me   I guess I must soon begin a
letter to some of Uncle's folks   You must think my
letter very disconnected but I have to leave off so often
to attend to other things   We found a sack of graham
crackers to day spoiled from damp   so we have to
throw them away. I wonder if you yet have got any

graham flour   if not, do there's a dear   I'm sure it
would be better than white for you   How does Caroline come on & how do the currant bushes look   Oh
every tree & spot around you is as vivid as tho I was
there yesterday   How I should enjoy going over to
Mrs Wrights to supper & see her clean house. I told
you in my last I would enclose a sprig off the "Lone
tree" but I forgot it   Will try & remember it this time
& then will sent a piece for Sarah Wright & Margaret
Coleman   you must tell them it the only tree we pass
for 200 miles   (Monday 15 [should be 14]) To day
we have passed some magnificent mountains & for a
considerable distance traveled along what seemed to
have been the bed of [a] river as there was all the
traces of water on the rocks   We camped about sundown but had poor grass   (Tuesday) Started this
morn about 4 O'clock   rode 6 miles then turned cattle
loose there being rich grass   staid about 1½ hours
Rickey's all passed but as we did not stop at noon we
passed them then resting   saw a dead mule in the
road   have come along a place where there were
immense round rocks like cannon balls the scenery wild
& beautiful   camped on the banks of the Platte   have
drove about 20 miles to day. Pa bought a cow of a man
the other [day?]   She had calved a few days previous
& seems an excellent cow   the man only asked $20 for
her   it was a great bargain we all think so now we
have 5 cows but there is so much bother to get them
milking (2 are dry) that I frequently have to by
milk   (Wednesday) To day we have been travelling
near all the distance through sandy roads as bad as
that little piece between Hicksons & Davenport   Oh
how tedious it did seem   we have got on a bad camp-

ing ground ½ mile from water & little or no grass &
the only wood is two wheels which we picked up here
There's a ferry near by on the Platte which is the last
we pass. the charges for crossing are enormous $5 for
each waggon & then extra for our horses & cattle
we however have no desire to go on the south side
(Thursday) To day we have come 26 miles without
any water excepting what we hauled as there was none
but alkali lakes between where we camped last night
& to night   the poor oxen seemed very much done
over as the roads were very sandy   one Alkali lake
we passed had a white substance (they say its saleratus)
all around the banks of the thickness of 6 or 8 inches
we picked some up   When we had come 4 or 5 miles
from it we passed a cow lying dead in the road from
drinking some of it   she was in a drove of cattle that
passed just before we did. We have camped to night
by a little spring but its as small & such crowds around
it (it being the only pure water for 26 miles) that it
takes a long time to get a bucket full however its the
only chance we have for some distance. we have now
joined in camp with a company from Dubuque   they
are all men   the Gent who takes them through was
constable of Dubuque   we joined them because we
shall soon be coming among the Crow Indians & its
best then to be in a large company   (Friday) Have
to night arrived on the Sweetwater river. took baby
to bath   it has a very rapid current   We are to night
in sight of "Independance Rock" & the Rocky mountains   we expect to drive but little to morrow so as
to recruit the cattle   have but poor grass to night &
no wood   (Saty) We have had a fine wild goose chase
to day after each other   In the morning we drove the

horse waggon to Independance Rock & staid there some
2 or 3 hours examining names which are inscribed in
every available place   Lilly & some others climbed
the summit but as sis was awake I had to remain below
most of our folks added their names to those already
there   Wilm. did not he said it looked too much
like hard work to clamber on the rough rock bare
footed for the sake of putting his name there   some
of the names are cut in the rock   others done with tar
white, red & black lead & some few with paint   I was
not certain I knew any of the persons put down though
there were many familiar   I only went on one side of
the rock as there was water so that I could not get all
round without riding   Our ox teams went on a head &
with the intention of only driving to good grass & then
lie by till Monday morn. We followed in the horse
waggon about 2 hours after & expected to come up with
them. we drove about 4 miles & then came in sight of
them but here we arrived at another natural curiosity
viz the "Devil's Gate" so we left the horse waggon to
continue on the road while Ma, Wm, Lill I & 2 or 3
young men walked up to the rock   it is a most sublime
sight almost worth going the whole distance to see
the river Sweetwater rushes through an opening in the
rocks which stand perpendiculary on each side to the
height of 400 feet   Oh how unbounded would have
been my gratification could you my dearest Polly have
stood by my side & gazed on the magnificent sight   I
wish I knew how to convey to your mind a representa-
tion of it but I cannot   You remember Mr Averill's
Panorama exhibiting in Davenport while I was with
you last time   Well he showed Independence Rock
also the Devil's Gate   we went to see it & she says it

was very exact in both representations   I bathed little
Sarah's feet & legs in the rushing waters   When you
go to Mrs Telfair's do get that book again & look at
the pictures of these 2 objects   I will now tell you
about our chase   When we left the rocks it was about
noon   we had to walk some distance before we reached
our horse waggon which was waiting for us   Numbers of tents were pitched on the banks of the "Sweet
Water" & we expected ours most likely ours were among
but not seeing them we enquired of different camps &
were told by all that they drove by between 11 & 12
that morn so were ahead. we therefore drove on looking out for them all the way our inner man admonish-
ing us that it was long since breakfast. well on & on we
rode till we began to be pretty certain that they had
turned off from the road & was therefore behind but
all whom we asked said no they were a head   We
were much surprised they had gone so far as it was
settled only to go 6 or 8 miles & I had quite a large
wash to do   Well we went 10 miles & saw no signs
of them & had nothing to eat, it was also near 5 O'clock
so we accepted the offer of a company named the "Bull
Heads" to camp with them that night   we had met
with them several times on the road & William was
slightly acquainted with 1 or 2 of them (they were
all from Iowa)   Well you may be sure we were glad
of our supper   I partook of biscuit, rice, stewed apples, & tea & felt considerably refreshed   the young
men were a fine set of fellows   one of our young men
was resolved to go still farther to see if our camp was
a head so he walked on some distance & came up to
Perrin's camp & on entering found Pa & our cook there
eating supper but most dead with fatigue   they were

of course mutually astonished at meeting. It appears Pa & the cook had visited the Devil's gate then went along on the mountains & when they enquired for their teams were told as we were that they were a head but the fun of it was that they came across some good wood & seeing but a poor chance for any along the road they gathered about enough to last over Sunday & packed it between them past all the camps expecting every one they came near was ours they carried the wood about 4 miles & then threw it away Then they came up to a man who said our tents were 2 miles back they walked back found to the contrary then went on & on till they fortunately met with Perrin whom we had not seen for 2 or 3 weeks & here our young man met with them it was only about a mile from where we had camped so after supper Pa returned to fetch Ma Lill & Richard to share with Mrs Perrin hospitality & so Wm, I, Thos, & 2 others stayed till morn with the "Bull Heads" Our cook & one other would go back to our own folks although they were so tired so they started about dark The young men all amused themselves with dancing after supper in which Wm joined as hearty as any. the cook of the company we had camped with amused us all much as he had found the previous day a bundle of woman's clothing which he had put on & had worn it all day, sun bonnet & all it caused considerable merriment all along the road & when dancing came off there was such a demand for this lady for a partner that Wm came for my saque dress & sun bonnet to wear Oh what guys the 2 did look but seemed well to enjoy themselves I sat looking at them till long after dark (Sunday morn) to day we drove up to where Pa Ma were Per-

rin's having gone a head   We camped on their ground
Ma, Wm, Lill & I have been in bathing in the "Sweet
Water" river. the Bull Heads have camped close by
us & keep us in food till our teams arrive   About
1 O'clock our folks caught up with us   they have
amused themselves much at our expense but however
it made a nice little change   (Thursday night) I have
not noted our progress since Sunday   It has been such
very cold weather that I have felt so little inclined
for writing   all Tuesday & Wednesday we rode along
side the Rocky Mountains & well indeed are they
named for they are a mass of solid rock   the roads
have been awfully sandy & we have passed much alkali
water   on Wednesday we counted 26 head of dead
cattle   we are very fortunate in not having lost any
of ours yet   To day we have passed several banks of
snow so you may guess we are in a high latitude
the mountains are covered with it & at noon we camped
alongside a large bank   to night we have camped near
the "Sweetwater" on such a pretty spot   such lots of
gooseberry bushes around   we have a man in our camp
taken very sick with Cholera   its not expected he will
live till morn   he has his family along with him. Ma
& I have just been to bathe in the sweetwater but Oh
it was cold as ice   we could only take 2 or 3 dips &
run out again   really what a strange country we are
in here   we bathing by the side of the snowbanks & in
sight of mountains covered with it whilst at the same
time the grass is good & gooseberries are growing in
abundance   I picked some to stew but they are none
bigger than currants   (Friday Morning) the sick man
is still alive but very bad, has severe cramps   Willm
has gone off to hunt a doctor for him   has returned
with one who thinks the man may recover   We have

to stay here all day on his account for as they travel
with us of course we would not leave them   Wm & I
have been all the morn picking gooseberries   what a
job we had   we got about a pint   I made 2 pies gave
1 to Ma   what a treat it did seem to do a bit of cooking again   I do long to get to housekeeping once more
but every thing I do seems to bring you my dear so
plainly before my eyes   Wm & I were talking of you
while picking gooseberries   We said if he got enough
to live on he should like to come back & settle down
near you for he loved you   Oh how pleased I was to
hear him talk so as I think there's still a hope of our
meeting   (Saty) The sick man is a trifle better   some
hopes are entertained of his recovery now   We have
only rode about 11 miles to day on his account   This
morn we arrived at the South Pass after which all the
water we see will be running to the Pacific   So we are
now on the other side of the world & about 4000 [7] feet
above the ocean   (Sunday) To day we drove a short
distance to a better camping place but still there's poor
grass except what is in swampy ground. We are camped
near Rickey's   Ma, Pa & some other attended service
at their camp this morn. Baby prevented me going
This afternoon Wm & I have been singing out of your
hymn book   it brought several round to join & we
have had a very pleasant sing   Since writing the above
I upset my ink and lost my pen consequently all my
writing operations have been suspended for some time
& we have journied on each day bringing something
fresh to notice   We arrived at Fort Bridger 113 miles
from Salt Lake City. at this place Pa traded off some
flour & an ox for a pretty little indian pony. the ox

---

[7] South Pass is really 7,412 feet altitude. Aubrey L. Haines, *Historic Sites
Along the Oregon Trail* (Gerald, Missouri, 1981), p. 235.

had been lame for some time his hoof was coming
off. Pa gave 7 bags of flour valued at $6 per hundred,
all considered it a good trade as he was very soon after
offered $60 for the pony he then concluded to ride
him on a head to Salt Lake City in order to find good
camping grounds also to see if employment could be
obtained for any of our men folks while we stay'd in
the City William had concluded to stay till Spring as
we were so tired of being in the crowd things were
so uncomfortable that we resolved to go the rest of the
way alone We all got to the City 3 days after Pa
started I was very much pleased with the appearance
of the place it was a great treat to see houses again
& I very much wished it might turn out for us to stay
there the winter Pa had spoken to a man [at] a mill
respecting William & he promised to engage him & his
team for the winter to haul lumber from the mountains
at $5 pr day William intends engaging in this as soon
as his cattle are recruited The day we arrived here
we camped opposite a boarding house so Pa immediately went over & engaged dinner for all our own family & Oh never did victuals look so nice before we
had green peas, potatoes, roast beef, chicken, bread,
butter, cheese & pie the bread & butter seemed the
greatest treat it looked so clean to what we had been
having & then the house was as trim as a little palace
but so unused were we to chairs that when we walked
in to the parlor we all seemed to prefer sitting on the
floor it really seemed the most natural I quite hated
the idea of going back to the waggons after being
in such a nice house [illegible][8] we succeeded in gaining information of a Mr Roberts (a Mormon) who

---

[8] All of the omitted words here are a result of a large blot of ink on the
paper. She mentions earlier having spilled the ink.

was next door neighbour to Pa in Iowa City but had
come to this place to live, so the day after our arival
we started out to find [?] as he had been here
some time (a Mormon had acted very [?] to our
folks in Iowa City) we thought he could wait till
William [?] We found him without much trouble
living in a pretty spot about 8 miles [?] the city
he was very glad to see our folks & wanted the whole
tribe [?] to his house to stay as long as we were
in the place, however we did not accept this kind offer
but William & I stayed all night in order to [?]
our stoping this winter Mr Roberts was very anxious
for Pa to stop & said it was [?] best for him to
proceede with the passengers & leave Ma & the family
here [?] then if successful in California, get a
home ready & send on for them in the Spring John
Richard & Thomas is left to take care of Ma & little
children John has the 2 horses & waggon to do team-
ing &c for their support & I'm in hopes the responsi-
bility will have a good effect on him Ma has a little
house in town & Wm & I are still with Mr Roberts &
expect in 2 or 3 weeks to go to the mill to live as
there's a house close by which we can occupy Wm &
John have again to work together at hauling for the
mill as there's plenty to employ both the machine at
the mill is principally for cutting shingles of which
large quantities are sold they also make some furniture our folks are to be paid in shingles which will
be as good as cash as theres plenty of sale for them &
they are assured they can easily make $6 or 7 a day
William has 2 yoke of cattle & a waggon Pa having the
remaining 2 waggons & oxen I really have so much
to tell about that I dont at all know where to keep
on I suppose you are aware that this valley is entirely

occupied by the Mormons or Latter day Saints   much
has been said about them making them out to be a dis-
grace to the earth but as far as we have seen they are
as hospitable & kind as any people I ever met with
I cannot say I should like to stay here altogether because there are none but Mormons, no other churches
at all & I cannot see as they do in many things   still
I do believe them to be Christians & it is truly wonderful to hear them account the dealings of God with
them   a more zealous people I never met wishing
every one they meet with among the Gentiles (as all
are called not belonging to them) to join their church
Last Saty was a great day with them the 24th of July
it being the 4th anniversary of their arrival in this valley   we went up to town to see the procession   it
really was very pretty indeed   they marched round
their tabernacle headed by 3 fine brass bands playing
lively tunes & all was as merry & happy as "a marriage
ball" in the first of the procession were 24 old ladies
(constituting their "board of Health")   they were
all dressed in black dresses with white net or muslin
squares over their shoulders (Oh they looked so nice
& neat) the formost carried a banner inscribed "Mothers in Israel, Our children are our Glory"   then came
a number of old men who were the bishops   I could
not see what was on their flags   then came 24 young
ladies dressed in white with light blue silk scarfs tied
across one shoulder & under the arm   they wore straw
hats trimed with blue ribbon their banner was inscribed "The virtue of Utah"   then were 24 little girls
in white frocks & light blue silk spencers straw hats
with a wreath of roses   then came a number of little
boys in white trowsers buff jackets & lastly a number

of men each one carrying some instrument used in his
trade one carried a little steam engine, he was an
engineer, another a little ship another a bust (suppose
he was a modeler) & so on altogether it was a very
pretty sight, the company all went into the tabernacle
a beautiful large building very plain & neat but a better one for accomodating an audience of 2,500 I never
saw. there are 4 large doors at each corner which makes
a good breeze through there are no galleries but the
seats all raise from the front of where the speakers
are I have been once on a Sunday the singing is so
nice its led by an English man who sings good old
english tunes the place is always full. The City contains a great number of English but what makes it so
beautiful is that the whole city & country is trenched
so that it can be quick watered at any moment the
water runs through every street in beautiful streams
their crops show the benefit of this irrigation nowhere
would things grow better than they do here all kinds
of vegetables are beautiful Respecting the pony Pa
bought he made a good trade having sold the flour at
the rate of $6 per 100 & here any quantity can be bought
for $3 per 100 but he had bad luck with his bargain
for on the 3rd morning after our arrival the pony was
found dead in the field so that was quite a loss to Pa
we could not tell what killed it unless the ride Pa had
taken him was too much or else he was to have eaten
some poison weed Pa however went on his journey
with the passengers having stayed about 10 days I
must now tell you who we met on Saty when going
to the celebration we had been sitting in Ma's house
a few minutes when in came John Richards bringing
Clarence Whiting & one of the Newby's we were

delighted to see them & I soon found they had letters
for me   I felt certain of a nice long one from you
dear Polly but to disappointment there was not a line
from any but English friends viz Mrs Shepperson Mrs
Scott & Jane Critchley & they all concluded not to tell
me anything in their notes as Uncle would tell me all
so between them Im but little wiser   Mrs Shep—
sent me a pretty neck ribbon & Jane said Mrs Grant
had given Uncle some pieces for baby which I suppose
you have got. I think Uncle might have sent me a letter giving me some account of his visit. William Newby
says the letters were given him the day after we left
however if any of you have sent letters to Sacramento
City as I directed Pa will send them on to us as there's
frequent communication between the 2 places   William has been harvesting & for 1½ days work at Cra-
dling he got 4 bushels of wheat   another lot he cra-
dled for half the grain   the general wages in the
harvest field is $2 per day   We are entirely without
everything for house keeping & every thing here is
very high   I will give you a list of some   Sugar 3 lbs
for a dollar   Coffee 40 cents, Tea $2   dried fruit 40
cts   Soap 50 cents a bar   so we have to be careful
with washing & they dont have grease enough to make
soft soap   Wood is $10 pr Cord it having to be fetched
from 8 to 20 miles there being none but what grows in
the Kanyons which are the openings between the Mountains   dry goods are also very high   common calico
25 & 30 cents pr yard, ribbons the cheapest $1   I am
glad I do not have my flannel gown covered with that
dress pattern as I still have it to make up   I have no
bonnet but my old Sun bonnet & use the parasol you
gave me. I think we shall learn to be saving while

here & that will be a great matter   Wm will not go
to California if he can make a good living here. he
says he will return to Iowa in 4 or 5 years if he makes
enough   this valley is a beautiful spot   we are about
8 miles from the mountains on one side & about 20
on the other   When it rains its wonderful to see the
clouds   they sometimes rest on the mountains more
than half way down   it looks so strange   We are 20
miles from the Salt Lake the waters of which are so
salt that from 3 barrels of water can be obtained one of
salt & its the most beautiful I ever saw so clear &
white   Clarence Whiting is going to stay here a while
& I think will engage in the mill Wm is going to work
for   The Newbys are gone on in good spirits   Wm
traded a yoke of his cattle for a yoke of ours as his
were foot sore & ours had got over it from the rest
of 2 weeks   O what fine feed is there here for cattle
they get very fat all winter on the grass which is as
good as hay. no one takes any more care of them in
winter than in summer excepting if they work their
oxen then of course hay has to be cut   Wm Newby
said Mr Willis was really talking of going to California next Spring but I rather guessed it would end
in talking   well if you should there's nothing to fear
in the road so far as we have come for its nothing so
bad as folks make out   more than 2 thirds of this distance is as good as a turnpike road   We had 2 mountains to descend some little distance from here which
were very steep & long & one little place we let down
with ropes but it sounds worse than it really is   We
had no breakdown at any place so think we had great
cause for thankfulness   we heard great talk of things
being thrown away on the road but we saw but little

that was of any good excepting stoves & there were
plenty of them   I never should think of taking one
as a bakeoven like yours with frying pan & iron pot,
to cook out of doors is far preforable to a stove   The
folks where we are staying drink wheat coffee & it
surely is the most nourishing drink I ever tasted   let
me beg of you to try it for yourself   it is so nice   use
it just the same as other coffee but its best to boil milk
in it   To give you some idea of the fertility of the soil
Ill just give you an instance   Mr Roberts tells us that
he found grow from one kernal of wheat *30* stalks each
stalk producing *50* kernals so if all yielded in that
manner they would beat the world   Potatoes are very
fine   no rot has at present appeared   They are culti-
vating the sugar beet & apparatus is on the road from
France to manufacture sugar   the people now make
their own molasses from it   I shall try to do so this
fall as its a very easy process   There's but little fruit
here of course at present   The bushes on the sides of
the mountains produce an excellent berry called the
service berry. all the inhabitants try to go to gather
them   Our folks are going to day   I'm to keep house
they take a tent & stay all night   the berries are about
the size of cranberries but are so sweet that when ripe
require no sugar   they dry them for winter use   I
wonder how your horse net speculation succeeds   we
have let Mr Roberts have ours & he is to make us a
good table for them so that will be pretty made as Pa
bought a table for Ma & gave $10 cash for it & its
nothing but a common kitchen table   furniture is very
dear indeed   Wm has ordered *3* chairs & a bedstead
for us to be made at the mill   the commonest bedsteads
are $11. we shall be some thing before we can afford
to get sheets   its fortunate I've got towels table cloths,

& pillow cases along with me   If we had known we should stay here we might have brought many of our things along which would have saved us a good bit. Clarence Whiting & the Newbys never met till they were crossing the last mountains   There's such a lovely creek close by here so surrounded by bushes that I go to bathe with sissy every day & sometimes twice   Sis has not yet cut a single tooth   I've not yet weaned her nor do I know when I shall   it will be such a job I dread it much   she wont stay with anyone 5 minutes if I'm near   I have to carry her when ever I go & she's such a great fat puss   She wears me out some times. I fear she's taken the hooping cough   its very much about & she coughs a little   she cannot yet walk alone but trots all over the room pushing her little chair in front of her. she still sucks those 2 fingers   We still sleep in the waggon   I much prefer it to a house Wm has taken the box of & it stands on the ground so that is all the house we possess   We have a tent which we shall use when we go to the mill   all the inhabitants have their waggon beds standing outside their houses to keep things in   The houses are all made of unburnt bricks   they call them "dobies"   imigrants are arriving every day   there's good chances of making money with cattle most of those that are now brought in are so poor that imigrants will trade off 2 yoke of poor cattle for one in good condition   well then the poor ones recruit in a few weeks with rest & good feed   Wm says he thinks he shall go to town & trade off his yoke for 2–last week we saw a man wanting to give a first rate mare for a yoke of cattle The cows here are quite a sight   they get so fat you never saw any so large   Pigs are rather scarce   I've only seen 2 or 3 since I've been here. Wm regrets he

did not try to bring a grain drill out here. they would
answer first rate & would be a fortune to any one that
had one for a pattern to get others made from

The writing on the side is very much smeared-over
but little Sissy did it   she stands by my knee jiggling
about all the time   I wish you could see her   I think
she looks so sweet, folks say she's pretty child   she
wore her red saque the other sunday. it was so much
admired. How I run on from one subject to another
but you must look over all defects   snow is to be seen
above the mountains although the weather is so hot
now. In the former part of this epistle I promised to
send a sprig of the Lone Tree   I found a piece but in
touching it it all clumbled to pieces so you must all take
the will for the deed. I've sent instead a few seeds of
cactus which we gathered on our road   I could not
send more as we only noticed one flower gone to seed.
you can dispose of them as you please   they must be
set in a very sandy soil & I think require but little
water   Mr Willis would do well at his trade here for
Mr Roberts has 2 wash tubs which he made himself &
he says thousands would be bought if they could be
obtained at $5 a piece & buckets also would fetch an
enormous price so that if you conclude to start for
California next spring why you can stay one winter
& get quite rich   the inhabitants make considerable
by going out some 50 or 60 miles to meet imigrants &
sell them butter vegetables & fish   one man came to
our camp with butter at 50 cents pr pound   we took
1½ pounds but it was last years butter so I should
think that paid them well   John Richard came from
town to day & tells us Ma has sold the cow Pa left
with her (the one he bought for $20) to a cabinet
maker who is to let her have a bedstead & 6 chairs

Well now Ive told you about all I can think of just
now & the mail goes out in a day or two. I find it leaves
every month for the states   I shall not write again till
I hear from you   I hope you will not fail to write soon
as you receive this & then tell me all the summer's
news   Give Mr Willis my kindest love tell him I think
much of returning to see him & you & your pretty house
so that he must not go to California for I want to settle
down near you – this is the wish of both William &
myself   give lots of love to Uncle & his folks   try
& get them all to write now I'm so far away   to Mrs
Wright & Sarah, Mrs Coleman &c &c give any pretty
message you can think of   I'd like to see them all very
much   hope I shall when I return to Rockingham
I wonder if Lydia is married yet   I intend to write
to Emma   perhaps shall do so by next mail   I wish
she was here to wean Sarah   If Ma was like most
grandmammas why she would take that trouble but its
useless to look to such a quarter   Well now dear sister
what can I say in conclusion   I can only wish & pray
that the God of peace may preserve us & permit us
once again to meet in this world & finally send us safe
in heaven   this is the earnest desire of your ever affectionate sister

Lucy Cooke
Utah Territory

Direct to me at Great Salt Lake City
William sends lots of love to you both
  he often talks of your home

end of Oct 1852

Dearest Polly
  Just to while away a Sunday afternoon I set me
down to write to you   I long have been wishing to

hear how you get along & quite expect a letter next
mail   O how often you are the subject of our conversation and still oftener do I wish I was seated on the
lounge by your side in that sunny room of yours telling you some of the wonders of travelling for you
know travellers do see wonders. I suppose you have
received my letter written from here soon after our
arrival so that I must only tell you our proceedings
since that time   I believe I sent word Clarence Whiting was going to winter here but he soon decided to
the contrary & went to California. But to relate of ourselves, William assisted Mr Roberts (the friend who
took us to his house) through his harvesting which took
up some time   he then went to cutting hay for our 2
yoke of oxen for as they have to be worked through
the winter they cannot be turned out to eat their own
food as others do   We lived in Mr R's family about
4 or 5 weeks & then pitched our tent opposite their
house so that I could cook for ourselves which we
found a vast deal more comfortable for its nice living
in a tent *in fine weather* but when the wind storms
come along then its trying for although ours is an
excellent tent still the dust you cannot keep out   We
lived thus about 6 weeks & then moved to the mill
where Wm was engaged to work & here we are at
present   We have quite a snug little one roomed log
cabin just as large as I want to have to keep clean
myself   it is close by the mill & 2 other houses so that
its far more lively than Tete de Mort but still the
folks are all Mormons which I dont like; but to return
to a description of our dwelling we have 4 shingle
blocks for seats also a rickety wash bucket which is
our seat for company   our mantelpiece ornaments are
(centre) that tin bottle I had made like yours, the tin

feeder a box of mustard Williams bowie knife his rasor strop & flute I often compare the things to yours on your mantelpiece Oh me Oh me what a difference!!!! what shall come to next We have no bedstead so sleep on the floor but I dont mind that at all indeed the whole furniture of our dwelling is as good as I care about for the place & sometimes we are pretty happy & at all times very snug as it has a nice open fire place & good shelves also 2 nice little windows. We have put our waggon cover over head for a ceiling which is the custom here We have no crockery at all, all tin ware & but little of that We have had many difficulties to contend with since we came in the valley for as William has only just commenced earning we have had to do without almost every thing for weeks I could not get any soap & twice washed with castile we have only had $1 worth of sugar 2½ lbs that lasted us 4 or 5 weeks no candles, indeed the only things we could get was flour & potatoes this seemed like hard living for us & very unthankful we frequently felt on sitting down to our frugal meals William has now commenced hauling for the mill & if he could keep staying at it we should soon have plenty but its such dreadful hard work he has injured his back several times with lifting logs so he had to lay up he only has 1 yoke of cattle has hired the others to a man who works with him. before the days were so short they could haul a load a day & chop it which would make about 2000 shingles & they had half for hauling. shingles sell for $10 pr 1000, so that is pretty good work Wm only cares to work ½ the time indeed none keep steady at it would be too hard on team & driver the Kanyon where they get the wood is only about 2 miles from here but then they have to go more

than ς miles up it which is an awful road   nothing
but rocks to go on   theres never a day but what several waggons break down in it   William has traded
off his waggon for a tremendous heavy one so that he
has only broken the reach twice & turned over once
folks come and borrow his waggon to fetch their loads
home when they have had a break down. the snow
begins to cover the mountains pretty freely now. We
expect next week to go to town to lay in our winter
groceries for the stores will be bought empty of such
things long before more can be brought and we have
already a nice lot of potaoes squash & sugar beets
these latter are not grown in the States   the seed has
been sent from France where sugar is made from them
they are delicious eating   We have also plenty of meat
now   as Wm bought a hind ¼ of beef of the man who
owns the mill   this we have salted down so that now
we are living much more comfortably only I do miss
groceries but Wm tries to cheer me by telling me he'll
get all I need in a little time now. We have all along
done better than Ma has in the city for John makes a
poor one at providing for a family though I dont think
he's lazy but they manage so poorly so that whenever
we go to see them they have nothing but bread & potatoes   now fortunately whenever they have come to
see us we've had a bit of butter or something different
to their fare   I often think of your nice preserves &
the sugar to [be] bought at 10 or 12 lbs for $1   Dear
Polly since writing the above I have rec[eived] your
letter written Sep 13th   Oh how delighted I was to
hear from you   I am the first that has heard from the
States   Ma was very anxious to hear if anything was
said about any of her friends but there was not   You

dont seem to have a very high opinion of the Mormons Neither have I & much will you be astonished (but perhaps not) when I tell you that about 5 weeks ago I witnessed the baptism of Ma she having joined the Mormon Church & on Sunday next John & Lill are to be baptized Oh dear my only fear is that she will influence my dear Wm. for myself I fear but little as regards that matter & at present Wm is very much opposed to them. I'm glad we live away from the city as that is a good excuse for our not attending their meetings often but Ma says we lose a great deal from not having that privilege for she does if absent from any one of them I will now look over your letter the first thing I notice is that poor "old bones" is dead how Wm did burst out laughing when I came to that part. And so Lydia is married. I wonder if she's a mother yet. This letter as you may suppose is a long while in hand having to be laid by for a week or 2 after every few lines are written & now I'm happy to say we heard from Pa in California. May recd 13 letters one of which was yours to me I now feel so full of news that I dont know how to do anything or what to tell you first We never recd a letter from Uncle so how very much I feel for poor Mrs Burnell in losing her dear babe he was a lovely child I thought do give my kind love & sympathy to her if she's returned from the east how often I wish I would have such as her for my friends here but they are not met in the every day walks of life do you think they are? I hope her dear babe is well & that it will be spared to her What fine times you seem to have had at C Williams's wedding I should like to have been among you just then Pa seemed to have a good time in get-

ting through   I dont think he lost any cattle tho' poor
things some nearly gave out crossing the desert   2
oxen laid down & moaned for water & after a while
Pa met with a chance to buy some at 75 cents a bucket which revived them considerably   he afterwards
passed a place where it was being sold for $5 a bucket
but fortunately he then had a supply   one cow gave
out & then would have had to leave her but they met
a relief train from Cal – who bought her & gave Pa
[ink blot]!! & a good breakfast for all his men with
feed for the cattle   so was not that pretty   well the
rest of the cows fetched $100 each & the oxen $100 a
yoke as they were very poor when they got in   Pa
visited many of the principal cities in the mining dis-
trict   things were very dull for want of rain which
would set all in motion again   he had not when his
first letters were written obtained any work but in his
last he stated he was engaged to superintend a farm
a short distance from S. F.   it is owned by a firm   on
that place there are 5 hired hands. Pa has a nice house
to live in a house keeper also a horse to ride, on which
he goes down to the Pacific to bathe every morn   his
salary is $75 for the 1st month   it was all he asked
he has no work to do only just to tell what is to be
done   We wonder how he manages as he is no farmer.
he says he took the situation with regard to Wm taking
it when we go on in spring he thought it would not
suit him & would be a home to go to at once which it
would. I think very likely Wm will go there for a
while   Pa had not recd Ma's letter about her joining
the Mormons so he dont know he's got to come back
here to live for Ma will not go on to California now
I guess he'll not hesitate to join them for he said be-

fore he left that he was almost a Mormon   He speaks very highly of California & its products   says he is about purchasing land for all his boys (Wm included) as farming is the most profitable way of getting a living   he wrote me a very kind letter said he did it to tell me he loves me. this perhaps he thought best from the fact of Wm & I having several disagreements with them on the road so much so that I think it unlikely either party will think as much of the other again now this dear M A I dont wish mentioned to any friends as nothing need ever be know[n] of it but we used sometimes to come to very high words so much as that Wm tried to get a waggon & team for us to travel alone but Pa was unwilling consequently we determined to stop at Salt Lake   But coming to California has many disagreeables   few very few companies get through without disagreeing & separating it is the most trying to a persons temper, even dear Pa I saw twice in a passion such a thing as I never witnessed before & thought it impossible almost   you will not wonder then that I was irritable   You know how much Wm & I thought of Mr Gilbert of Moline & that Mr & Mrs Hubbard were in company with him (the latter kept house for him in Moline) on their way to Cal—   well even they had to separate   Mr & Mrs H remain here till spring   we expect to go in company then   In the former part of this letter I said we expected soon to go town to make our first purchases for housekeeping   we have been & will relate what we got   the shingles William got $8 a thousand for *cash* which is a very scarce article here   We bought at the tin shop a small bread pan $1½ a small camp kettle (sheet iron with lid) $2, tin coffee or tea pot

like the one you use in common $1 lastly a little tin
bucket with lid $1 so that was $5½ in as many minutes
Then we went to the store & bought 12 lbs of sugar
at 40 cents 5 lbs coffee 40 cents ½ lb tea $2 ½ gal
molasses at $3 pr gal, 1 lb saleratus 40 cents, 2 bars
soap 50 cents a pretty linsey dress for me 50 cents pr
yard   3 yds calico at 25 cents to make sis apron   ½
a quire of paper 50 cents   lastly a pair of buckskin
mittens for Wm $1½ pr   Oh what a little compass
all the things went in & yet cost so much   We also got
a nice piece of beef with some beautiful suet for pud-
dings Wm being very fond of them   We bought a
lump of tallow 25 cents pr lb   this we use for *pie crust*
& candles   is it not handy   Since I commenced this
letter Wm has traded off his 2 yoke of cattle for a span
of horses & harness so now we drive our own horse
team & go where & when we please   he has also traded
off the heavy waggon for a lighter one   one of the
horses is older than Wm likes & is blind in one eye so
we are about changing him off for one which Wm
& indeed most folks that have seen him thinks is a very
fine animal but shall have to pay a high price for him
i e the blind horse & 5000 shingles but Wm thinks
him worth it   We shall then have a good horse team
to go to California with which will fetch considerable
there though after all we may go on with oxen for
Wm says he shall propose to Pa for him to send him
money to buy up cattle & then deliver them to Pa free
of expenses in Cal— Wm having the use of them to
haul flour to sell in Carson Valley that being a scarce
article there. We have had a heavy snow storm   the
mountains are covered in white   Wm is now unable
to do any hauling until the snow packs down   he &

2 others have been up in the mountains to day with
their cattle to try & cut a road through so as to continue working but they returned without doing it as
the snow was in many places breast high so that nothing
more can be done until the snow will bear. They saw
5 mountain sheep on the rocks & could have easily
have shot them had they had guns along — their horns
are much than an ox's horns   some young men are
going up on the mountains tomorrow to shoot them
as they are not likely to be far from where they were
to day. Bears are often seen & frequently killed   Mr &
Mrs Hubbard live 9 miles back in the mountains
there's a lumber mill up there which he has built. I
have never been to see them. Wm has been there often
as he has to go near there to get shingle timber. Pa sent
Ma a lot of new music so as we had no piano we all
went to the Governor Brigham Young to try it over
he is very friendly indeed said Wm must let him know
when we next came in town as he would invite a gent
(a comic singer from England) to meet him at his
house   I have not said a word about dear little Sissy.
she is not weaned yet & I guess I shall not do so till
spring   she does not talk yet & has not run about more
than a month   She has 8 teeth all cut since she was a
year old & strange she cut her eye teeth first   She's a
cunning puss   knows all we say   tell Mrs Wright
she has 2 great faults which I am continually whipping
her for   one is poking her fingers into the bread when
set to rise   the other is opening my box & sitting on
the top of things & twice she did her occasions in it.
I've just made her a little black watered silk hood
out of that bonnet of mine. she wears that red de laine
dress and a petticoat made of that piece left of Jemima

Parkhursts cloak   I saved that nice quilted skirt you
gave her & shall when there is cold weather shorten it
for her while that piece of red flannel will make her
a best dress   that place on her head has only just
healed up   I'm hoping it will not break out again.
she's a great hand to kiss. every meal she has to smack
her lips to Wm & I & when no one else is in the room
she toddles off to kiss the cat   every time a dog barks
she trots to the door clapps her hands & kisses having
seen us do so when cattle were in the yard. She always wears the pretty red saque when dressed in best.
its not at all dirty yet   I find her cloak very useful
wonder how old she'll be when you next see her for I
cannot think it will be a very distant period   Wm
often wishes we were back & says he'll return as soon
as he gets any more than he came with. I always fancy
I'd like to live somewhere near Morey's farm   If I
was anxious I know Wm would send me to you in
Spring & he start on to California alone but I think
we had better keep on together now I've got this far
With regard to clothing Ive been poorly off having
bought no bonnet since I've been here   That old pink
calico sun bonnet has been the only one I've had so
have worn it Sundays & week days until it was really
so mean looking I cant use it no longer   I then made
another out of a piece of an old lilac dress I brought
from England & that is what I'm wearing now   tho I
shall make a black silk hood soon as I get a good pattern which will last till we arrive at the El Dorado
then I no longer dress as a poor woman   Of course
had I know[n] we should winter here would have
brought several things which I left behind   my old
cloak would have been worth at the very least $10

I've nothing to wear now but the green shawl as Ma
cut the cloak she lent me to make Eddy clothes so that
when I go out riding I have to bundle up in a com-
forter by the way in the former part of this letter
I said we slept on the floor Thomas has since made
us a bedstead of course its all in the rough just hewed
out still it does well enough for here so long as we're
leav[ing] I care so little for appearances for there's
no one here I care a snap for Wm sold his good thick
over coat at Kanesville for $3 as he was told there'd
be no use for it & we never passed a night on the road
but what it would have been a comfort & now it would
be of great service but I guess he'll do without one as
they are so dear here he therefore wears a waterproof
blanket (one Pa bought in Kansville) with a hole cut
in the centre for his head to go through this is the
Spanish fashion in California Pa says the Chinese are
as plentiful there as Americans & they adhere to their
own customs such as eating rice with chop sticks &c
&c My dear little pet is now asleep Wm is gone to
town with Mr Alexander the gent who owns the mill
so Ive again sat down to write a few lines it seems
as tho I'd never get through your letter as I have to
tell you all I can knowing that you will be pleased to
read it I'm sorry you had but a poor crop of fruit this
last season. I thought so much about it as we have none
at all here except dried apples & peaches which are
40 cents pr lb Wm bought us 8 lbs of the latter You
say in your letter that you'll get the LeClaire folks
writing to me but no letter at present has arrived I
intend writing to them this mail if I can also to Mrs
Hill Dubuque As to English letters I dread beginning them as I know not how to condense what I've

to tell friends & have not time to write long letters
dear Mrs Shep— I shall regret if she never hears
again from me it will seem as tho I was unmindful
of all her kindnesses I fear she'll soon leave this
world I should hardly say *fear* for to her it will
be intrinsic gain many in the humble walks of life
will remain to mourn her loss & so Mr Shep— is not
dead as you surmised how is it she has not mentioned
him in her few last letters When we first met with
Mr Gilbert of Moline just after we crossed Missouri
for the last time he gave me a letter from his sister a Mrs. Thompson wife of judge Thompson from
Michigan she with 2 interesting little girls came
to board at Mr Gilberts a week or 2 before we left
there I never had much conversation with her as she
seemed a very retiring lady & seldom left her room
but at meal times well after I left there & Wm returned to settle up affairs with Deere Tate & Gould
just after Sissy's birth he stayed a day or two at Mr
Gilberts & met this Mrs Thompson again & had considerable conversation with her. The cholera was about
in Moline & around proving very fatal which alarmed
Mrs T— she being a very delicate lady & moreover
her husband was absent at Chicago. Wm tried to cheer
her up & comfort her mind which so touched her
heart that he an impenitant should seek to administer
comfort to a Xtian (which she is) it touched a cord
(to use her own expression) in her heart which has
often vibrated when bowed before the mercy seat in
prayer Oh dear M A its is a beautiful letter she wrote
I think I must inclose it for your perusal as I'm sure it
will give you pleasure to know of any left behind who
have offered up prayer for me & mine if I do inclose
it I must omit sending Mrs Shep's this time but will

take good care of it & send it next opportunity or perhaps if I write I will send it in theirs. That will be
better. I've written to Mrs Thompson this mail in
which letter I tell her of you & beg her to visit you
I wish she may as from her letter you can see she's a
sincere Xtian & a real lady in her gentle unassuming
manners You must take care of her letter & return it
when you next write for I prize it much for when
feeling cast down from seeing nothing but worldly
characters around I read this letter it raises my
thoughts & feelings heavenward Oh there's so little
here that looks to me like Christianity no one mentions their Maker's name unless in oaths Why am I
placed here Oh when shall I hear the voice of a
Xtion minister. These & all such feelings come over
me when I think of you & the many privileges which
(compared with me) you have & why should I so weak
in the faith be removed from all these I wonder what
you'll say when I tell you the Mormons are building
a theatre & that it will belong to the church it's to
be opened at Xmas. Ma is one of the actress's she has
been voted in by the committee in 3 different plays
of course all the performances will be strictly moral
in this respect it will differ from all others the kind
& you know many persons (of which Ma is one) are
of the opinion that if carried on aright much good
might tonight from the stage this the Mormons are
professing to aim at it remains to be proved how
far they will fall I feel sure you will not coinside
with their notion Ma is teaching school for a quarter
until the Music Hall is finished she is then to have
a room assigned her to teach Music. Brigam Young
has bought a superior English Piano & Melodion for
her use in the Hall. John is now employed by Brigham

in hauling wood from his Kanyon which is close by
he has $2½ pr day & Brigham keeps his horses so he
only has to drive to the house for them   a col'd man
takes them & unharnasses & that's all he has to do
with them   Wm talks of going to Brigam to get a
similar birth if he cannot get shingle stuff but I hope
he will not have to do it as I want to keep him from
working in town   Thomas works in the mill by us
he does not seem to like the Mormons though as he's
Ma's favorite of course she's anxious he should be
connected to her faith   How strange it does seem
that they should think it right to have so many wives.
they say the more children a man has the more will
be his glory here after & that the bible states that in
the last days 7 women shall cleave to one man to be
called by his name to take away their reproach. I dont
know how many Brigam has   there are various reports
but none but his first wife is seen at his house   the
others are all kept in little log cabins near his dwelling
the doctrine would not suit me for if I was married
to a man I would not be kept in the back ground
the[y] profess to have had revelations from God to
adopt his "Plural System" as its termed   I think most
of the men have more than one, some 5 or 6   Wm told
Ma the men were a perfect set of whoremongers he
thought. she reproved him very much for saying so
said he did not understand it yet

   The house where she lives there are 3 wives of one
man. he has just gone to England on his way to Prussia
on a mission & the day before he left he married a
widow so that he has 4 now & his daughter told me
he had 2 more some where but that they had left for
her father would never keep a woman if she was not
satisfied   The other night Wm & I went to a party

there were some young ladies there   I enquired who
they were of the mistress of the house   she replied
they were her husbands wife's children   how strange
it seemed to me but there are many of the Mormons
themselves who cannot believe the doctrine is right &
according to their talk if when Pa returns Ma should
live with him before he joins their church she would
be living in adultery   the boys plague her about this
I must really now conclude   give our very kindest
love to your dear husband with a kiss from me & wishing you to write soon   I remain your affectionate sis
                                        Lucy Cooke
This is finished on the 27th of November having been
in hand about 5 weeks

[Added note on flap 1 of outside sheet:]

I dont expect you will get this much before spring
as the mails are so delayed on account of the snows
still they have to leave every month   if they return
when reaching Weber river which I'm told they do
& that that is the way this letter will go   What did
Fanny say in her letter & have you heard anything of
Beatie's

[Added note on flap 2 of outside sheet:]

I dont know if I've sent any kind messages to Davenport & Rockingham friends   if not be sure & give
them   tell Mrs Wright Sis sucks her fingers as much
as ever & [it] dont seem they look different from the
others   I hope Sarah Wrights will not marry Sargent

                          Great Salt Lake Utah Terty
                                      Jan 30/53
Dearest Sis
    It seems such a long long time since I heard from
you that I got quite uneasy and wonder why you don't

write   I have only just this moment thought of writing to you & shall now have to look sharp or shall not get it off in time to mail   I cannot write a decent letter now as I feel in such constant excitement about leaving here that I cant settle to nothing   Oh how I wish I was back with you   I am so sick & sick at heart of this Mormon country   We have no Sunday whatever   Oh it seems so sad. Mr & Mrs Hubbard of Moline have been sharing our little cabin for the last 2 months & will until we start for Cal   you may guess we are pretty crowded. we have 2 bedsteads, each with only 1 leg as they are poles drove in the wall   we can scarcely turn round   still we get along very well for the circumstances   Mr & Mrs H lived about 9 miles up in the Kanyon till the snow fell so deep as to make it impossible to stay so we offered them part of our dwelling & well they accepted it as it was the means of savings their lives. After they left their shanty in the Kanyon some men went to cut timber up there & occupied a cabin close by Hubbards. the wind blew very hard so as to cause the fireplace to smoke so they went over to Hubbards the house being empty & engaged in baking bread when a snow slide or avalanche came down from the mountain & buried the house so as not to leave the slightest sign of a dwelling   There were 3 men in the company but providentially one had just stepped out & was walking down the road when he heard a tremendous crash & on turning round saw what had happened   he was a lone so could do nothing   he accordingly ran down to a mill about 2½ miles & obtained help to return & dig for his 2 companions. they at length succeeded in finding one, quite dead, apparently instantaneously by the falling of a

rock which partly formed the fireplace as he was just
turning the bread they dug some hours & could find
nothing of the other man at length gave up the search.
when some others came & dug being determined not
to leave till they found him they at last heard a call
from under the snow but it was so indistinct as not
to give the least idea of where to find the sufferer they
left the house & commenced digging out of doors for
an hour or two then went back & after working a
length of time came to a boot they scarcely dared to
hope they might find him alive they moved it and
what was their joy to find it move again of course
they lost no time in getting him out he was lying his
full length with his arms extended over his head &
so had laid 6 hours one of the poles of the house
over his hands which hurt them pretty bad. he had
no chance to move an inch after he was knocked
down, poor fellow he was quite sensible all the time
but thought his hour was come as he was getting
quite overcome with sleep when they found him The
neighbors treated him very kindly & as quick as they
could get into the valley came for a team to fetch him
& the corpse out William took his horses the next
day & brought them out of the Kanyon The young
man was not able to do any thing for some weeks but
has now recovered They belong to a company from
Farmington Ill. on their way to California & were
engaged to put up a mill in the Kanyon under Mr
Hubbards superintendance the man that was killed
left a wife & 5 children in Farmington what sad
news for them! there are frequently snow slides when
the wind is high it makes me so uneasy sometimes
when William is in the Kanyon. one day as he was

driving up one came down within a few yards of his
horses heads it filled the road completely so that
he had to turn round & return home   But all the talk,
work, & trading is for California   the emigrants all
seem so tired of the valley   We are wishing to start
with the 1st emigration which will be beginning of
March   Mr & Mrs Hubbard have engaged their
passage through with a family   We tried to do the
same but. could not so I expect we shall go on with
our own waggon that is if we can get a young man to
help drive & do chores   I believe I wrote that we
had sent to Pa to send means to buy cattle for us to
take through but we cannot wait to hear from him
William has had so poor a chance to work that he
wants to leave as quick as possible   I have not written to any friends in England yet & really dont know
when I shall get an opportunity & there I must pay
postage to them which I cannot until we get where
cash is paid for work. every dime we see has to go
for victuals   Pa sent a gold dollar for each of us as
a Xmas gift   We had to spend our 2 for meat & sissys
went for a pair of shoes for her   I felt quite bad at
having to part with them   he also sent Ma a very
rich brocade silk dress, some silk velvet for a bonnet,
ribbon, gloves &c &c a pair of gloves for me also. he
is doing first rate   Oh what a treat it will be to get
where provisions are reasonable. We have been without sugar and tea for some time, however Wm managed to get a store order for $6 so he got that out in
tea, coffee & sugar, but it bought but little. still we
try to be thankful for small favors   Since I commenced this the gent has called who is going to take
Hubbards through & he still seems to think he will

take us I wish they may. they are a nice family &
he is I think a Christian man which would to me be
a great comfort they expect to be 4 months on the
road as they have to stop in Carson Valley perhaps
4 or 5 weeks but there is plenty of employment there,
gold mining &c &c I have not seen Ma since Xmas
day we rode up there to see her but I feel so different to her to what I used now she has turned Mormon & stage actress. the theatre is in full operation
now Wm went last week. he says it was first rate but
I hope never to countenance it here or in any other
place. The Mormons are great for parties think of
nothing else in winter I have been to several amongst
the neighbours & at Xmas I was engaged to write
invitation tickets for a ball given by the person Wm
works for they gave a first rate supper which was
a treat to us

Hubbards had two nice little pigs they were fat-
tening to use on the road but as they have hired their
passage do not need them then, so we killed one the
other morn before breakfast as we were quite out of
meat & had been some time it weighed 56 lbs the
other is a trifle larger but it will readily sell for $10
when we start. We are trying to sell every thread of
clothes we can. Wm sold his best coat for 400 lbs of
flour. Several want to buy my satin dress which I
have offered for a good cow. Ma wants to buy it but
I dont care for her pay as it would be trust I hope
I shall have a letter from you before we leave but I
fear its doubtful Oh how different I hope things
will be in California I think we'll never trouble
Salt Lake again though the Mormon Patriarch when
giving Lilly her blessing (according to their custom)

prophesied that Wm & I should join their church
He also said Lilly would live to see the coming of
Christ We rather doubt these things I must now
close as the men are wanting my letter to go to town
I shall write again before we start which I hope will
be in 4 or 5 weeks Sissy is quite well I am trying
to wean her she has not nursed in the day time for
a week but I cannot dry up the milk easily.
I swapt that calico dress which I had unmade at your
house to Mrs Hubbard for a black alapacca dress
made as she wanted a calico so I made considerable
by that trade I shall be glad of a black dress on the
road I am quite out of under clothes & cannot get
anything in the city. theres not a yard to be bought
Mrs Hubbard gave me a large night dress of hers to
make me 2 chemises so dont you think we are hard
up We'll want every thing new when we get to our
journey end
Try & get Uncles folks to write to me as I seem so
far from all my friends give my kindest love & a
kiss to your dear husband Wm sends lots of big love
to you all including LeClaire friends
I had such a job to get a pair of shoes for sissy & at
last had to cut the tops off a pr of mens boots & get
the shoe maker to make them he charged a *dollar*
there were none in the stores
   Well dearest sister farewell I trust we'll meet again
in this world *I think we shall*

Yours Very Affectionately
Lucy Cooke

South Mill Creek
   If I get to Cal I'll pay the postage on my letter but
at present we are so poor I cannot Thomas bought

a little rocking chair for Ma last week   it was like
that little one of yours   he paid $7 for it!!

Great Salt Lake City   Utah Ter
March 12/53

My dear Sister
  I am now with Ma paying her a last visit preparatory to leaving for California   She has just received
quite a budget of news from Pa among which was a
letter from Pa to William & one for me. Mine contained a letter from Uncle dated Sep 7th which he
sent by Mr Bratton[?]   there was nothing particular
in it as Uncle doubted if it would ever reach me
I wrote to you some 2 months ago but its so uncertain
when you will get my letters on account of snow still
I wished to let you know when I started   we are so
rejoiced to have the time for leaving come, being so
tired of the valley   Pa is very anxious to have all the
family come as he has a very good berth & is doing
fine   his employers also wish the family to come on &
promise to do great things for them   I guess they will
Ma will go but not until July or August as Ma has
just commenced giving music lessons so she will have
to finish the quarter   Pa wants Wm there much as
there are chances for him to have the management
of a farm belonging to merchants in the city   Pa has
the entire charge of everything   does just as he thinks
best. he says he found the chickens getting rather numerous on the place so he took 150 to the city for
which he got $300 !! & $2½ pr doz for the eggs. Flour
was selling at $50 pr 100   he says he never before
witnessed so much wealth & poverty as it is to be met
with in San Francisco   I shall try & enclose my letter

from him which will give you further particulars
Well now with regard to our going we have paid our
passage thro with a family who stayed here last fall
on their way to Cal   We give them a yoke of oxen &
a waggon for our 2 selves & $30 for Sissy for which
Wm drives 2,3rds of the way   I have nothing to do
but mind Sarah so I think we may be more comfortable
than when last on the road   We have a wide track
wagon with projections at the sides   our bed is the
whole width & will remain all day as at night so that
we can lie down when ever disposed   Mr & Mrs
Hubbard go in the same company   We are to be
taken to Sacramento city & shall there have to take
steamboat to San Francisco   We shall have to stay in
Carson Valley some 4 or 5 weeks till the mountains
are passable   doubtless we have a dreary time before
us & there is considerable danger from Indians when
near our journeys end. all go well armed   Wm has a
brace of pistols & bowie knife but still I trust we shall
see no occasion for blood shed   the Lord is able & I
pray that he may be willing to protect us all our journey through   I'm thankful to say our healths have
been fine all winter   I was weighed last week & would
you believe I've gained 17 lbs since on the Missouri
Rvr & I then weighed 115 lbs   I now weigh 132! so
I'm in first rate condition   dear Sarah weighs 25 lbs
so she's pretty chunky   I've not quite weaned her
yet   she nurses on going to sleep at night   I had considerable trouble in drying up my milk at first but its
no trouble now   I wish she was weaned. she's such a
great fat girl   dont talk yet except to say pa pa, go,
stop it. I've just cut up that green shirt you gave me
to make her a petticoat on the road its so nice & warm

for the little puss   Oh how often I wish you could
see her   she's just getting so cunning but if we all
are spared a few years you will see us back as this
is our first desire & prayer and it's our intention to
return   I've been quite busy preparing for our journey have pulled my three comforters to pieces   had
them washed   you will perhaps remember 2 were lined
with white which was filthy dirty   I have to taken the
linings for pr of sheets & used instead that comfort
you made before I was married   the red flannel binding I've saved & used for binding several things   so
glad to have clean & sweet bed clothes again   I've sold
my satin dress to get Wm an overcoat which is a good
broadcloth very heavy & well lined also bound with
silk binding   in fact it's much too good for our purpose being valued at $25   still he needed one so bad
& my frock was only in my way & of no use till we
got to Cal   I can then get another quite as cheap   I
got a new figured alpacen dress besides the cost $1¼
pr yard   I needed a second best dress to wear when
at our journeys end   My black silk is about done for
i e the waist is   I'm delighted to say our boxes have
arrived at Pa's   he had to pay $50 freight   my chest
the hassock was off but Pa thinks nothing was gone
2 of the cups 1 saucer & a salt was all that was broken
I so long to see them again   We have all been to the
governors [9] twice   lately he treated us all exceeding
kind wished us to go bid him good bye before we left
he has lent Ma one of his pianos a very handome one
she has 3 pupils   I'm quite disappointed at not hearing from you before I leave as I shall now not hear till
I arrive in San Francisco which will doubtless be 4

---

[9] Brigham Young.

months in the meantime dear M A you have my
fervant prayers & best wishes

March 22nd   Dearest M A   We are expecting to
leave to day   its beautiful weather   We have been
out visiting every day for the last 2 weeks   Wm went
to bid the president good bye yesterday   he gave him
his blessing & said he would prosper   We have met
with much kindness among the Mormons & shall
always have reason to speak well of them   I enclose
a scrap of paper Pa sent respecting the mails & if I
can get a letter to enclose I will do so   Wm desires
kind love. be sure to give my best to dear brother Willis   I often wonder how his health is   I long to hear
O I had most forgot to tell I've just met with some
Bedford folks living here   the lady Mrs Smith (a mil-
liner) knows the Hills well   Martha & her were
married at the same time. wife was apprenticed to
Mrs T— to learn the business   I really must now conclude as I have to get my things ready for the wagon
we expect soon   with much love & best wishes to yourself Uncles folks & all friends   I remain your affectionate Sis

                                        Lucy Cooke
I need not tell you pen is bad   you can see it
[Written addition on flap #1 of folded letter]
    As soon as we get to Cal & have a dime to help
ourselves with I shall pay postage   I hate to make you
do it all the time but we are so poor
    Ma has treated us very kindly while staying with her.
[Written addition on flap #2 of folded letter]
I have just finished a saque for myself made out of
a summer coat of Pa's   Ive lined it with a blanket Ma
gave me   its so nice & warm I had nothing to wear

but my little green shawl & we expect some very cold
weather   I enclose Pa's letter to me & ½ a sheet of
Willms for you to see the picture   Sissy is waking so
I can say no more except how much I think of you &
love you dearly   Yours ever

Lucy

This letter commenced latter part of April 1853
My dearest Marianne

As I am again on the road I shall try to give you
an account of our travels tho I daresay I shall not do
so as regular as I did last season   We left Salt Lake
City on 31st March tho this you will know before as I
mailed a letter to our Uncle on that day   We have
now been on the road about 3 weeks 1 week of which
we laid bye as we were on good feed & no use to hurry
as we cannot cross goose creek mountains (on account
of snow) for some weeks   I have very much enjoyed
being out on the road again   Oh it is so nice so much
preferable to living in the Valley & I can assure you
we live "first rate." hitherto its so nice to have women
manage affairs   things look so much sweeter   I dont
know that the folks we are now with have more variety
than Pa had last year but they make it seem better
we often have pies & to night for supper we had fried
sausages, eggs, bread, butter boiled cabbage, tea &c
&c   its so nice to have such an abundance of milk
also butter & eggs. We have potatoes but not many
however I must not write too much about our eating
but give an account of other things. We have a very
comfortable waggon & all to ourselves pleasant   most
of the loading is under the bed & but 2 meat barrels
in front which have clean flat lids so they make me

nice tables   then theres room to move about comfortably Oh how different to the huddled up way
we were in last season   still the main point is not so
good as then i e the cattle Pa had fine, very fine
teams & now we have very light ones being mostly
cows & in poor condition from the exceedingly hard
winter   our wagon has only 2 yoke, 1 of oxen 1 of
cows   all Pa's wagons had 4 yoke. the passengers seem
sure we cannot take all 4 waggons thro' We crossed
Bear River last week on a little raft of 9 small logs
theres always a ferry there in the season but as we
were very early in leaving the valley we arrived there
before the ferryman and not bin willing to wait his
arrival some agreed to procure logs from the mountains & build a raft which was just large enough to
take on 1 waggon at a time   there were between 20 &
30 crossed in this way. then the cattle had all to swim
across which was a tiresom job the river being so wide.
I met with a trifling accident in crossing. When our
waggon was put on the raft it was thought I might
as well go over at same time not inside as that was
not safe so I was told to stand by the hind wheel
Sarah was in my arms   the raft was let loose from
shore & owing to the wagon not being pushed far
enough on it backed of into the water sending the
raft & some portion of my legs under water   I was
much scared as the jerk had made sis fall back over
my arm   I thought my child was gone   I screamed
Oh my child but William who was on with me threw
his arms round my back & caught her & held us both
tight in his arms to the wheel until they pulled us back
to shore   every one praised me for the courage I dis-
played as I never spoke except the above sentence.

they said if it had been any other woman she would
have screamed all the time. Well the hind part of
the wagon was all under water but we were in hopes
it had not gone high enough to hurt anything they at
length got it out & sent it over first rate tho I remained
behind to go in a skiff (belonging to the ferryman
which the folks found hid on an island) at length
we all got over safe, but could not get our cattle to
swim across after having had them driven into the
water twice, poor things what trouble they seemed
in they all clung together by the bank of the River
while some 30 or 40 men were hallowing & whipping
them with all their might we were obliged to let them
come out & remain on the other side till morning it
being most dark In the morn they were again sent
in & after being beaten for about ½ an hour they swam
over We then thought our difficulties were over for
a while but we presently came to another stream which
we were told would be bridged but found it had swollen to a wide river & no bridge visible. they after con-
sultation took one wagon bed off & sent the waggon
to Bear river for the skiff while they were gone I
thought it a good opportunity to clean out my waggon
& dry any thing got wet the night before when lo on
opening my box which was under the bed found the
contents saturated with water I cried with vexation
but finding it did no good set to work & took everything out & hung up to dry my towels & tablecloths
were all wringing wet & so stained also Sissy's white
clothes which I had no nicely starched & ironed ready
for her use on arriving at Sacramento I was really
vexed you may be sure for instead of having a box of
clean linens its all stained & dirty but suppose the

affair was a trifle for this journey but now to return
to crossing this stream which is set down in the guide
as being the worst (on account of mud) to cross in all
the journey the skiff arrived waggons were emptied
of heavy things which were sent over on the skiff & a
man undertook to wade & swim the river to ascertain
its depth he managed to walk pretty well the water
not coming in its deepest places higher than his arm-
pits the cattle were therefore sent over & it was
thought best for men to take the wagons in the water
& draw them partly over having found part of the
bridge by walking round with poles which however
was not safe for oxen so Wm & some 5 or 6 others
waded the water up to the waists from noon till near
sun down taking the wagons about ½ way & then a
man with a yoke of cattle was wading the other side
to draw them out then there was a job to pack all
the wagons again Oh the pleasures of going to see
the Elephant!! [10] I wish you could have seen the men
in the water with the wagons they made such noises
as tho it was very funny for my part I was glad when
it was over

May 1st Its now dear M A a long time since I began
this since we have changed again having left the company we started with & joined one which had been
travelling near us for a while We left the former
because they expected William to do camp duties i e
fetch wood water &c &c this he wanted not to do
having paid his passage (& plenty more persons think)
to have such things done for us as there were plenty
of hands in the family to do chores Willm helped

10 "The Elephant" was a term used for the overland trail either to Oregon
or to California. Shirley Sargent has edited James Hutchings' Journal
to California as *Seeking the Elephant, 1849* (Glendale, California, 1980).

with the milking & took his turn in churning but as
they expected more & said he could not go with them
unless he did chores he at once drew out his wagons
& yoke of cattle & joined the other company who take
us thro' for the same. as far as teams are concerned
we have made an excellent change the man we are now
with having as fine a set of cattle as could be got   he
brought them all through last season from Chicago
Oh they are such pictures & so fat   then he has loose
cattle which is a great advantage being never obliged
to work any but those which feel first rate   The company we first joined could only travel very slow &
such a job it was when we come to a mud hole or hill
on account of the cows being so poor   the company
we now joined concluded to leave them as we could
travel so much faster so we left them   they talked of
waiting a week where they then were camped   Mr
Holly the gent we are now with has with ours 6 wagons 37 head of cattle & 3 horses   his wife rides in a
horse wagon as we did last year. directly we joined
him he put 3 yoke of fine large fat oxen on our wagon
which is lightly loaded having but 5 sacks of flour
besides our own clothes   I assure you its some what
different to riding behind cows   why we go right
right along thro mud, mountain, snow or anything that
happens to come next so as I before said as far as teams
are concerned that's the principal thing we have made
a happy change but we live very poorly   the bacon
they have is awfully musty & no vegetables nothing
but bacon bread & dish cloth coffee   I missed the milk
& butter so much but Wm tried around the camp to
get the former & has got a cow to milk keeping the
milk for his trouble   so as long as the folks travel

with us I'm well off for milk   I have now got 5 lbs
of butter which is as choice as gold   I got it of our
folks when we left them   I should not have got it but
I had a new pair of leather shoes I bought in the valley for $3 as one of their women folks was most bare-
foot. they were glad to get them so paid me ½ in
butter at 30 cents pr lb   it was a mutual accomoda-
tion for I did not need the shoes   I think I told you
or Uncle there were 3 single men in our first company
well they left & joined this one for the sake of getting
through quicker   we crossed Goose creek mountains
about 9 days ago   we had to double teams through
some of the snow drifts & got over them in 1 day with
out so much difficulty though 1 or 2 of the ascents
were almost perpendicular   my waggon seemed as
tho it was going to stand on end   I rode all the time
for it was a very disagreeable day   the snow was falling fast & wind blowing as hard   however when we
got down in the valley we found quite pleasant weather
but on looking back could see it still snowing on the
mountains we had just crossed. Last Friday it snowed
hard   we camped as soon as we could get a spot but
it was so comfortless the ground being covered with
snow & no wood but sage brush & that a long way
off   we all 3 went to bed to keep warm & slept away
the time as much as we could & with the exception of
2 wagons which have gone a head to establish a ferry
on the Humboldt   we are the first company on the
road tho there's plenty behind us   To day being Sunday we have camped for the day   there's another
company just come near us to camp   they have a 1000
head of sheep along so we shall try & keep a head of
them   How I wonder if you have come into the sheep

raising business We meet Indians every day now &
to day there's a party come & camped on the opposite
side of the creek I dont know what thats done for
some say they're watching the sheep the Indians we
hitherto have met do not appear hostile tho there's no
trading for buckskin with them as they will take nothing but "caribee" i e guns or ammunition for them.
this we wont trade as either of them might be used
to our own disadvantage The weather is very cold
we are surrounded all the time with snow clad mountains What a comfort my flannel gown is to me in
the day time I hold Sis in it & at night sleep in it.
I've weaned Sis some 3 or 4 weeks . She made no fuss
about it Oh she looks so well her cheeks are red &
purple with health She tries to talk catches hold of
both corners of my bonnet & holds quite long conver-
sations in my face I say yes, yes, yes, all the time &
so on she talks tho not one word do I understand
She still sucks her fingers I dont yet try to brake her
of it notwithstanding Mrs Wrights counsels Oh what
a comfort the little puss is to me I cannot think how
I go on without her she's up to every trick I know
Pa will make a great fuss with her & so would you
if she was near you May 14th I'm not very regular
in writing our travels but when a person has been so
many weeks & months on the road it seems an old
story. We have now been travelling on the Humboldt
river some days the weather is much warmer quite
hot at noon We have seen some 8 or 10 graves this
last day or 2 so suppose its unhealthy in hot weather
One grave we passed was that of a young man who was
shot by an Indian while on guard (this the board of
the grave informed us) he lived 2 days. We have seen

but few of this new Indian tribe "Diggers" they are
very shy & back in the willows along the banks of the
river we saw 3 day before yesterday but they were
across the river we however were anxious to have
a nearer interview as they were said to be so different
to other tribes so bread was thrown in the water to
induce them to swim over to us they were very unwilling to come but at last they did & rather put
some of us modest females to the blush they being
perfectly naked except a "breech clout" i e a strip of
rag between their legs. they had little or no forehead
& no eyebrows when they found we were amicably
inclined they followed us some miles & took dinner
with us & one we found at our camp next morn before breakfast. yesterday we had to camp soon after
starting for a cow is lost to day we have come about
8 miles & have again stopped for the same cause but
suppose will go on in 2 or 3 hours the calves are to
be carried in the waggons for a few days. We crossed
the bridge I mentioned above (but then called it a
ferry) Wm paid for our waggon going over as Mr
Holly was going to ferry the stream using one of the
waggon beds for a boat but as that leaked so much &
the risk seen of wetting our things besides the trouble
of taking everything out of our wagon we preferred
paying the toll of the bridge which was very reasonable the ferryman charged us but $1½ as we had to
pay ourselves the usual toll being $3 Mr Holly
after gave Wm 75 cents towards it as it did n't cost
us much Holly had also to treat his men with $5
worth of whiskey for going in the water & they dropt
over a bag of sugar weighing 100 lbs it nearly all
got wet as he would have been better to have paid the

toll & gone over without losing a day's time. I had a
chance to trade with the Indians while our folks were
getting over the stream I swapt one of my small
blankets for a pretty robe of prairie dog skins I think
there are 10 in it all nicely sewed together my blanket
was getting quite old I wonder the Indian was willing to trade for his robe is new & will look so pretty
over me when in a buggy riding but they think so much
of a blanket another Indian had some beautiful mink
skins tied over his shoulders & under his arm it caught
my eye as being enough to make a nice flat boa so I
got an old red flannel shirt of Williams that he was
quite willing to swap for. its a nice piece there are
3 skins in it but only 2 tails so would now have but one
at each end or none at all! if I made it round of course
2 tails would be sufficient but I prefer it flat If you
had not so good a boa I most certainly would keep it
for you It's just like one Mrs Drew had. dont you
think I got a bargain! Well then a young man in one
company traded for some wild cat skins one of which
he made me a present its nice & will make a pretty
muff, as it's such beautiful long soft fur not unlike fox
skin I intend keeping it for you as I think you will
value it I shall be sure to find a chance to send it
I remember you had just got a black muff which you
must make last till this reaches you I've also had a
present of a large wolf skin so I'm set up for fur Oh
what dreadful plains we have had to go through lately
the mud at the banks of some of the forks of the Humboldt was so deep that in one place a yoke of our large
cattle had to be put to 1 wagon & then it was a dreadful pull the chains broke pretty fast. yesterday Wm
called me out of my wagon to come & see an ox down

in the mud nothing could be seen but the top of his
back & head his nose was quite covered I often
wonder what you'd do in crossing such places Almost
every week & sometimes twice we have to place boards
on the projection of our wagons & put all the loading
on them for the streams we cross come quite a piece
up our waggon box but every stream brings us nearer
our journeys end. yesterday while camped some Indians
were with us & our company think they have persuaded
2 to go with us they have kept close by ever since &
one who is I think ½ Spanish seems very proud of
the idea he has had his hair cut & looks quite civilized having on a red flannel shirt & his legs covered
with the sleeves of another the other Indian is dressed
in skins & lots of ornaments Should they continue
with us we are likely to less trouble with any of the
tribe Oh what a loss I'm at to know how to amuse
myself for tho I have little sewing yet its nothing that
must be done & what I cannot well do while riding my
principal job is to sew bosom & wrist 2 of Wms shirts
I might knit but have only red yarn which I bought
for Sis & its too near summer to commence woolen
socks If I only had some muslin how nicely I could
be preparing our under clothes for we are all quite
destitute & it will be such a job when we get to Cal.
I have no night dress at all sleep in a col[ore]d saque
Sissy will have no clothes when we get through she
now wears a little red flannel dress made out of the
piece you saw & that green quilted skirt which on warm
days is too heavy but I have no fears of getting things
when we arrive at Pa's for he'll set us up in all we
want I'm sure of that It seems quite providential
he went on last year for we all have a home & some-

thing to expect now so different to going unknown. Oh
if I could but see my dear Marianna & have a long
talk with her how happy I should feel. still I look
forward to such a season as not at all unlikely my
earnest desire is that we should end our days near
each other & I think we shall

Carson Valley June 5/53

Dearest Sis

We arrived here about a week ago & shall be detained until early part of July not being able to cross
the Sierra Nevada mountains with wagons on account
of snow

Willm is hired out at mining $50 pr month & board,
which is $2 pr day   I am helping round the house of
Willm employers so that I get my own & Sissy's board
free which is considerable   its a tavern & store where
we are stoping but only the mistress of the house to
do the work so as she [?] very pleasant young
woman we get along first rate & have such nice living
I have a chance to send this to Sacramento to mail
so send it off in a hurry

We are all well   give our kindest love to Mr. Willis
& accept the same from yours ever   affectionately

There are 20 boarders here most of them working
in the mines

Write to San Francisco & when I get there will
write again not quite in such a hurry.

Index